Handbook of Graphs and Networks in People Analytics

Handbook of Graphs and Networks in People Analytics

With Examples in R and Python

Keith McNulty

CRC Press
Taylor & Francis Group
Boca Raton London New York

CRC Press is an imprint of the
Taylor & Francis Group, an **informa** business

A CHAPMAN & HALL BOOK

First edition published 2022
by CRC Press
6000 Broken Sound Parkway NW, Suite 300, Boca Raton, FL 33487-2742

and by CRC Press
4 Park Square, Milton Park, Abingdon, Oxon, OX14 4RN

CRC Press is an imprint of Taylor & Francis Group, LLC

Library of Congress Cataloging-in-Publication Data

Names: McNulty, Keith, author.
Title: Handbook of graphs and networks in people analytics : with examples in R and python / Keith McNulty.
Description: First edition. | Boca Raton : CRC Press, [2022] | Includes bibliographical references and index.
Identifiers: LCCN 2021059612 (print) | LCCN 2021059613 (ebook) | ISBN 9781032211244 (hbk) | ISBN 9781032204970 (pbk) | ISBN 9781003266815 (ebk)
Subjects: LCSH: Human capital. | R (Computer program language) | Charts, diagrams, etc.
Classification: LCC HD4904.7 .M398 2022 (print) | LCC HD4904.7 (ebook) | DDC 658.300285--dc23/eng/20220303
LC record available at https://lccn.loc.gov/2021059612
LC ebook record available at https://lccn.loc.gov/2021059613

ISBN: 978-1-032-20497-0 (pbk)
ISBN: 978-1-032-21124-4 (hbk)
ISBN: 978-1-003-26681-5 (ebk)

DOI: 10.1201/9781003266815

Typeset in LM Roman
by KnowledgeWorks Global Ltd.

Publisher's note: This book has been prepared from camera-ready copy provided by the authors.

Contents

Notes on data used in this book

For R and Python users, each of the data sets used in this book can be downloaded individually by following the code in each chapter. Alternatively, if you intend to work through all the chapters, all data sets can be downloaded in advance by installing the onadata package.

For R users, this can be installed as follows:

```r
# install onadata package
install.packages("onadata")
library(onadata)

# see a list of data sets
data(package = "onadata")

# find out more about a specific data set ('karate' example)
help(karate)
```

For Python users, use `pip install onadata` to install the package into your environment. Then, to use the package:

```python
# import onadata package
import onadata as ona
import pandas as pd

# see a list of data sets
ona.list_sets()

# load data into a dataframe
df = ona.karate()

# find out more about a specific data set ('karate' example)
ona.karate().info()
```

Technical note for R users

This book uses the new native pipe operator |> which was introduced in R version 4.1.0. Users using an older version of R, or who wish to use the alternative pipe operator %>% can simply replace this in all code. However, an appropriate library containing %>% will need to be loaded, such as `magrittr`, `dplyr` or `tidyverse`.

Foreword by Professor Jeff Polzer

We all understand that when it comes to getting things done in organizations, "who you know" matters. This truism only scratches the surface, though, of how deeply our social networks affect everything we do. They shape our day-to-day opportunities through every meeting, email, and serendipitous encounter, just as each interaction in turn alters our networks. We strengthen some relationships, develop new ones, and let others languish. We spend lots of time and attention focusing on our immediate relationships, and for good reason; they are a source of joy and psychological fulfillment, while helping us do our jobs and achieve our goals.

If we give most of our attention to our direct relationships, however, we miss an important part of the social structure in which we are embedded. After all, it's not just who we know, but who our friends and colleagues know that helps us succeed. These more distant, indirect connections are hard to discern, and our accuracy diminishes when we try to evaluate these indirect ties or make sense of how they fit into a larger picture. Though hidden from our direct line of sight, this social structure has a powerful influence on what we, and our organizations, can achieve.

This is where Keith McNulty's new book on network analysis comes into play. He draws on a rich tradition of social science to distill what we know about networks and clearly explain how to analyze and apply network data to organizational challenges. Network researchers have identified powerful patterns that are easily overlooked from any one person's vantage point, from in-depth studies of relationships among small groups of employees, to intricate analyses of teams embedded in organizational networks, to cross-firm investigations of interlocked boards of directors, among many others. The beauty of network analysis is that it allows seemingly simple dyadic connections between individuals to be knit together into an entire social structure. This approach allows us to zoom in or out to answer questions at different levels of analysis, whether about the centrality of a specific individual or the centralized structure of an entire organization.

The time is ripe for organizations to embrace network analyses to understand how connections among employees are helping or hurting their ability to achieve their goals. As companies have come to understand the value of using network techniques in their core business, such as Google using links between websites to organize internet searches, or LinkedIn using ties between platform users to guide job searches, they have started to experiment with using network concepts and methods to address their workforce challenges. The availability of new digital sources of data and ever-growing computational power, coupled with the well-documented rigor of network methods, hold great promise for understanding how employee networks function.

Some companies at the forefront of this field incorporated network analyses into their toolkits years ago, in many cases importing and adapting methods from academic research via their newly minted people analytics teams. Other organizations, however, have not yet considered this approach or have encountered obstacles along the way. While most managers, for example, intuitively understand the basic importance of "networking," some still view rigorous network analysis as an esoteric subject. Others may struggle to decide what sources of employee data to use—whether from digital communication platforms, surveys, or HR information systems—or how to gather and prepare the data for this type of analysis without violating employee privacy and trust. As a result of these challenges, the gap between what is possible and what is currently in practice remains wide, in part because those poised to do this work may not appreciate the extent to which network methods are adaptable and versatile.

This book aims to bridge this gap, laying out the foundational building blocks of networks in terms of the concepts, terminology, data, analyses, and code, complete with hands-on examples of real use cases. It is exciting and inspiring to see the way McNulty explains network methods, as he unpacks the distinct elements and analytic steps to make them transparent. This makes it easier for readers to see how these elements fit together and apply to organizational challenges, sparking new ideas for innovative solutions. By demystifying this topic, McNulty empowers people to find their own solutions and engage in more productive conversations, regardless of who is writing the actual code or running the analyses. This book can help to democratize network analysis and improve the level of data fluency in organizations more generally. Considering the benefits of understanding network analysis, it is easy to see why top business schools now include it in their curriculum, whether in a course on People Analytics or in other domains.

With a clearer understanding of network methods in hand, the potential applications for this approach should excite not only those in human resources and people analytics, but also managers who are trying to help employees work together in a more productive and sustainable way that improves both individual and collective welfare. Virtually every organization is trying to juggle the demand by some employees to work remotely, while others anxiously wait to return to the office, creating the need to design hybrid arrangements that satisfy everyone. Communication and collaboration networks are at the very heart of these questions, whether the goal is to execute current projects, spur innovation, or improve employee well-being. Companies are now using network analyses to help with challenges that include socializing new hires, cultivating an environment of inclusion and belonging, preventing collaboration overload and burnout, and planning office utilization. Beyond these types of organizational concerns, scientists across disciplines are using these tools to tackle the world's most pressing problems, from mapping the spread of infectious disease to understanding the social conduits of political polarization. All of these issues, and many more, are amenable to network approaches. This valuable book can help you examine these challenges from new angles and design fresh approaches to address them.

Jeff Polzer
December 2021

__Jeffrey T. Polzer__ is the UPS Foundation Professor of Human Resource Management in the Organizational Behavior Unit at Harvard Business School. He studies how people collaborate in teams and across organizational networks to accomplish their individual and collective goals. He has ongoing projects in collaboration with a number of organizations, often working with members of their people analytics groups on problems of mutual interest. He has taught a variety of courses in the MBA, Executive, and Doctoral Programs at HBS, and published his research in numerous top management and psychology journals.

Introduction

One evening in early 2014, I settled down in front of my computer to catch up on some of my family tree research. This was my second major sprint at digging into the stories of my predecessors. The previous sprint was back in 2001 with some weekend trips to the family records center in London. Back then, over the course of a year or so of dedicated effort on my part, I had slowly managed to find information on my immediate ancestors dating back to the late 1800s.

This second sprint had been very different. Over the course of only a few weeks, I had created an extensively deep and wide family tree with some branches going all the way back to 17th century England. On this particular evening I was in for a real surprise. As I logged in the Ancestry website, I had a hint waiting for me asking me to click on another member's family tree where we seemed to have a common ancestor. I duly clicked, confirmed the common ancestor and then followed this new tree down to the present day. One of the names I saw when I got there was Alan S. P. Rickman.

A quick check of the family tree details against his Wikipedia biography revealed that this was *the* Alan Rickman—the star of the *Harry Potter* movies, the original *Die Hard*, and many other big-screen classics. He had always been one of my favorite British actors, but now I learned that he was my second cousin too. My latest attempt at genealogical research was proving a truly amazing experience for me. I had never imagined that I could progress so quickly and discover such rich and surprising information.

Why was my second sprint at genealogy so much more productive than my first? Of course, part of the reason was the digitization revolution, which meant that there were more historic documents available instantly to me electronically than was the case a decade before. But the biggest reason why I could make so much more rapid progress was because I was no longer doing this alone. I was, in fact, part of a huge open network graph created by millions of family history researchers. When that hint appeared that led me to my new-found famous cousin, an edge was connected from the nodes in my family tree to the nodes of Alan Rickman and his ancestors. It had been hundreds of these edges over the previous months that had allowed me to reach so far and wide into my own ancestral history. Thirteen years earlier when I last tried this, that graph simply did not exist.

Like it or not, nowadays most of us are a part of at least one big graph which has come into existence in the early years of the 21st century. When you connect with someone on Facebook or LinkedIn or follow someone on Twitter or Instagram, you are casting out yet another edge in a gigantic graph. Maybe genealogy is not your thing and you prefer music, or books, or knitting? Don't worry, there's a graph for all of those too where you can connect with people of the same interests and share your passion and knowledge. If you are stuck in a traffic jam and your car is at a standstill, you may be contributing to the value of an edge on numerous GPS navigation graphs and thus helping some other person avoid your pain.

The technology of graphs is all around us and enables so many of the ways in which we live our lives today. That same technology is also available to us at no cost as an analytic tool to allow us to better understand network structures and dynamics in the fields of science, technology, economics, sociology and psychology, to name just a few. It is available to academics and practitioners alike and can be used on problems ranging from a very small network analysis which takes a few minutes on a laptop, to massive scale network mining requiring days or weeks of processing time.

But here's the problem: few people really know how to do network analysis. It is still considered by many as a deep specialism or even a 'dark art.' It shouldn't be. More academic students and researchers should know how to apply graph theory and methods to their work. More business analytics professionals should know how to store and analyze data that is not in traditional rectangular form and which focuses on connection rather than transaction. More companies and organizations should be thinking about how their data can be structured and analyzed to tell them more about how people, skills and knowledge connect and how this can influence key positive and negative institutional outcomes. What's more, they should not need expensive and inflexible network analysis and visualization software offered by vendors to do this, when the best tools are freely available open source and just require a little bit of programming skill to make full use of them.

This book aims to make the field of graph and network analysis more approachable to students and professionals by explaining the most important elements of theory and sharing common methodologies using open source programming languages like R and Python. It does so by explaining theory in as much detail as is necessary to support analytical curiosity and interpretation, and by using a wide array of example data sets and code snippets to demonstrate the specific implementation and interpretation of methodologies. Those who start the book will learn about simple but important steps like creating graphs from data sources and visualizing them intuitively. Those who finish the book will learn about important measures like graph density and centrality and useful algorithms for partitioning graphs and identifying communities in complex populations. As you will see as you read on, these methods have many exciting applications. In organizational settings—my personal speciality—they can be applied to problems of onboarding new hires, encouraging diverse collaboration and interaction, finding efficient communication strategies, identifying new organizational structures that better reflect the flow of work, detecting intensely collaborative groups, connecting individuals with common interests, finding potential leaders and many other problems.

There is no way that this book could be a complete overview of graph theory and methods—at least not without the printer running out of ink. There are many, many elements of graph theory and methodology that are not covered in this book. My focus has been primarily on teaching the most critical elements for those who will use graphs in a sociological, psychological or organizational context. This book will improve over time, so if you feel I have missed anything very important, or if you spot errors or have any other suggestions, please do get in touch by leaving an issue on the book's Github repository[1]. If you use the contents of this book or any examples from it for teaching purposes, you don't need to ask my permission to do so, but I would ask that you reference this book as the source.

It just remains for me to thank various people and groups who helped me make this book a reality. Various individuals have contributed to making this book better by reading early drafts, or by trying out code, offering encouragement or suggesting new examples, in particular: Liz Romero, Rachel Ramsay, Christopher Belanger, Jenna Eagleson and Bennet Voorhees. Nothing in this book would be possible without the fantastic packages that exist in languages like R and Python for working with graphs, and so the authors and contributors of open source packages like `igraph`, `networkx`, `ggraph`, `pyvis`, `visNetwork` and `networkD3` deserve thanks. I am grateful to the Stanford Network Analysis Project (SNAP) and the SocioPatterns collaboration[2] for the data sets they make available to the public, many of which I have used as examples in this book. As always, my thanks go to all the developers who work on the `rmarkdown` and `bookdown` R packages which allow me to write and format these technical books with much less complexity than would otherwise be the case.

For me there is no doubt that network analysis is the most exciting, most fun and fastest developing field in People Analytics. I hope you have as much fun learning from this book as I did writing it.

Keith McNulty
October 2021

---

[1] https://github.com/keithmcnulty/ona_book
[2] http://www.sociopatterns.org/

1

Graphs Everywhere!

If you have ever been lucky enough to pay a visit to the vibrant city of Kaliningrad on the Baltic coast, it's likely to have been a trip you remember. An unusual exclave of the massive Russian Federation, you cannot get to the remainder of Russia from Kaliningrad over land without crossing through at least two other countries. Things have landed this way, like they always do, because of the cards dealt by history. The strategic importance endowed to Kaliningrad owing to its prime coastal position placed it in the center of a geopolitical 'tug-of-war' which saw it change hands on numerous occasions over the centuries. By the end of the Second World War, as Stalin cast his eye over the ruins of Europe, he considered the city far too strategically important to be left in the hands of any other Eastern Bloc state, and so—despite the physical separation—it was duly deemed to be Russia's sovereign territory.

As you might expect, Kaliningrad has only been so named since it became part of the USSR in 1946. Prior to this, and stretching back to the Middle Ages, it was known as Königsberg—the King's Mountain—in honor of King Ottokar II of Bohemia (c.1233-1278). Steeped in glorious and tragic history, the city is rich in museums, castles, cathedrals and monuments from its past. But for mathematicians like me, Königsberg is perhaps best known for a simple, unassuming puzzle that occupied the minds of many a renaissance intellectual in the 17th and 18th centuries—a problem which, it could be argued, laid the foundations for the highly connected world we live in today.

1.1 The Seven Bridges of Königsberg

The city once known as Königsberg is separated in two by the path of the Pregel River. As the Pregel breaks toward the Baltic Sea, two islands form a part of the city. This leads to a city comprised of four land masses: the two mainland masses on either side of the river (known as Altstadt-Loebenicht and Vorstadt-Haberberg), and the two island land masses (Lomse and Kneiphof). In the 1700s, a total of seven bridges connected these land masses[1]. Figure 1.1

---

[1] Only two of these bridges still survive today

DOI: 10.1201/9781003266815-1

is a suitably historic map of the situation. The island on the left is Kneiphof and the island on the right is Lomse. The beautiful dress worn by the lady in the foreground of this picture is large enough so that one of the seven bridges is entirely covered by it, but you can see the other six.

FIGURE 1.1: The Prussian city of Königsberg circa 1600 from *Civitates Orbis Terrarum*, Vol.III (credit: Historic Cities Research Project)

The puzzle went like this: is it possible to devise a walk where you would set foot on all four land masses while crossing all seven bridges only once? There was a strong hunch from trial and error that the answer was no—the problem was how to prove this mathematically. No effective techniques had yet been discovered to allow such a proof.

Enter Leonhard Euler, an 18th century Swiss mathematician who spent the majority of his life in St. Petersburg and Berlin. A prolific original thinker, Euler is considered by many as the greatest mathematician of all time. It is impossible to study mathematics even at high school without being constantly exposed to Euler's work. He popularized the greek letter π to denote Archimedes' constant ratio between the circumference and diameter of a circle. He formalized the letter i to denote the imaginary number $\sqrt{-1}$ and he defined the exponential constant e which is known as *Euler's number*. Living between two cities on either side of Königsberg at the time of the problem of the seven bridges, he set about finding a solution. The one he discovered is both a testament to the beauty of mathematical proof and the first use of the concept of a graph to solve a mathematical problem.

The first thing Euler did—as any good mathematician will always do—is strip the problem of all its extraneous information and reduce it to its most minimal form. The problem merely requires one to set foot on a land mass. It is not concerned with what route one takes while on that land mass. Therefore, we can represent each of the four land masses as dots. We can then draw lines between the dots to represent the bridges. This, he reasoned, leads to a diagram like that in Figure 1.2. The picture can be drawn in infinitely many ways, but it will always be four dots connected by seven lines in the same configuration.

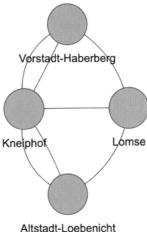

FIGURE 1.2: A minimal representation of the *Seven Bridges of Königsberg* problem

First, Euler observed that if one starts their journey at a certain place and crosses all seven bridges once, there must have been eight total visits to places. This is because we start at a place, and every time we cross a bridge, we add another place to our walk. So if we cross seven bridges, we must visit eight places (including repeat visits to a place).

Euler then looked at any situation where you have a place P connected to other places by an *odd number* of bridges. If there was one bridge and it was crossed once, we would only be in place P once—either at the beginning or end of the journey. If there were three bridges and all were crossed once, place P would have been visited twice no matter where we started. If there were five bridges, place P would have been visited three times. If there were n bridges, place P would have been visited $\frac{1}{2}(n+1)$ times.

Now Euler calculated how many place visits this would mean in total for Königsberg. Since Kneiphof has five bridges to other places, if all were crossed once Kneiphof would have been visited three times. The other three places each have three bridges connecting them, so any such walk would result in two visits to each place. Adding all this up, this means that if a walk existed through all four places where every bridge was used only once, there must be nine total place visits. Since this contradicts Euler's earlier observation that such a walk must involve only eight place visits, we must conclude that such a walk does not exist.

Euler's proof was the first time a graph like the one in Figure 1.2 was used to solve a problem. The solution also involved concepts that would later become critical in the study of graphs. Euler set up the places as *vertices* or *nodes* of the graph, and he set up the bridges as *edges*. The proof depends on a conclusion about the number of edges connected to a vertex, which later became known as the *degree* of a vertex. The proof required the study of *walks* or *paths* through the graph. The requirement that a walk could only use each edge once became known as an *Euler walk* (or *Eulerian path*) and various algorithms exist today to calculate Euler walks for problems such as constructing DNA sequences from their fragments[2]. Little was Euler to know the Pandora's Box he had opened.

> **Thinking ahead:** If you know how to load a graph object into R or Python, you could try to load the `koenigsberg` data set from the onadata package or download it from the internet[3] and create a graph from it. You could use your software to calculate the degrees of the vertices of the graph. For example in R, if you have the data loaded into an `igraph` object, you can use `igraph::degree()` to get a vector showing you the degrees of each vertex. There is even a package called `eulerian` in R which has a function `hasEulerianPath()` which determines whether an Euler walk exists in a given graph.

1.2   Graphs as mathematical models

Graphs and networks have existed long before Euler, and probably since the beginning of time itself. They exist physically, such as in a spider's web, in the electrical wiring of your home or in the molecules that make up the universe. Since the time of Euler, graphs have also existed conceptually as the best way we can describe many complex systems, and in this book we will focus on the use of graphs to describe systems related to people, groups, organizations or other similar societal constructs. Before we jump into our core topic, it is worth taking a few moments to appreciate how fundamental graphs are to both science and to everyday life by discussing a few examples of the practical use of graphs to solve problems.

Whenever objects move physically through a network structure, it makes sense that graph theory will be of great use in solving problems of routing and

---

[2]In fact, Euler extended his proof to consider any graph and concluded that if an Euler walk exists in a graph, then the number of vertices with odd degree is either 0 or 2. For a fascinating write-up of Euler's original proof, see Paoletti (2006)

[3]https://ona-book.org/data/koenigsberg.csv

optimization. An obvious example of this is whenever a route is planned on Google or Apple Maps, or on a SatNav system. When you search a driving route to a given destination, the underlying calculation involves streets and roads as edges and intersections as vertices. The fastest routes are calculated based on stored properties of the edges such as the road length, road speed limit and live traffic information. The underlying graphs are updated over time with edges switched on and off according to information on road closures[4]. It doesn't just have to be road networks of course. Rail, air and other forms of transport networks make great use of graph theory. Maybe you are sitting on a train while reading this book and, if you are, have a look around you for the route map and you'll see a graph right there. Essential public services such as the management of sewerage networks are an example of one of the less glamorous fields where graph theory is essential to operational calculations and decisions. If there is a sudden cold snap in a city and roads need to be de-iced, the problem of how to get around the city in an efficient way, saving resources by minimizing the route while still covering all critical areas sounds like a puzzle Euler himself would have loved.

Nowadays, objects that move through networks are often electronic in nature, such as bytes of code or electrical currents. National and local power grids are managed with the help of graph theory. Communications networks, telephone, satellite, cable and internet are all networks where nodes are connection points such as junctions or receiver points and edges can be visible in the form of underground or undersea cables or invisible in the form of signals sent through the air or into space.

In the sciences, graphs are essential as models of biological, chemical or physical processes or phenomena. Chemical Graph Theory (CGT) deals with the applications of graph theory to molecular problems. In condensed matter physics, graph theory is essential in quantitatively modeling atomic structures. In biology and biochemistry, graphs are important in understanding the spread of disease in epidemic models, in the study of genomics and DNA, in the neuroscientific modeling of brain functioning and in the ecological modeling of species migration. In the computational sciences, huge progress has been made in the storing of data thanks to databases that have a graph-like structure, and many of the latest algorithms used in Machine Learning operate through graph-like structures like trees or neural networks. In linguistics, graphs have facilitated great advances in how we understand natural language as a collection of discrete words and phrases that are related to each other. The list goes on and on.

Arguably, the area where graphs have impacted our daily lives the most in recent decades is in the development of online communities which depend on them. Social networks like Facebook, Twitter, LinkedIn, Instagram and many others use graphs to connect people in ways that have fundamentally changed

---

[4]Such networks are known as *temporal networks*.

lives and livelihoods. Friendships and acquaintances happen today between people who have never and often will never meet physically. Countless relationships, marriages and families have been brought into existence. Long lost families separated by adoption or abandonment have found each other again. Job opportunities have been created and filled. Individuals with common interests have been connected irrelevant of where they are located. The positives and negatives of this rapid and paradigm-shifting rise in social networking are vigorously debated, but what cannot be denied is that they would not exist without graph theory.

1.3   Graph theory in the analysis of people and groups

In the social sciences and in the study of people and groups, the increasing prevalence of network data and the ability to analyze it using graph-theoretic methods have opened up rich and continuously developing veins of research that encompass both academic and enterprise settings. Much of the work that is done can be grouped into a few different study areas.

1.3.1   The study of connection

In most organizations, institutions and societal groups, connection is considered a critical facilitator of happiness, motivation, productivity and progress. The psychological concept of *belongingness*, which describes a human need to connect, affiliate and be accepted by others, is an important element of Maslow's Hierarchy of Needs. Empirically, greater social connection has been associated with positive effects on mental and physical health, cognitive functioning, life expectancy and even wound healing (Holt-Lunstad (2018)). Conversely, lack of connection—or loneliness—is of research interest because of its potential negative effects on mental well-being, productivity and workplace performance. A meta-analytic review of the relationship between social relationships and mortality risk concluded that lack of social connection carries a higher risk of premature mortality than obesity (Holt-Lunstad et al. (2015)). In workplace settings, practitioners and academics are showing an increasing amount of interest in connection and how it affects performance, productivity and employee retention. Empirical research has demonstrated links between friendship at work and improved work engagement and productivity (Rath (2006)), and social interaction at work (whether work-related or otherwise) has been associated with improved outcomes (Olguin et al. (2009)).

The ability to analyze connection in the workplace and in society-at-large will become increasingly important as we move further into the 21st century. The variety of data that could represent connection is expanding. Connection between people can now be defined by in-person interaction, electronic transaction and even assumed connection through overlaps in geographic location or in work or personal activities. Strong analytic techniques will be necessary to support evidence-based practice, because not all measures of connection are meaningful to the outcomes being researched and, even when they have been shown to be meaningful, resulting interventions do not always have the expected effects (for example, a study by Feld & Carter (1998) demonstrated that deliberate attempts to increase interracial contact in American schools actually ended up causing greater racial segregation).

1.3.2　The study of information flow

General fascination with how information propagates through networks dates from the earliest chain letters in the late 19th century (Solly (2020)). Those of us who are old enough may remember receiving letters in the mail asking to send the message onward to a specified number of individuals, and promising that this will generate thousands of replies within a few weeks. Figure 1.3 is an example of one of these letters used as a way to generate money in Texas in 1935.

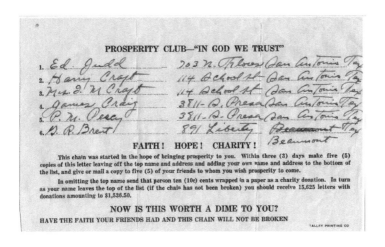

FIGURE 1.3: Chain letter from Texas in 1935 (credit: Daniel W. VanArsdale)

More recently, information flow between people has been fundamentally transformed by the digital age, with potential reach and speed of transmission massively enabled by technology. Today, the study of the propagation of information in networks has many purposes including the development of emergency alert strategies, the prevention of fraudulent activities, the defense of public health or the protection of the integrity of criminal justice processes. Although this area of research is still in its infancy, models which are not dissimilar to those used in biology and epidemiology are employed (for example, Hafnaoui et al. (2019)). The likelihood of messages propagating can depend on the characteristics of the network, the nature of the message and the node which is propagating it (popularity, credibility), and the receptiveness of the onward nodes to the message. The term 'viral' has entered our lexicon to describe rapid electronic message propagation in the last decade or so. The effect of message propagation on the development of networks is also of great research interest—for example, what nature and frequency of message propagation leads to rapid network growth?

Currently, research of this nature is mostly confined to academics working with social media data, but there is substantial value to be gained from its application in workforce settings. An increasingly distributed workforce with lower levels of geographic concentration will mean that organizations will need to more effectively manage important, urgent or time-sensitive communication with their workforce and this will require greater intelligence on how information propagates effectively and efficiently in their specific environments.

1.3.3   The study of community, diversity and familiarity

Distance in a network—which we will define more precisely in later chapters—can be representative of likely similarity or familiarity (or lack thereof) between individuals, which allows for mathematical models to support the study of community and diversity. Algorithms for calculating distance and diameter in a network help determine how 'tight' groups are and allow some measurement of inter- and intra-group interaction. Community detection algorithms involve graph partitioning to help identify 'pockets' of highly connected individuals in large networks. This is of great interest in the field of sociology, but also it has applications in other areas such as the study of common purchasing behaviors among customers, and the study of common interests among academics or writers (Lu et al. (2018)).

Increasing focus on diversity as a positive influencer of organizational outcomes in recent years means that the ability to measure distance and identify community structures in networks will be of high utility, particularly in complex organizational contexts. Use cases can range from highly strategic questions of organizational design to highly tactical questions of meeting attendance or group membership. Current trends away from physical co-location of employees and the rise of more virtual organizational structures will likely result in greater requirements for analysis of remote and electronic interaction in order to determine whether imposed structures genuinely reflect the way people work. Effective use of these techniques can even be valuable in the coordination of large professional or social events, where subgroups can be identified to maximize in-group distance in order to better ensure a more diverse mix of employees in professional or social activities.

1.3.4 The study of importance, influence and attachment

While the concept of vertex/node importance or centrality has been a fundamental tenet of graph theory for a long time, the rise of social networks seems to have turbo-charged its relevance in research and analytics. The rise of the 'influencer' as a highly connected and influential member of a network has entered deeply into social consciousness in the past decade, and the study of how followership is generated through the forming of attachments between members of networks is one of the more rich veins of sociological research currently. The idea of preferential attachment or the *Matthew Effect* describes an accumulated advantage over time, where those with more attachment attract yet more[5]. It has been believed that social networks show similar properties to scale-free networks which obey a power law distribution of the degree of their vertices/nodes; see Figure 1.4.[6] In fact, the most recent research indicates that scale-free networks exist rarely and that social networks are at best weakly scale-free (Broido & Clauset (2019)), or may not exhibit any notable preferential attachment behavior at all (Fisher et al. (2017)).

Of course, any organization, institution or place of work can be considered a social network and there will be individuals that command greater or less attachment according to their tenure, seniority, skills or general popularity. Understanding this in an organizational context can lead to insights about leadership and followership and help us better determine the influence of followership on recruitment and attrition. Different types of centrality such as degree, betweenness, closeness and eigenvector centrality can imply different roles of individuals in terms of their importance and influence in their network.

---

[5]So named because of a segment of the Gospel of Matthew in the New Testament: "For to every one who has will more be given, and he will have abundance; but from him who has not, even what he has will be taken away."

[6]In a scale-free network, the proportion of vertices/nodes of degree k takes a shape similar to $k^{-\alpha}$ where usually $2 < \alpha < 3$.

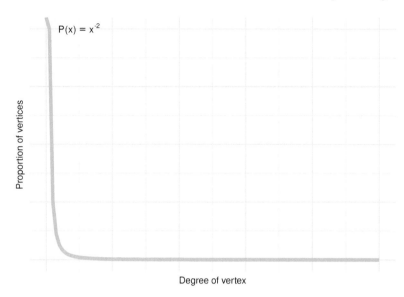

FIGURE 1.4: Power law distribution of vertex degrees in a scale-free network for $\alpha = 2$, showing a mass concentration toward low-degree vertices and an exclusive tail of vertices with high degree. This has been believed to be a consequence of preferential attachment in networks.

> **Thinking ahead:** If you know how to, load up the graph of Zachary's Karate Club via the `karate` data set in the `onadata` package or by downloading the edgelist from the internet[7]. See if you can find some functions to calculate the degree centrality, betweenness centrality, closeness centrality and eigenvector centrality of the various individuals in the network. If you compare the results, you should discover that centrality can mean different things depending on how you define it.

1.3.5   Graphs as data sources

As use cases for network analytics mature, and as more and more organizations seek to understand their networks better, traditional rectangular-style databases will become increasingly challenging to work with. Consider a desire to analyze whether two salespeople in an organization are connected through serving the same customer in the same month. Depending on how data is currently stored in systems, this could easily end up being a lot more

---

[7]https://ona-book.org/data/karate.csv

complicated and computationally expensive than it needs to be. Sales records may need to be joined to customer records, which may then need to be re-joined back to sales data. This may need to be done repeatedly to eventually obtain the required view of the data. Traditional rectangular databases are stored to keep records of transactions, not of connections.

Many organizations are turning to graph databases to store data about relationships and to allow much faster query and calculation whenever the unit of analysis is connection. A graph database is designed to store information about connected objects like people or organizational units in its vertices, and information about relationships in its edges. Such databases suit data that already comes in the form of a graph edgelist such as information on communication or interaction, but it is also becoming more common to transform other forms of data to be loaded into a graph database in order to query relationships that are otherwise not easy to see[8]. Social media engines and many knowledge-based resources like Wikipedia are supported by graph databases, and these sorts of databases are also becoming more commonly found in enterprise settings. They have helped solve some high-profile problems. For example, the International Consortium of Investigative Journalists (ICIJ) used a graph database to load document metadata from the *Panama Papers* document leak. Stored in this format the metadata exposed various complex networks of offshore tax arrangements.

All of the topics mentioned above will come up to a greater or lesser degree in the content of this book, and from time to time there will even be diversions into a few other use cases outside of the people analytics domain in order to help illustrate the broader applications of methods. As this book is intended to be more of a technical manual than a work of philosophy, we will be coming at this entire topic from the point of view of methodology and we will be focusing more on the *how* than the *why*. That said, some of the examples we use will clearly point to the motivation of the analysis and how each methodology can be useful in practice. As enthusiastic readers progress through the technical material and work through the examples chapter by chapter, I expect that they will quickly grasp the potential for application of these methods in their work or study.

1.4 Purpose, structure and organization of this book

This book is targeted at technical practitioners who need a thorough grounding in the storage, visualization and analysis of network data. It requires an elementary knowledge of the R or Python programming languages. As I am

---

[8]We will look at examples of how to do this in Chapter 4 of this book.

first and foremost an R programmer, most of the content of this book will be primarily demonstrated in R, but efforts have been made to ensure that Python implementations have been demonstrated wherever possible, albeit more briefly in most places. If you are a Python programmer, I would recommend that you are open to reading the sections that use R code as they will often help you build a better understanding of the work through the more thorough descriptions and discussions contained therein. If you have never programmed before, you may find the introductory R tutorial chapter in my previous book (McNulty (2021)) useful as a starting point.

If you are not a technical practitioner, this book can still be useful to you, as it contains considerable detail on concepts, methods and use cases related to network analytics in organizations, and it gives guidance on the interpretation of network analysis and statistics. You will just need to be willing to tolerate the various code blocks that will appear as part of the technical instruction.

Various downloadable data sets are used throughout this book, and in some cases I point to other sources of data outside the book for those who are interested in further exploration, particularly of very large network data. Data sets are introduced and described at various points as they are used, and many of them are used multiple times in the book to illustrate different methodologies.

Most chapters end with a set of discussion questions and data exercises, and I strongly encourage the reader to engage with these in order to put their learning into practice. Often, it is through taking on these exercises that readers discover some of the common pitfalls of working with graph data structures, and better to learn these pitfalls now than to find out about them in high-stakes or more urgent situations.

Readers will have already noticed the 'blue boxes' that appear in this chapter, and they will be a regular feature throughout this book. They are optional, and generally encourage readers to 'think ahead' or 'play around' with some of the ideas or methods introduced. These blue boxes are intended to make the book more fun and to encourage experimentation as a way of learning, especially for more competent technical practitioners. Occasionally, they try to thread together related concepts that appear in different chapters of the book, so that readers can get a better sense of how some of the theory and methodology fit together.

This chapter can be considered preliminary. From Chapter 2 onward, this book takes the following structure:

- Chapter 2 introduces the simple elements of graph theory including how to define a graph, types of graphs, vertex and edge properties and the ways in which a graph can be described mathematically. It then proceeds to demonstrate how to create graph objects in R or in Python and how to start working with them.

- Chapter 3 looks at the various options for how to visualize graphs in R and in Python. It goes through a variety of technical options for static and dynamic visualizations of graphs and how to customize the appearance of graphs for various purposes.

- Chapter 4 looks at how data can be transformed to be used in a graph structure, which is an important workflow element in making graphs useful for analysis. Two substantial examples are used to illustrate how to transform rectangular data into an edgelist for a graph and how to scrape document information for use in graphs.

- Chapter 5 examines the topic of paths and distance in graphs, introduces related concepts such as graph diameter, and demonstrates some common methods such as Dijkstra's shortest path algorithm. The utility of these concepts is illustrated through two examples: facilitating workplace introductions and generating diverse employee groupings.

- Chapter 6 examines the topic of vertex importance and centrality in graphs. It discusses different types of centrality and their meaning and usefulness in a network analytics context, and it shows various methods for calculating and graphically illustrating centrality in graphs. These metrics are then put to use on an example network of office workers.

- Chapter 7 looks at community and clique detection. It covers various options for how to identify communities in graphs, how to describe communities and how to illustrate them effectively. A high school network and a Twitter network of politicians are used to illustrate how to detect communities and how to describe them using ground truth network properties.

- Chapter 8 deep dives into some common statistics used in analyzing networks, in particular related to similarity, assortativity and attachment.

- Chapter 9 introduces the concept of graphs as databases and provides some examples of how to design and use graph databases for the purpose of network analytics. Examples include how to query the open access Wikidata knowledge graph and how to work with a Neo4J graph database natively and via R and Python. This can be considered an extension chapter for those who are interested.

- Chapter 10 is a set of practice exercises and data sets designed to give the reader an opportunity to put some of the learning from earlier chapters into practice. These exercises are ideal for class assignments or project work.

2

Working with Graphs

When we think of a graph, we usually think of a diagram of dots and lines. Indeed, as we have seen in Chapter 1 of this book, the very concept of a graph came into existence in the 1700s when a mathematician tried to solve a problem diagramatically. It makes sense that we think about graphs in this way, because it is intuitive, easy to communicate and in many cases a diagram helps us better address the problem we are solving. However, a diagram is only one way of describing a graph, and it is not particularly scalable. It is easy to draw a diagram for a graph of a few nodes and edges like in our *Bridges of Königsberg* problem, but what if our problem involved thousands of nodes and millions of edges? Most interesting graphs which we will want to study will be more complex in nature and will contain many hundreds or thousands of nodes and many more edges, and diagrams of graphs of that size are not always useful in helping us solve problems.

In this chapter we will gain a basic understanding of graphs and how to construct them so that we can work with them analytically. We will introduce the most general way of describing a graph mathematically, and we will then discuss how different types of graphs can be defined by placing more conditions on the most general definition. We will go on to look at the different options for how a known graph can be described, including edgelists and adjacency matrices. Equipped with this understanding, we will then learn how to create graph objects in R and in Python. Unlike the larger examples which we will introduce in later chapters, the data and examples we will use in this chapter are simple and straightforward to work with. The focus here is to make sure that the basic structures and definitions are understood before proceeding further. Readers should not skip this chapter if they intend to fully understand the methods and procedures that will be introduced in later chapters.

2.1 Elementary graph theory

The way that graphs are created, stored and manipulated in data science languages like R and Python bears a strong resemblance to how they are

DOI: 10.1201/9781003266815-2

defined and studied algebraically. We will start this section with the general mathematical definition of a graph before we proceed to look at different varieties of graphs and different ways of representing graphs using data.

2.1.1 General definition of a graph

A graph G consists of two sets. The first set V is known as the *vertex* set or *node* set. The second set E is known as the *edge* set, and consists of pairs of elements of V. Given that a graph is made up of these two sets, we will often notate our graph as $G = (V, E)$. If two vertices appear as a pair in E, then those vertices are said to be *adjacent* or *connected* vertices.

Let's use an example to illustrate this definition. Figure 2.1 is a diagram of a graph G_{work} with four vertices representing four people. An edge connects two vertices if and only if those two people have worked together.

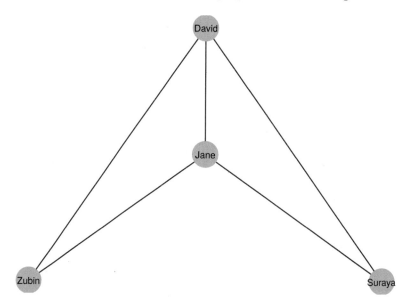

FIGURE 2.1: A graph G_{work} consisting of four people connected according to whether they have worked together

Our vertex set V for the graph G_{work} is:

$$V = \{\text{David}, \text{Suraya}, \text{Jane}, \text{Zubin}\}$$

Our edge set E for the graph G_{work} must be notated as pairs of elements of the vertex set V. You can notate this in many ways. One example for how you may notate the edge set is the formal set-theoretic notation:

$$E = \{\{\text{David}, \text{Zubin}\}, \{\text{David}, \text{Suraya}\}, \{\text{David}, \text{Jane}\},$$
$$\{\text{Jane}, \text{Zubin}\}, \{\text{Jane}, \text{Suraya}\}\}$$

An alternative notation could also be used such as:

$$E = \{\text{David} \longleftrightarrow \text{Zubin}, \text{David} \longleftrightarrow \text{Suraya}, \text{David} \longleftrightarrow \text{Jane},$$
$$\text{Jane} \longleftrightarrow \text{Zubin}, \text{Jane} \longleftrightarrow \text{Suraya}\}$$

It doesn't really matter how you choose to notate the vertex and edge sets as long as your notation contains all of the information required to construct the graph.

> **Thinking ahead:** If you already know how to load graphs in R or Python, you might want to take a look at a graph object now, and you will see how the object is structured and defined around the two set structure $G = (V, E)$. For example, try to create a graph from the data for the *Bridges of Königsberg* problem using the `koenigsberg` edgelist in the `onadata` package or downloaded from the internet at `https://ona-book.org/data/koenigsberg.csv`. Take a look at the vertex set or the edge set to see how they contain the structures discussed here.

The relationship that we are modeling using our edges in the graph G_{work} is reciprocal in nature. If David has worked with Zubin, then we automatically conclude that Zubin has worked with David. Therefore, there is no need for direction in the edges of G_{work}. We call such a graph an *undirected* graph. In an undirected graph, the order of the nodes in each pair in the edge set E is not relevant. For example, David $\longleftrightarrow$ Zubin is the same as Zubin $\longleftrightarrow$ David.

A graph where direction is important is called a *directed* graph. As an example, let's consider a graph G_{manage} with the same vertex set of four people but where an edge exists between two people if and only if the first person is the manager of the second person, as in Figure 2.2.

Clearly, direction matters in this graph, and therefore we may wish to notate the edge set E for G_{manage} as:

$$E = \{\text{Suraya} \longrightarrow \text{David}, \text{David} \longrightarrow \text{Zubin}, \text{David} \longrightarrow \text{Jane}\}$$

Note that it is still possible in a directed graph for the edges to point in both directions. While that is unlikely in the case of G_{manage} because the manager

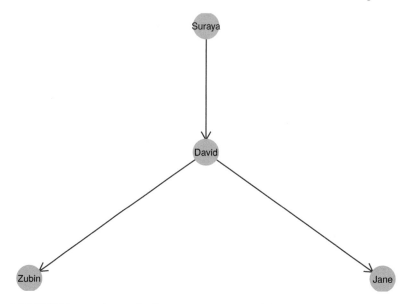

FIGURE 2.2: A graph G_{manage} consisting of four people connected according to whether one person manages another

relationship usually only operates in one direction, imagine another graph G_{like} where an edge exists between two people if and only if the first person has listed the second person as someone they like. It is perfectly possible for edges to exist in both directions between two vertices in a graph like this. For example, it may be that Jane likes Zubin and Zubin likes Jane. However, it is important to note that in such a graph, Zubin $\longrightarrow$ Jane and Jane $\longrightarrow$ Zubin are considered two *different* edges.

> **Thinking ahead:** The graphs G_{work} and G_{manage} are called **simple graphs**. A simple graph cannot have more than one edge between any two vertices, and cannot have any 'loop' edges from one vertex back to itself. As we are about to learn, not all graphs are simple graphs.

2.1.2 Types of graphs

Equipped with our general definition of a graph, we can now define different varieties of graphs by adding or allowing certain conditions on the edges of a general graph. There are many such varieties, but here are a few of the more common graph types.

A **multigraph** is a graph where multiple edges can occur between the same two vertices. Usually this occurs because the edges are defining different kinds of relationships. Travel routes are common examples of multigraphs, where each edge represents a different carrier. For example, Figure 2.3 is a graph of flights between the San Francisco (SFO), Philadelphia (PHL) and Tucson (TUS) airports based on a data set from December 2010. The graph is layered onto a map of the United States. Philadelphia to Tucson is not a common route and is only offered by one carrier in one direction, while there are multiple carriers operating in both directions between Philadelphia and San Francisco and between San Francisco and Tucson.

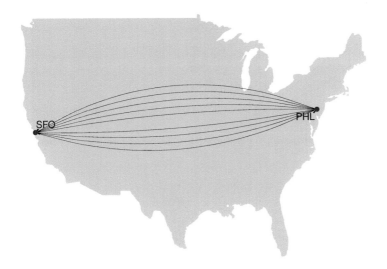

FIGURE 2.3: Carrier routes operating between three US airports in December 2010

Multigraphs are also commonly used when individuals or entities can be related to each other in different ways. For example, imagine if we were to combine our G_{work} and G_{manage} graphs from Section 2.1.1 into one single directed graph depicting both 'worked with' and 'manages' relationships. It might look like Figure 2.4.

Many large graphs used in practice are multigraphs, as they are built to capture many different types of relationships between many different types of entities. For example, a graph of an organizational network might contain vertices which represent individuals, organizational units and knowledge areas. Multiple different types of relationships could exist between individuals (such as 'worked with,' 'manages,' 'published with'), between individuals and organizational units (such as 'member of' or 'leader of'), between individuals and knowledge areas (such as 'affiliated with' or 'expert in') and all sorts of other possibilities.

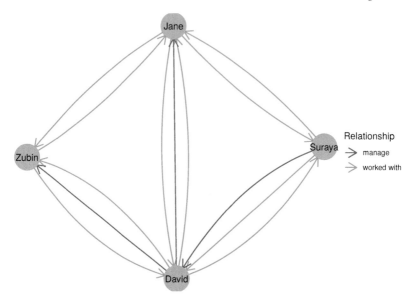

FIGURE 2.4: Graph depicting different types of relationships between individuals

Pseudographs are graphs which allow vertices to connect to themselves. Pseudographs occur when certain edges depict relationships that can occur between the same vertex. Imagine, for example, a graph G_{coffee} which takes our four characters from G_{work} in Section 2.1.1 and depicts who buys coffee for whom. If David goes to buy Zubin a coffee, there's a good chance he will also buy himself one in the process. Thus, you can expect the following edge set:

$$E = \{\text{David} \longrightarrow \text{Zubin}, \text{David} \longrightarrow \text{David}\}$$

An example of where pseudographs frequently occur might be in the analysis of financial transactions. Let's imagine that we have a graph of three vertices representing different companies A, B and C, where an edge represents a bank transfer from one company to another on a certain day. If a company holds multiple bank accounts, such a graph might look something like Figure 2.5. An edge which connects a vertex to itself is usually called a *loop*.

A **complete graph** is a graph where all pairs of vertices are connected by an edge. Let's go back to our four characters in G_{work} from Section 2.1.1. You may notice that only one pair of these characters have not worked together. Let's assume that we return a month later and update our graph, and it seems that Zubin and Suraya have now worked together. This means our graph becomes a complete graph as depicted in Figure 2.6.

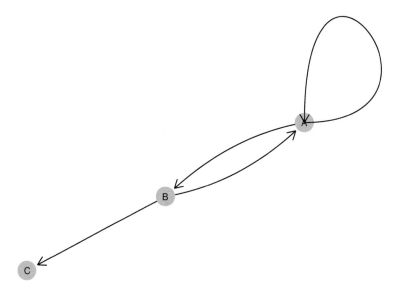

FIGURE 2.5: Pseudograph representing bank transfers between three companies A, B and C with a loop on vertex A

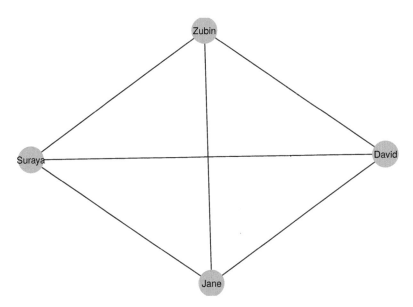

FIGURE 2.6: Updated version of G_{work} with one additional edge to make it a complete graph

Complete graphs are rare and not very useful in practice, since if you already know that a relationship exists between every pair of vertices, there is not a lot of reason to examine your graph or put it to any practical use. That said, in the field of Graph Theory, it can be important to prove that certain graphs are complete in order to support important theoretical results.

> **Thinking ahead:** While entire graphs which are complete are rarely useful in practice, it is often useful to identify sets of vertices inside graphs which together represent a *complete subgraph*. Such a group of vertices is known as a *clique*, and we will look at clique discovery in a later chapter.

Bipartite graphs are graphs that have two disjoint sets of vertices, such that no two vertices in the same set are connected. Imagine we were to add three new individuals from another department to our G_{work} vertices, and redefine our relationships so that an edge means that two individuals worked with each other across departments. Then the new graph G_{new} may look like Figure 2.7, with the distinct sets of vertices representing individuals in different departments.

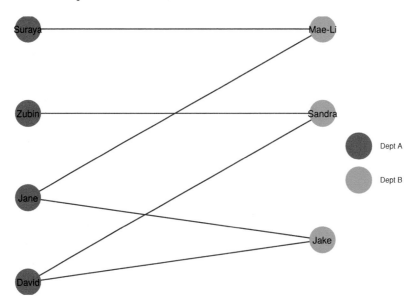

FIGURE 2.7: A bipartite graph G_{new} showing individuals in different departments A and B working across departments

Extending the idea of bipartite graphs, k-**partite graphs** are graphs which have k disjoint sets of vertices, such that no two vertices in the same set are connected.

Trees can be regarded as vertices connected by edges, and so trees are graphs. For example, our graph G_{manage} in Section 2.1.1 is a tree because it displays a hierarchical management structure between individuals. For a graph to be characterized as a tree, there needs to be *exactly* one path between any pair of vertices when viewed undirected.

Usually, trees are graphs where the edges represent some sort of hierarchical or nested relationship. Figure 2.8 shows a tree graph of the author's favorite boy bands, where an edge indicates that the vertex below is a member of the vertex above. It seems like five is the magic number for a great boy band.

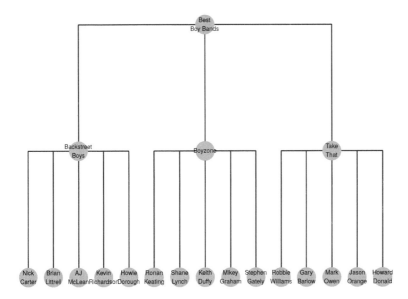

FIGURE 2.8: Membership of the exclusive class of the author's favorite boy bands can be represented as a tree graph

2.1.3 Vertex and edge properties

In Section 2.1.1 we learned that a graph $G = (V, E)$ consists of a vertex set V and an edge set E. These sets are the minimum elements of a graph—the vertices represent the entities in the graph and the edges represent the relationships between the entities.

We can enhance a graph to provide even richer information on the entities and on the relationships by giving our vertices and edges *properties*. A vertex property provides more specific information about a vertex and an edge property provides more specific information about the relationship between two vertices.

As an example, let's return to our directed pseudograph in Figure 2.5, which represents bank transfers between companies A, B, and C. In this graph, we only know from the edges that transfers took place, but we do not know how much money was involved in each transfer, and in what currency the transfer was made. If we wanted to capture this information, we could give each edge properties called `amt` and `cur` and store the transfer amount and currency in those edge properties. Similarly, we don't know a great deal about the companies represented by the vertices. Maybe we would like to know where they are located? If so, we can create a vertex property called `loc` and store the location in that vertex property.

Figure 2.9 shows this enhanced graph with the vertex and edge properties added diagramatically.

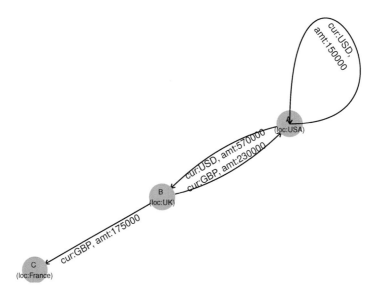

FIGURE 2.9: Graph of bank transfers between companies A, B and C with additional information stored as vertex and edge properties

Alternatively, we can notate properties as additional sets in our graph, ensuring that each entry is in the same order as the respective vertices or edges, as follows:

$$G = (V, E, V_{\text{loc}}, E_{\text{cur}}, E_{\text{amt}})$$
$$V = \{A, B, C\}$$
$$E = \{A \longrightarrow A, A \longrightarrow B, B \longrightarrow A, B \longrightarrow C\}$$
$$V_{\text{loc}} = \{\text{USA}, \text{UK}, \text{France}\}$$
$$E_{\text{cur}} = \{\text{USD}, \text{USD}, \text{GBP}, \text{GBP}\}$$
$$E_{\text{amt}} = \{150000, 570000, 230000, 175000\}$$

Note that the vertex property set V_{loc} has the same number of elements as V and the associated properties appear in the same order as the vertices of V. Note also a similar size and order for the edge property sets E_{cur} and E_{amt}. This notation system allows us to provide all the information we need in a reliable way for any number of vertex or edge properties.

> **Thinking ahead:** If you know how to, load up the graph of romantic relationships in the TV Series *Mad Men* using the `madmen_edgelist` data set from the `onadata` package or by downloading it from `https://ona-book.org/data/madmen_edgelist.csv`. Try to create a graph that contains the `Married` edge property and then try to query your graph to determine which relationships were marriage relationships.

One of the most common edge properties we will come across is **edge weight**. Weighted edges are edges which are given a numeric value to represent an important construct such as edge importance or connection strength. This can often be used to simplify otherwise complex graphs, and will be frequently used in calculations related to centrality and community. As an example, returning to our flights graph in Figure 2.3, instead of creating an edge for each carrier, we could simplify our graph by creating one edge per route and giving it a weight according to the number of carriers on that route. Such a graph would look like Figure 2.10.

2.1.4 Representations of graphs

So far in this chapter we have seen two common ways of representing a graph. The first, and most well-known, way is a diagram. The second is an algebraic structure $G = (V, E)$ consisting (at a minimum) of a vertex set V and an edge set E. As we discussed at the beginning of this chapter, diagrams are useful for visualizing und understanding small graphs, but less useful for storing graph data and working with large graphs. When working with graphs in the field of data science, the two most common sources of graph data will be edgelists and adjacency matrices.

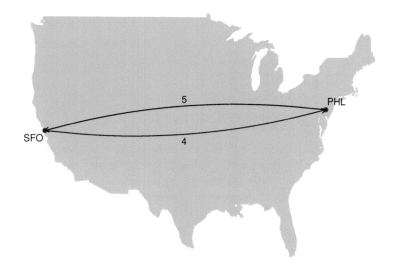

FIGURE 2.10: Simplifying the flights graph using weighted edges to represent the number of carriers on each route. Edge thickness represents weight.

An **edgelist** is the edge set E in our graph $G = (V, E)$. If we don't care about *isolates*[1], then our vertex set V can be derived directly from E. This means that the edgelist is all that is needed to build a graph provided you are happy to ignore isolates. It is common that an analyst is happy to ignore isolates because we are often only interested in the connections or relationships in the data. Let's look at an example.

Recall our edge set E in the graph $G_{\text{work}} = (V, E)$ from Section 2.1.1:

$$E = \{\text{David} \longleftrightarrow \text{Zubin}, \text{David} \longleftrightarrow \text{Suraya}, \text{Suraya} \longleftrightarrow \text{Jane},$$
$$\text{Jane} \longleftrightarrow \text{Zubin}, \text{Jane} \longleftrightarrow \text{Suraya}\}$$

Since by definition each edge in E must be a pair of vertices from V, and since we are not concerned about isolates (in fact, we know they don't exist in this case), we can obtain the vertex set V by simply listing the unique vertices from the pairs in E. Therefore, we can construct V to be

$$V = \{\text{David}, \text{Suraya}, \text{Jane}, \text{Zubin}\}$$

---

[1] Isolates, also known as singletons, are vertices which are not connected to any other vertices. Many real-life graphs contain isolates which will often be removed in order to better focus on connected components.

and we now have obtained everything we need for our graph from the edgelist.

Edgelists typically take the form of two columns of data, usually labelled 'from' and 'to' or 'source' and 'target.' Therefore, our edgelist for G_{work} would look like Table 2.1.

> **Playing around:** If you still have the *Bridges of Königsberg* data loaded as a graph in R or Python from earlier, you should be able to generate its edgelist easily. Try to find the right function to use to do this within your package of choice.

An **adjacency matrix** is a square matrix with the vertices indexing the rows and columns, and where the (i, j)-th entry of the matrix represents the number of edges from vertex i to vertex j. As an example, using our graph G_{work} again from Section 2.1.1, the adjacency matrix would look like this:

	David	Jane	Zubin	Suraya
David	0	1	1	1
Jane	1	0	1	1
Zubin	1	1	0	0
Suraya	1	1	0	0

Adjacency matrices are also commonly written in *sparse form*, without the use of zeros. For example:

	David	Jane	Zubin	Suraya
David	.	1	1	1
Jane	1	.	1	1
Zubin	1	1	.	.
Suraya	1	1	.	.

An adjacency matrix for an undirected graph like G_{work} is symmetrical on its diagonal, since the existence of an (i, j) edge automatically implies the existence of a (j, i) edge. However, a directed graph may not have a symmetrical

TABLE 2.1: Edgelist for G_{work}

from	to
David	Zubin
David	Suraya
David	Jane
Jane	Zubin
Jane	Suraya

adjacency matrix. Here is the adjacency matrix for our G_{manage} graph from Section 2.1.1.

	David	Jane	Zubin	Suraya
David	.	1	1	.
Jane	.	.	.	.
Zubin	.	.	.	.
Suraya	1	.	.	.

If a graph is a pseudograph, then the diagonal entries may be greater than zero, and multigraphs can have entries that are any non-negative integer. Here is the adjacency matrix for our flight network graph in Figure 2.3:

	SFO	PHL	TUS
SFO	.	4	4
PHL	5	.	1
TUS	2	.	.

> **Thinking ahead:** Again, with the *Bridges of Königsberg* graph loaded in R or Python, you can turn it into an adjacency matrix easily. Try to find the right function for this in your package of choice. Note that in packages like `networkx` in Python, the format is slightly different and is called an *adjacency list*.

2.2 Creating graphs in R

In this section we will use some of the examples from the previous section to learn how to create graph objects in R using the `igraph` package, and to examine the structure of these objects. A strong understanding of how graph objects are structured will make it easier for us to do more advanced manipulation and calculations involving graphs later in the book.

2.2.1 Creating a graph from an edgelist

Let's start by manually creating an edgelist for our G_{work} graph from Section 2.1.1 as a dataframe in R. We can see this edgelist in Table 2.1. Remember that G_{work} is an undirected graph, so we do not need to worry about edge direction when we create this edgelist.

```
(gwork_edgelist <- data.frame(
  from = c("David", "David", "David", "Jane", "Jane"),
  to = c("Zubin", "Suraya", "Jane", "Zubin", "Suraya")
))
```

```
##      from      to
## 1 David   Zubin
## 2 David  Suraya
## 3 David    Jane
## 4  Jane   Zubin
## 5  Jane  Suraya
```

This looks right. Now we are going to load the `igraph` package and use the function `graph_from_edgelist()` to create an undirected graph object from this edgelist. This function expects to receive the edgelist as a matrix, and so we will need to convert our `gwork_edgelist` dataframe to a matrix before we use it in the function.

```
library(igraph)
```

```
gwork_edgelist <- as.matrix(gwork_edgelist)
gwork <- igraph::graph_from_edgelist(el = gwork_edgelist,
                                     directed = FALSE)
```

We now have our G_{work} graph in memory. Before we go any further, let's take a look at it.

```
gwork
```

```
## IGRAPH 6f60680 UN-- 4 5 --
## + attr: name (v/c)
## + edges from 6f60680 (vertex names):
## [1] David --Zubin  David --Suraya David --Jane   Zubin --Jane   Suraya--Jane
```

Let's start with the string `UN--` on the first line of the output. This string describes the type of graph this is. The letter `U` denotes an undirected graph, and `N` denotes a graph with named vertices. The two other properties, which we will discover later, are currently not present and so are represented by the dashes `--`. Next we have the number of vertices (4) and edges (5), followed by two further dashes.

On the next line, the attributes of the graph are listed. In this case there is just one attribute `name`, which is a vertex attribute of character type—denoted by (v/c). Finally the edges of the graph are given using the vertex names. Note that there is no direction to these edges, so they are denoted with --.

Let's try the same thing but this time with our directed graph G_{manage} from Section 2.1.1.

```
gmanage_edgelist <- data.frame(
  from = c("Suraya", "David", "David"),
  to = c("David", "Zubin", "Jane")
)


gmanage_edgelist <- as.matrix(gmanage_edgelist)
(gmanage <- igraph::graph_from_edgelist(el = gmanage_edgelist,
                                        directed = TRUE))
```

```
## IGRAPH b6375e9 DN-- 4 3 --
## + attr: name (v/c)
## + edges from b6375e9 (vertex names):
## [1] Suraya->David David ->Zubin David ->Jane
```

We see a similar output to gwork, except we now have a directed graph, donated by D in the first line, and we see that the edges are now denoted with direction using ->.

2.2.2   Creating a graph from an adjacency matrix

Similarly, we can create a graph from data provided in an adjacency matrix. Let's manually create an adjacency matrix for our flights graph in Figure 2.3, and then we can use the graph_from_adjacency_matrix() function in igraph to create a graph object from the matrix.

```
# create 3x3 adjacency matrix
adj_flights <- matrix(c(0, 5, 2, 4, 0, 0, 4, 1, 0), nrow = 3, ncol = 3)
rownames(adj_flights) <- c("SFO", "PHL", "TUS")
colnames(adj_flights) <- rownames(adj_flights)

# create multigraph from adjacency matrix
(flightgraph <- igraph::graph_from_adjacency_matrix(
  adjmatrix = adj_flights,
  mode = "directed"
))
```

```
## IGRAPH f207d8e DN-- 3 16 --
## + attr: name (v/c)
## + edges from f207d8e (vertex names):
## [1] SFO->PHL SFO->PHL SFO->PHL SFO->PHL SFO->TUS SFO->TUS SFO->TUS SFO->TUS PHL->SFO PHL->SFO
## [11] PHL->SFO PHL->SFO PHL->SFO PHL->TUS TUS->SFO TUS->SFO
```

We see the expected directed multigraph with 3 vertices and 16 edges. If we wish to create the weighted graph in Figure 2.10, we add `weighted = TRUE` to the arguments.

```
# create weighted graph
(flightgraph_weighted <- igraph::graph_from_adjacency_matrix(
  adjmatrix = adj_flights,
  mode = "directed",
  weighted = TRUE
))
```

```
## IGRAPH b24dc33 DNW- 3 5 --
## + attr: name (v/c), weight (e/n)
## + edges from b24dc33 (vertex names):
## [1] SFO->PHL SFO->TUS PHL->SFO PHL->TUS TUS->SFO
```

We now see a graph with only 5 edges, but we see the addition of `W` in our graph type, indicating a weighted graph. We also see a new edge property of numeric type called `weight`. In situations where we want to simplify multiple edges to single edges without worrying about weight, the `simplify()` function in `igraph` works well. By default, `simplify()` will collapse multiple edges to a single edge and remove any loop edges from vertices to themselves in order to create a simple graph[2].

```
(flightgraph_simple <- igraph::simplify(
  flightgraph
))
```

```
## IGRAPH 298d46f DN-- 3 5 --
## + attr: name (v/c)
## + edges from 298d46f (vertex names):
## [1] SFO->PHL SFO->TUS PHL->SFO PHL->TUS TUS->SFO
```

2.2.3 Creating a graph from a dataframe

As we noted in Section 2.1.4, edgelists are usually sufficient to descibe a graph when isolates are not of concern. The function `graph_from_edgelist()` works

---

[2]If you only want to do one of these—such as remove loops but not multiples—you can set this in the function arguments using `remove.multiples = FALSE` or `remove.loops = FALSE`.

fine for this purpose, but it is lacking in flexibility when graphs contain isolates or where vertices have properties that you would ideally like to load on creation. The function `graph_from_data_frame()` allows you to create a more flexible graph directly from dataframes containing the required data.

Let's create our bipartite graph G_{new} from Figure 2.7 using this function. At a minimum, this function requires a dataframe of edges, and will also accept a dataframe of vertices if needed.

```
# edge dataframe
edge_df <- data.frame(
  from = c("David", "David", "Jane", "Jane", "Zubin", "Suraya"),
  to = c("Sandra", "Jake", "Mae-Li", "Jake", "Sandra", "Mae-Li")
)


# vertex dataframe
vertex_df <- data.frame(
  name = c("David", "Jane", "Zubin", "Suraya",
           "Sandra", "Jake", "Mae-Li"),
  Dept = c(rep("A", 4), rep("B", 3))
)


# create graph
(gnew <- igraph::graph_from_data_frame(
  d = edge_df,
  directed = FALSE,
  vertices = vertex_df
))
```

```
## IGRAPH 9a6fcf1 UN-- 7 6 --
## + attr: name (v/c), Dept (v/c)
## + edges from 9a6fcf1 (vertex names):
## [1] David --Sandra David --Jake  Jane --Mae-Li Jane --Jake  Zubin --Sandra Suraya--Mae-Li
```

> **Playing around:** The functions in this section are not the only functions in the `igraph` package that build graphs from data, but they are by far the most commonly used ones. By typing `?graph_from` in your R console and looking at the functions that autocomplete, you can see some of the other functions that build graphs from data. Try playing around with them if you are curious.

2.2.4 Adding properties to the vertices and edges

Vertex and edge properties can be added to a new graph at the point of creation or can be added progressively to an existing graph. To add properties at the same time as creating a graph, simply include these properties as columns in the edge or vertex dataframes in the `graph_from_data_frame()` function. Let's recreate our financial transaction graph including the edge and vertex properties from Figure 2.9.

```r
# dataframe of edges and properties
edge_transfers <- data.frame(
  from = c("A", "A", "B", "B"),
  to = c("A", "B", "A", "C"),
  cur = c("USD", "USD", "GBP", "GBP"),
  amt = c(150000, 570000, 230000, 175000)
)

# dataframe of vertices and properties
vertex_transfers <- data.frame(
  name = c("A", "B", "C"),
  loc = c("USA", "UK", "France")
)

# create graph
(gtransfers <- igraph::graph_from_data_frame(
  d = edge_transfers,
  directed = TRUE,
  vertices = vertex_transfers
))
```

```
## IGRAPH 6c01bfc DN-- 3 4 --
## + attr: name (v/c), loc (v/c), cur (e/c), amt (e/n)
## + edges from 6c01bfc (vertex names):
## [1] A->A A->B B->A B->C
```

We see that the additional edge properties cur and amt and the vertex property loc have been included in the graph. The codes immediately following these properties represent the property type and the data type. We can see that loc is a vertex property of character type (v/c), cur is an edge property of character type (e/c) and amt is an edge property of numeric type (e/n).

> **Playing around:** An arbitrary number of properties can be added
> to the vertices and edges of a graph. If you label one of the prop-
> erties as `weight` and if that property is numeric, this will change
> the type of your graph to W, a weighted graph. Try playing around
> with this by changing the name of the `amt` column to `weight` in
> `gtransfers`. Also, earlier we introduced the `simplify()` function in
> `igraph`. The `simplify()` function helps turn a graph with multiple
> edges or with loops into a simple graph. However, be careful when
> using this function if your graph has properties stored in the edges
> which you need to preserve. Play around with using this function on
> the `gtransfers` graph above and see what happens. Experiment with
> the `edge.attr.comb` function argument to try to control how the at-
> tributes are dealt with when collapsing the edges.

You can view the vertex and edge sets of a graph using the V() and E()
functions, respectively.

```
V(gtransfers)
```

```
## + 3/3 vertices, named, from 6c01bfc:
## [1] A B C
```

```
E(gtransfers)
```

```
## + 4/4 edges from 6c01bfc (vertex names):
## [1] A->A A->B D->A B->C
```

To see specific properties or attributes within the vertices or edges, the $
operator can be used.

```
V(gtransfers)$name
```

```
## [1] "A" "B" "C"
```

```
E(gtransfers)$amt
```

```
## [1] 150000 570000 230000 175000
```

Vertex and edge properties can be written into an existing graph directly
in this way, providing the properties have the correct length and order. As
an example, here is another way of creating our weighted flights graph from
Figure 2.10.

```r
# create unweighted graph from routes edgelist
edge_routes <- data.frame(
  from = c("SFO", "SFO", "PHL", "PHL", "TUS"),
  to = c("PHL", "TUS", "SFO", "TUS", "SFO")
)

edge_routes <- as.matrix(edge_routes)

flightsgraph <- igraph::graph_from_edgelist(
  el = edge_routes,
  directed = TRUE
)

# add weights as an edge property
E(flightsgraph)$weight <- c(4, 4, 5, 1, 2)

# view flightsgraph
flightsgraph
```

```
## IGRAPH 499227a DNW- 3 5 --
## + attr: name (v/c), weight (e/n)
## + edges from 499227a (vertex names):
## [1] SFO->PHL SFO->TUS PHL->SFO PHL->TUS TUS->SFO
```

We see a weighted graph has been created by adding a `weight` property to the edges of an unweighted graph.

A bipartite graph can be created by giving the vertices a `type` property according to the two disjoint sets of vertices. Let's use our G_{new} bipartite graph again as an example, which we generated earlier as the gnew object. In our vertex set, we can define our `type` property to be the same as the department property `Dept`.

```r
V(gnew)$type <- V(gnew)$Dept

gnew
```

```
## IGRAPH 9a6fcf1 UN-B 7 6 --
## + attr: name (v/c), Dept (v/c), type (v/c)
## + edges from 9a6fcf1 (vertex names):
## [1] David --Sandra David --Jake  Jane --Mae-Li Jane --Jake  Zubin --Sandra Suraya--Mae-Li
```

We can see that our graph gnew now has the final of the four graph types: B meaning bipartite.

> **Playing around:** Hopefully you can now see that there are many ways to construct your graph. Try using the `graph_from_data_frame()` function to create gnew as a bipartite graph at the point of creation.

2.3 Creating graphs in Python

In this book we will use the `networkx` package in Python to create graphs. A version of the `igraph` package is also available in Python, but `networkx` contains more convenient functions for building graphs from existing data.

2.3.1 Creating a graph from an edgelist

A graph can be constructed from an edgelist in a Python dictionary. Let's create our undirected graph G_{work} from Section 2.1.1.

```python
import pandas as pd
import networkx as nx

# create edgelist as dict
gwork_edgelist = dict(
  David = ["Zubin", "Suraya", "Jane"],
  Jane = ["Zubin", "Suraya"]
)

# create graph dict
gwork = nx.Graph(gwork_edgelist)
```

To view the edges or vertices/nodes, these can be seen as attributes of the gwork object.

```python
# see vertices as list
list(gwork.nodes)
```

```
## ['David', 'Jane', 'Zubin', 'Suraya']
```

```python
# list some edges
list(gwork.edges)[0:3]
```

```
## [('David', 'Zubin'), ('David', 'Suraya'), ('David', 'Jane')]
```

A graph can also be constructed from an edgelist in a Pandas DataFrame. By default, the edgelist needs to have the columns `source` and `target`[3].

```
gwork_edgelist=dict(
  source=["David", "David", "David", "Jane", "Jane"],
  target=["Zubin", "Suraya", "Jane", "Zubin", "Suraya"]
)

#create edgelist as Pandas DataFrame
gwork_edgelist = pd.DataFrame(gwork_edgelist)

# create graph from Pandas DataFrame
gwork = nx.from_pandas_edgelist(gwork_edgelist)
```

By default these functions use a `Graph()` class to create an undirected graph. Various methods exist to check the type of graph. For example:

```
gwork.is_directed()

## False

gwork.is_multigraph()

## False
```

To create our directed graph G_{manage}, we use the `DiGraph()` class.

```
gmanage_edgelist=dict(
  David=["Zubin", "Jane"],
  Suraya=["David"]
)

# create directed graph
gmanage=nx.DiGraph(gmanage_edgelist)

# check edges
list(gmanage.edges)

## [('David', 'Zubin'), ('David', 'Jane'), ('Suraya', 'David')]
```

---

[3]These columns can also be named differently and identified via the `source` and `target` arguments in the `from_pandas_edgelist()` function.

```
# check directed
gmanage.is_directed()
```

```
## True
```

2.3.2   Creating a graph from an adjacency matrix

The function `from_numpy_matrix()` allows the construction of a graph from an adjacency matrix created using `numpy`. Let's construct our directed multigraph for flight carriers from Figure 2.3 in this way.

```
import numpy as np
```

```
# create adjacency matrix
adj_flights = np.reshape((0,4,4,5,0,1,2,0,0), (3,3))
```

```
# generate directed multigraph
multiflights = nx.from_numpy_matrix(adj_flights, parallel_edges=True,
create_using=nx.MultiDiGraph())
```

```
# name nodes
label_mapping = {0: "SFO", 1: "PHL", 2: "TUS"}
multiflights = nx.relabel_nodes(multiflights, label_mapping)
```

```
# check some edges
list(multiflights.edges)[0:3]
```

```
## [('SFO', 'PHL', 0), ('SFO', 'PHL', 1), ('SFO', 'PHL', 2)]
```

To generate the graph with only single weighted edges as in Figure 2.10, simply change the `parallel_edges` argument and use the `DiGraph()` class. This will map the entries in the matrix to a `weight` edge attribute.

```
# create with single weighted edges
multiflights = nx.from_numpy_matrix(adj_flights, parallel_edges=False,
create_using=nx.DiGraph())
```

```
# name nodes
label_mapping = {0: "SFO", 1: "PHL", 2: "TUS"}
multiflights = nx.relabel_nodes(multiflights, label_mapping)
```

```
# check edges
list(multiflights.edges)
```

```
## [('SFO', 'PHL'), ('SFO', 'TUS'), ('PHL', 'SFO'), ('PHL', 'TUS'),
   ('TUS', 'SFO')]

# check weights of edges
[multiflights.edges[i]['weight'] for i in list(multiflights.edges)]

## [4, 4, 5, 1, 2]
```

2.3.3   Adding vertex and edge properties to a graph

The easiest way to add attributes to the vertices and edges is to use the
`set_node_attributes()` and `set_edge_attributes()` functions, respectively.
Vertex/node attributes must be passed as a dict with the nodes as keys. Let's
build our financial transactions graph as in Figure 2.9.

```
# create dict of edgelist
transfer_edgelist = dict(
  A = ["A", "B"],
  B = ["A", "C"]
)

# create directed graph
transfer=nx.DiGraph(transfer_edgelist)

# view vertices
list(transfer.nodes)


## ['A', 'B', 'C']

# add attribute loc to vertices
loc_attributes = dict(A = "USA", B = "UK", C = "France")
nx.set_node_attributes(G = transfer, name = "loc",
values = loc_attributes)

# check
[transfer.nodes[i]['loc'] for i in list(transfer.nodes)]


## ['USA', 'UK', 'France']
```

Note that multiple attributes can be set at once by passing a dict of dicts.

```
# view edges
list(transfer.edges)
```

```
## [('A', 'A'), ('A', 'B'), ('B', 'A'), ('B', 'C')]
```

```
# add attributes to edges
transfer_attributes = {
  ('A', 'A'): {"cur": "USD", "amt": 150000},
  ('A', 'B'): {"cur": "USD", "amt": 570000},
  ('B', 'A'): {"cur": "GBP", "amt": 230000},
  ('B', 'C'): {"cur": "GBP", "amt": 175000}
}
```

```
# set edge attributes
nx.set_edge_attributes(G = transfer, values = transfer_attributes)
```

```
# check
[transfer.edges[i]['cur'] for i in list(transfer.edges)]
```

```
## ['USD', 'USD', 'GBP', 'GBP']
```

```
[transfer.edges[i]['amt'] for i in list(transfer.edges)]
```

```
## [150000, 570000, 230000, 175000]
```

While this may look tedious and manual, as we move into adding common properties like node centrality or edge weight to graphs, we will find these to be easy to set because of built-in functions that automatically index their output by the vertices or edges. For example, we have already seen in Section 2.3.2 that the function `from_numpy_matrix()` automatically sets a weight according to the number of edges when we set the argument `parallel_edges` to `False`. Also, if you have edge properties as columns in your Pandas edgelist, you can automatically import them into your graph by setting `edge_attr = True` in the `from_pandas_edgelist()` function in `networkx`.

> **Playing around:** As with the `igraph` package in R, the `networkx` package in Python contains a whole host of ways to import data into a graph. While the methods outlined here are likely to be the most common, it's worth taking a look at some of the other functions such as `from_dict_of_dicts()` or `from_dict_of_lists()` to see what is available to you.

2.4 Learning exercises

2.4.1 Discussion questions

1. Describe the two sets that make up a graph.

2. If a graph has no vertices, then it has no edges. Why is this statement true? Is the converse of this statement true?

For each of the following real-world cases, what kind of graph would be the best choice: a pseudograph, multigraph, k-partite graph or tree? Also state whether it should be directed or undirected.

3. A graph of academic collaboration where vertices represent people and an edge represents a published paper with both vertices as authors.

4. A graph where each vertex represents a soccer player and an edge exists if both vertices have played on the same team at the same time.

5. A graph where the vertices are geographical cities, countries and continents and an edge exists if one vertex is geographically located in another.

6. A graph where the vertices are a group of colleagues and where an edge exists between vertex A and vertex B if at least one email message has been sent from colleague A to colleague B.

7. A graph where the vertices are world cities grouped by continent, and an edge exists between two cities if an intercontinental flight exists between those cities.

8. What criteria must a graph satisfy to be called a tree?

9. Give two different ways to construct the graph described in Question 3 above.

10. Can you think of three things in your everyday life that could be represented by graphs? What would the vertices and edges represent? What kinds of graph would be best for each case?

2.4.2   Data exercises

Load the `koenigsberg` edgelist from the `onadata` package or load it as a dataframe from the internet[4]. This is the edgelist for the *Bridges of Königsberg* problem we looked at in Chapter 1. Use your software of choice for the following exercises.

1. Create a graph object using this edgelist. Ensure that it is undirected.
2. By exploring the graph object you just created, determine how many vertices and edges are in this graph. Does this make sense given the original problem tackled by Euler?
3. Obtain a list of the names of the vertices in this graph.
4. Find a function or method in your graph package to create the adjacency matrix or adjacency list for this graph. Check the output to see if it makes sense.

Load the `pizza` data set from the `onadata` package or load it as a dataframe from the internet[5]. This data set represents requests made by Reddit users on a thread called *Random Acts of Pizza* or *ROAP*, and is part of a larger data set used for research purposes[6]. The `requester` column represents users who made requests for pizza, and the `responder` column represents users who read the request and responded to the request by giving pizza[7]. Other columns represent the request ID and data on the requester at the time the request was made.

5. Use an appropriate method to create a graph object using the `requester` and `responder` columns in this data set.
6. Use the information contained in the graph object to determine how many pizza requests were fulfilled.
7. Determine using the information in the graph whether anyone fulfilled more than one pizza request.
8. Using an appropriate method, add the other columns in the `pizza` data set as edge properties.
9. Use the edge properties of your graph object to determine which request ID had the largest number of requester votes.
10. Use the edge properties of your graph object to determine which request ID had the largest number of requester subreddits.

---

[4] https://ona-book.org/data/koenigsberg.csv
[5] https://ona-book.org/data/pizza.csv
[6] Althoff et al. (2014)
[7] This data set is only a small subset of the full data set, which included many requests which were not fulfilled. As we all know, a free pizza is a rare thing!

3

Visualizing Graphs

Now that we have learned how to define and store graphs, it's time to take a look at ways of visualizing them. As we noted in earlier chapters, visualization is an important tool that can make graphs and networks real to others. But visualizations are not always effective. Graphs can be laid out and visualized in many different ways, and only some of them will effectively communicate the inferences or conclusions that the analyst is inviting others to draw about the phenomena being represented in the graph.

While a graph is made up of vertices and edges, there are many other factors that will impact how the graph appears. First, there are cosmetic matters of vertex size, edge thickness, whether or not vertices and edges are labelled, colored and so on. Second, there are matters of layout—that is, where we position vertices relative to each other in our visualization. As an example, recall our simple four vertex undirected graph G_{work} from Section 2.1.1. Figure 3.1 shows two different ways of visualizing this graph, where we make different choices on vertex size and on graph layout[1].

The choices of how to visualize a graph are wide and varied, and we will not be covering every single permutation and combination of cosmetics and layouts in the chapter. Instead, we will focus on learning how to control the most common options. This will equip readers well not just for work we do later in this book, but also for when they need to visualize graphs they create as part of their work or study. We will also cover a variety of graph visualization programming package options in R and Python.

In this chapter we will work with a relatively famous graph known as *Zachary's Karate Club*. This graph originates from a piece of research on a karate club by social anthropologist Wayne W. Zachary[2], and is commonly used as an example of a social network in many teaching situations today. The graph contains 34 vertices representing different individuals or actors. The karate instructor is labelled as 'Mr Hi.' The club administrator is labelled as 'John A.' The other 32 actors are labelled as 'Actor 2' through 'Actor 33.' Zachary

---

[1]The right-hand visualization uses the degree centrality of the vertices to scale their size—we will learn about this later. The layouts are also different. The left-hand visualization uses a grid layout, while the right-hand visualization uses a metric multidimensional scaling (MDS) layout.

[2]Zachary (1977)

DOI: 10.1201/9781003266815-3

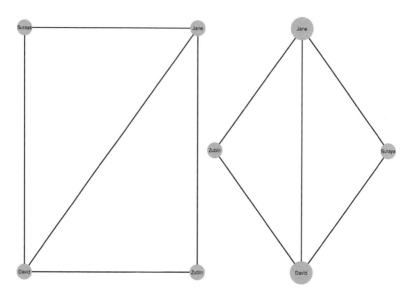

FIGURE 3.1: Two different ways of visualizing the G_{work} graph

studied the social interactions between the members outside the club meetings, and during his study a conflict arose in the club that eventually led to the group splitting into two: one group forming a new club around the instructor Mr Hi and the other group dispersing to find new clubs or to give up karate completely. In this graph, an edge between two vertices means that the two individuals interacted socially outside the club.

3.1 Visualizing graphs in R

Let's load the karate graph edgelist in R from the onadata package or from the internet[3], and check the first few rows.

```
# get karate edgelist data as dataframe
karate_edgelist <- read.csv("https://ona-book.org/data/karate.csv")

head(karate_edgelist)
```

---

[3]https://ona-book.org/data/karate.csv

```
##      from       to
## 1 Mr Hi  Actor 2
## 2 Mr Hi  Actor 3
## 3 Mr Hi  Actor 4
## 4 Mr Hi  Actor 5
## 5 Mr Hi  Actor 6
## 6 Mr Hi  Actor 7
```

Now let's use our edgelist to create an undirected graph object in igraph.

```
library(igraph)

(karate <- igraph::graph_from_data_frame(karate_edgelist,
                                         directed = FALSE))
```

```
## IGRAPH 6c5eef9 UN-- 34 78 --
## + attr: name (v/c)
## + edges from 6c5eef9 (vertex names):
##  [1] Mr Hi --Actor 2  Mr Hi --Actor 3  Mr Hi --Actor 4  Mr Hi --Actor 5  Mr Hi --Actor 6
##  [6] Mr Hi --Actor 7  Mr Hi --Actor 8  Mr Hi --Actor 9  Mr Hi --Actor 11 Mr Hi --Actor 12
## [11] Mr Hi --Actor 13 Mr Hi --Actor 14 Mr Hi --Actor 18 Mr Hi --Actor 20 Mr Hi --Actor 22
## [16] Mr Hi --Actor 32 Actor 2--Actor 3  Actor 2--Actor 4  Actor 2--Actor 8  Actor 2--Actor 14
## [21] Actor 2--Actor 18 Actor 2--Actor 20 Actor 2--Actor 22 Actor 2--Actor 31 Actor 3--Actor 4
## [26] Actor 3--Actor 8  Actor 3--Actor 9  Actor 3--Actor 10 Actor 3--Actor 14 Actor 3--Actor 28
## [31] Actor 3--Actor 29 Actor 3--Actor 33 Actor 4--Actor 8  Actor 4--Actor 13 Actor 4--Actor 14
## [36] Actor 5--Actor 7  Actor 5--Actor 11 Actor 6--Actor 7  Actor 6--Actor 11 Actor 6--Actor 17
## + ... omitted several edges
```

We can see that we have an undirected graph with 34 named vertices and 78 edges.

3.1.1 Native plotting in igraph

The igraph package allows simple plotting of graphs using the plot() function. The function works instantly with an igraph object, using default values for its various arguments. As a starting point, we will use all of the default values except for the layout of the graph. We will set the layout of the plot initially to be a random layout, which will randomly allocate the vertices to different positions. Figure 3.2 shows this default plot for our karate network.

```
# set seed for reproducibility
set.seed(123)

# create random layout
l <- layout_randomly(karate)
```

```
# plot with random layout
plot(karate, layout = l)
```

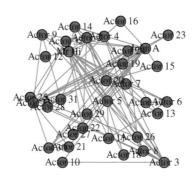

FIGURE 3.2: Basic default plot of `karate` network

Playing around: The previous code chunk fixes the positioning of the vertices on our `karate` graph. By setting a random seed, we can ensure the same random numbers are generated each time so that this precise plot is repeatable and reproducible. Then the `layout_randomly()` function calculates random x and y coordinates for the vertices, and when we use it in the `plot()` function, it assigns those coordinates in the plot. As we learn about layouts later in the chapter, we will use this technique a lot. If you like, try playing around with other layouts now. A couple of examples are `layout_with_sugiyama()` and `layout_with_dh()`. Remember to always set the same seed whenever you generate a graph layout calculation to ensure that your visualization in reproducible by yourself or others.

Looking at Figure 3.2, we note that the labeling of the vertices is somewhat obtrusive and unhelpful to the clarity of the graph. This will be a common problem with default graph plotting, and with a large number of vertices the plot can easily turn into a messy cloud of overlapping labels.

Vertex labels can be adjusted via properties of the vertices. The most common properties adjusted are as follows:

- `label`: The text of the label
- `label.family`: The font family to be used (default is 'serif')
- `label.font`: The font style, where 1 is plain (default), 2 is bold, 3 is italic, 4 is bold and italic and 5 is symbol font
- `label.cex`: The size of the label text
- `label.color`: The color of the label text
- `label.dist`: The distance of the label from the vertex, where 0 is centered on the vertex (default) and 1 is beside the vertex
- `label.degree`: The angle at which the label will display relative to the center of the vertex, in radians. The default is `-pi/4`

Let's try to change the vertex labels so that they only display for Mr Hi and for John A. Let's also change the size, color and font family of the labels. The output can be seen in Figure 3.3.

```
# only store a label if Mr Hi or John A
V(karate)$label <- ifelse(V(karate)$name %in% c("Mr Hi", "John A"),
                          V(karate)$name,
                          "")

# change label font color, size and font family
# (selected font family needs to be installed on system)
V(karate)$label.color <- "black"
V(karate)$label.cex <- 0.8
V(karate)$label.family <- "arial"

plot(karate, layout = l)
```

Now that we have cleaned up the label situation, we may wish to change the appearance of the vertices. Here are the most commonly used vertex properties which allow this:

- `size`: The size of the vertex
- `color`: The fill color of the vertex
- `frame.color`: The border color of the vertex
- `shape`: The shape of the vertex; multiple shape options are supported including `circle`, `square`, `rectangle` and `none`

We may wish to use different vertex shapes and colors for our actors compared to Mr Hi and John A. This is how this would be done, with the results in Figure 3.4.

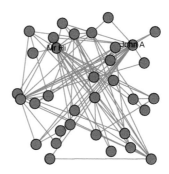

FIGURE 3.3: Adjusting label appearance through changing vertex properties

```
# different colors and shapes for Mr Hi and and John A
V(karate)$color <- ifelse(V(karate)$name %in% c("Mr Hi", "John A"),
                          "lightblue",
                          "pink")

V(karate)$shape <- ifelse(V(karate)$name %in% c("Mr Hi", "John A"),
                          "square",
                          "circle")


plot(karate, layout = l)
```

In a similar way, edges can be changed through adding or editing edge properties. Here are some common edge properties that are used to change the edges in an igraph plot:

- color: The color of the edge
- width: The width of the edge
- arrow.size: The size of the arrow in a directed edge
- arrow.width: The width of the arrow in a directed edge
- arrow.mode: Whether edges should direct forward (>), backward (<) or both (<>)

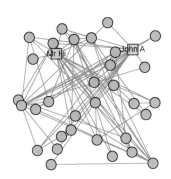

FIGURE 3.4: Adjusting vertex appearance through changing vertex properties

- lty: Line type of edges, with numerous options including solid, dashed, dotted, dotdash and blank
- curved: The amount of curvature to apply to the edge, with zero (default) as a straight edge, negative numbers bending clockwise and positive bending anti-clockwise

Note that edges, like vertices, can also have a label property and various label settings like label.cex and label.family. Let's adjust our karate graph to have blue dashed edges, with the result in Figure 3.5.

```
# change color and linetype of all edges
E(karate)$color <- "blue"
E(karate)$lty <- "dashed"

plot(karate, layout = l)
```

> **Playing around:** Usually, getting your graph looking the way you want takes some trial and error and some playing around with its properties. Try further adjusting the karate graph using some of the other properties listed.

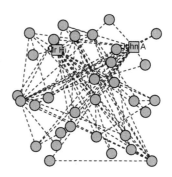

FIGURE 3.5: Adjusting edge appearance through changing edge properties

3.1.2   Graph layouts

The layout of a graph determines the precise position of its vertices on a
2-dimensional plane or in 3-dimensional space. Layouts are themselves algorithms that calculate vertex positions based on properties of the graph. Different layouts work for different purposes, for example to visually identify
communities in a graph, or just to make the graph look pleasant. In Section
3.1.1, we used a random layout for our karate graph. Now let's look at common alternative layouts. Layouts are used by multiple plotting packages, but
we will explore them using igraph base plotting capabilities here.

There are two ways to add a layout to a graph in igraph. If you want to keep the
graph object separate from the layout, you can create the layout and use it as
an argument in the plot() function, like we did for Figure 3.2. Alternatively,
you can assign a layout to a graph object by making it a property of the
graph. You should only do this if you intend to stick permanently with your
chosen layout and do not intend to experiment. You can use the add_layout_()
function to achieve this. For example, this would create a karate graph with
a grid layout.

```
# check whether existing karate graph has a layout property
karate$layout
```

```
## NULL
```

```
# assign grid layout as a graph property
set.seed(123)
karate_grid <- igraph::add_layout_(karate, on_grid())

# check a few lines of the 'layout' property
head(karate_grid$layout)

##       [,1] [,2]
## [1,]    0    0
## [2,]    1    0
## [3,]    2    0
## [4,]    3    0
## [5,]    4    0
## [6,]    5    0
```

We can see that our new graph object has a layout property. Note that running add_layout_() on a graph that already has a layout property will by default overwrite the previous layout unless you set the argument overwrite = FALSE.

As well as the random layout demonstrated in Figure 3.2, common shape layouts include as_star(), as_tree(), in_circle(), on_grid() and on_sphere(). For example, Figure 3.6 shows the circle layout for our karate network, and Figure 3.7 shows the sphere layout.

```
# circle layout
set.seed(123)
circ <- layout_in_circle(karate)
plot(karate, layout = circ)


# sphere layout
set.seed(123)
sph <- layout_on_sphere(karate)
plot(karate, layout = sph)
```

Thinking ahead: Notice how the circle and sphere layouts position Mr Hi and John A very close to each other. This is an indication that the layout algorithms have established something in common between these two individuals based on the properties of the graph. This is something we will cover in a later chapter, but if you want to explore ahead, and you know how to, calculate some centrality measures for the vertices in the karate graph—for example degree centrality and betweenness centrality.

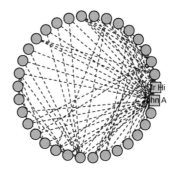

FIGURE 3.6: Circle layout of the karate graph

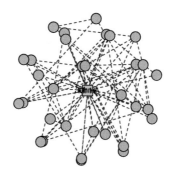

FIGURE 3.7: Sphere layout of the karate graph

Force-directed graph layouts are extremely popular, as they are aesthetically pleasing and they help visualize communities of vertices quite effectively, especially in graphs with low to moderate edge complexity. These algorithms emulate physical models like Hooke's law to attract connected vertices together, at the same time applying repelling forces to all pairs of vertices to try to keep as much space as possible between them. This calculation is an iterative process where vertex positions are calculated again and again until equilibrium is reached[4]. The result is usually a layout where connected vertices are closer together and where edge lengths are approximately equal.

For Zachary's Karate Club study, which was a study of connection and community, we can imagine that a force-directed layout would be a good choice of visualization, and we will find that this is the case for many other network graphs we study. There are several different implementations of force-directed algorithms available. Perhaps the most popular of these is the Fruchterman-Reingold algorithm. Figure 3.8 shows our `karate` network with the layout generated by the Fruchterman-Reingold algorithm, and we can see clear communities in the karate club oriented around Mr Hi and John A.

```
# F-R algorithm
set.seed(123)
fr <- layout_with_fr(karate)
plot(karate, layout = fr)
```

The Kamada-Kawai algorithm and the GEM algorithm are also commonly used force-directed algorithms and they produce similar types of community structures as in Figures 3.9 and 3.10, respectively.

```
# K-K algorithm
set.seed(123)
kk <- layout_with_kk(karate)
plot(karate, layout = kk)
```

```
# GEM algorithm
set.seed(123)
gem <- layout_with_gem(karate)
plot(karate, layout = gem)
```

As well as force-directed and shape-oriented layout algorithms, several alternative approaches to layout calculations are also available. `layout_with_dh()` uses a simulated annealing algorithm developed for nice graph drawing, and `layout_with_mds()` generates vertex coordinates through multidimensional

---

[4]Note that this means that the process is usually computationally expensive on large graphs and can easily freeze up your machine if you are not careful.

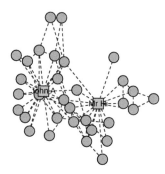

FIGURE 3.8: Force-directed layout of the `karate` graph according to the Fruchterman-Reingold algorithm

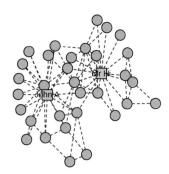

FIGURE 3.9: Force-directed layout of the `karate` graph according to the Kamada-Kawai algorithm

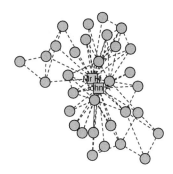

FIGURE 3.10: Force-directed layout of the `karate` graph according to the GEM algorithm

scaling based on shortest path distance (which we will look at in a later chapter). `layout_with_sugiyama()` is suitable for directed graphs and minimizes edge crossings by introducing bends on edges[5].

Finally, there are three layout algorithms that are suited for large graphs with many thousands or even millions of edges. One of the biggest problems with visualizing large graphs is the potential for 'hairballs'—that is, clumps of connected nodes that are so dense they cannot be usefully visualized. `layout_with_lgl()` uses the Large Graph Layout algorithm which tries to identify clusters of vertices and position the clusters before positioning the individual vertices to minimize the chance of hairballs, while still adhering to the principles of force-directed networks. `layout_with_drl()` and `layout_with_graphopt()` also use efficient force-directed algorithms which scale well on large graphs.

---

[5]The multigraph visualization in Figure 2.4 was generated using the Sugiyama layout algorithm.

Playing around: Try laying out the karate graph using these various algorithms and observe the different appearances. If you are interested in experimenting with a larger graph, and you have enough computing power that it won't freeze your machine, load the wikivote edgelist from the onadata package, or download it from the internet[6]. This network represents votes from Wikipedia members for other members to be made administrators. Create a directed graph object, and lay it out using layout_with_graphopt(). To help with your visualization, remove the vertex labels, set the node size to 0.5 and set the edge arrow size to 0.1. When you plot this, you should see a great example of a hairball, as in Figure 3.11.

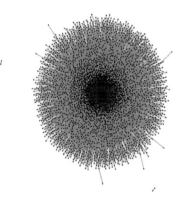

FIGURE 3.11: Example of a hairball generated by trying to visualize a large network of Wikipedia votes for administrators

In the absence of any information on layout, the plot() function in igraph will choose an appropriate layout using a logic determined by layout_nicely(). If the graph already has a layout attribute, it will use this layout. Otherwise, if the vertices have x and y attributes, it will use these as vertex coordinates. Failing both of these, layout_with_fr() will be used if the graph has fewer than 1,000 vertices, and layout_with_drl() will be used if the graph has more than 1,000 vertices. Thus, the plot defaults to a form of force-directed layout unless the graph attributes suggest otherwise.

---

[6]https://ona-book.org/data/wikivote.csv

3.1.3 Static plotting with `ggraph`

The `ggraph` package is developed for those who enjoy working with the more general `ggplot2` package, which is a very popular plotting package in R[7]. As with `ggplot2`, `ggraph` provides a grammar for building graph visualizations. While the native capabilities of `igraph` will suffice in R for most static graph visualizations, `ggraph` could be considered an additional option for those who prefer to use it. It also integrates well with `ggplot2` which allows further layers to be added to the graph visualization, such as a greater variety of node shapes and the ability to layer networks onto geographic maps with relative ease.

To build an elementary graph using `ggraph`, we start with an `igraph` object and a layout, and we then progressively add node and edge properties as well as themes and other layers if required. To illustrate, let's generate a relatively basic visualization of our `karate` graph using `ggraph` as in Figure 3.12. Note that it is customary to add the edges before the vertices so that the vertices are the top layer in the plot.

```
library(igraph)
library(ggraph)

# get karate edgelist
karate_edgelist <- read.csv("https://ona-book.org/data/karate.csv")

# create graph object
karate <- igraph::graph_from_data_frame(karate_edgelist,
                                          directed = FALSE)

# set seed for reproducibility
set.seed(123)

# visualise using ggraph with fr layout
ggraph(karate, layout = "fr") +
  geom_edge_link() +
  geom_node_point()
```

This is not particularly appealing. However, we can play with properties to improve the appearance, and we can move to a minimal theme to remove the grey background and add a title if we wish, as in Figure 3.13.

```
set.seed(123)
ggraph(karate, layout = "fr") +
  geom_edge_link(color = "grey", alpha = 0.7) +
```

---
[7]To learn `ggplot2` as a foundational package, Wickham (2016) is highly recommended.

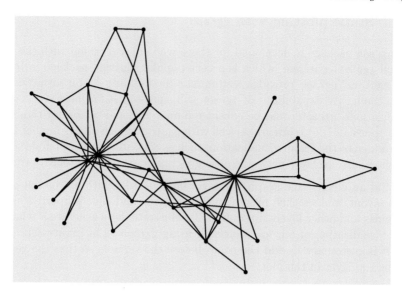

FIGURE 3.12: Elementary visualization of `karate` graph using `ggraph` and the Fruchterman-Reingold algorithm

```
geom_node_point(color = "blue", size = 5) +
theme_void() +
labs(title = "Zachary's Karate Club Network")
```

Like in `ggplot2`, if we want to associate a property of the nodes or edges with a property of the plot, we can use aesthetic mappings. For example, let's give Mr Hi and John A the property of "leader" in our graph, and then ask `ggraph` to color the nodes by this property, as in Figure 3.14.

```
V(karate)$leader <- ifelse(
  V(karate)$name %in% c("Mr Hi", "John A"), 1, 0
)

set.seed(123)
ggraph(karate, layout = "fr") +
  geom_edge_link(color = "grey", alpha = 0.7) +
  geom_node_point(aes(color = as.factor(leader)), size = 5,
                  show.legend = FALSE) +
  theme_void() +
  labs(title = "Zachary's Karate Club Network")
```

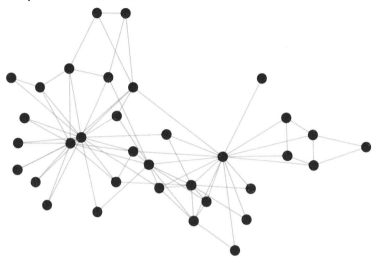

FIGURE 3.13: Elementary visualization of `karate` graph using node and edge geom functions

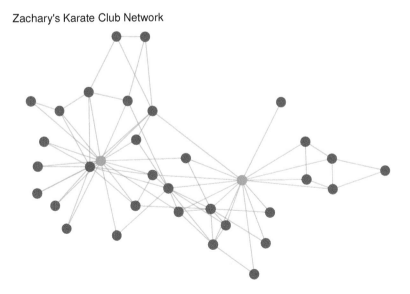

FIGURE 3.14: `karate` graph with `leader` property used as an aesthetic

As a further example of using ggraph, let's look at a data set collected during a study of workplace interactions in France in 2015[8]. Load the workfrance_edgelist and workfrance_vertices data sets from the onadata package or download them from the internet[9]. In this study, employees of a company wore wearable devices to triangulate their location in the building, and edges were defined as any situation where two employees were sharing the same spatial location. The edgelist contains from and to columns for the edges, as well as a mins column representing the total minutes spent co-located during the study[10]. The vertex list contains ground-truth data on the department of each employee. We will create a basic visualization of this using ggraph in Figure 3.15.

```
# get edgelist with mins property
workfrance_edgelist <- read.csv(
  "https://ona-book.org/data/workfrance_edgelist.csv"
)


# get vertex set with dept property
workfrance_vertices <- read.csv(
  "https://ona-book.org/data/workfrance_vertices.csv"
)


# create undirected graph object
workfrance <- igraph::graph_from_data_frame(
  d = workfrance_edgelist,
  vertices = workfrance_vertices,
  directed = FALSE
)


# basic visualization
set.seed(123)
ggraph(workfrance, layout = "fr") +
  geom_edge_link(color = "grey", alpha = 0.7) +
  geom_node_point(color = "blue", size = 5) +
  theme_void()
```

As it stands, this graph does not tell us much, but a couple of simple adjustments can change this. First, we can adjust the thickness of the edges to reflect the total number of minutes spent meeting, which seems a reasonable measure of the 'strength' or 'weight' of the connection. Second, we can color

---

[8]Génois & Barrat (2018)

[9]https://ona-book.org/data/workfrance_edgelist.csv and https://ona-book.org/data/workfrance_vertices.csv

[10]This data set has been further processed from the original data set, including limiting the edges to those where the total co-location time was at least 5 minutes.

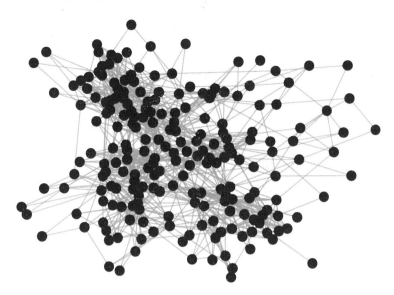

FIGURE 3.15: Connection of employees in a workplace as measured by spatial co-location

code the nodes by their department. The result is Figure 3.16. We can now see clusters of highly connected employees mostly driven by their department.

```
set.seed(123)
ggraph(workfrance, layout = "fr") +
  geom_edge_link(color = "grey", alpha = 0.7, aes(width = mins),
                 show.legend = FALSE) +
  geom_node_point(aes(color = dept), size = 5) +
  labs(color = "Department") +
  theme_void() +
  labs(title = "Spatial co-location of employees in a workplace")
```

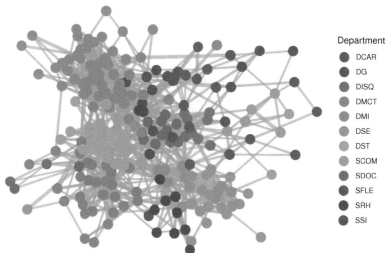

FIGURE 3.16: Connection of employees in a workplace with edge thickness weighted by minutes spent spatially co-located and vertices colored by department

Thinking ahead: The graph we have just created in Figure 3.16 shows how we have detected a community partition of our vertices. It's relatively clear that individuals in the same department are more likely to be connected. Community detection is an important topic in Organizational Network Analysis which we will study later in this book. It's not always straightforward to identify drivers of community in networks, but we will learn about a number of unsupervised community detection algorithms which will partition the graph into different community groups. As an example, Figure 3.17 shows the results of running the Louvain community detection algorithm on the workframe graph with mins as the edge weights. You can see that the communities detected are strongly aligned with the departments in Figure 3.16.

ggraph visualizations can work relatively easily with other graphics layers, allowing you to superimpose a graph onto other coordinate systems. Let's look at an example of this at work. Load the londontube_edgelist and londontube_vertices data sets from the onadata package or download them

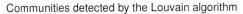

Communities detected by the Louvain algorithm

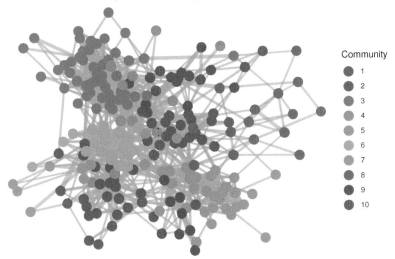

FIGURE 3.17: Clusters of employees as detected by the Louvain unsupervised community detection algorithm. Note the cluster similarity of communities with the departments in the previous graph.

from the internet[11]. The vertex set is a list of London Tube Stations with an id, name and geographical coordinates longitude and latitude.

```
# download and view london tube vertex data
londontube_vertices <- read.csv(
  "https://ona-book.org/data/londontube_vertices.csv"
)
head(londontube_vertices)
```

```
##    id         name latitude longitude
## 1  1   Acton Town  51.5028   -0.2801
## 2  2      Aldgate  51.5143   -0.0755
## 3  3 Aldgate East  51.5154   -0.0726
## 4  4   All Saints  51.5107   -0.0130
## 5  5     Alperton  51.5407   -0.2997
## 6  7        Angel  51.5322   -0.1058
```

The edge list represents from and to connections between stations, along with the name of the line and its official linecolor in hex code.

---

[11] https://ona-book.org/data/londontube_edgelist.csv and https://ona-book.org/data/londontube_vertices.csv

```
# download and view london tube edge data
londontube_edgelist <- read.csv(
  "https://ona-book.org/data/londontube_edgelist.csv"
)
head(londontube_edgelist)
```

```
##    from  to          line linecolor
## 1    11 163 Bakerloo Line   #AE6017
## 2    11 212 Bakerloo Line   #AE6017
## 3    49  87 Bakerloo Line   #AE6017
## 4    49 197 Bakerloo Line   #AE6017
## 5    82 163 Bakerloo Line   #AE6017
## 6    82 193 Bakerloo Line   #AE6017
```

We can easily create an `igraph` object from this data and then use `ggraph` to create a visualization using the `linecolor` as the edge color between stations, as in Figure 3.18.

```
# create a set of distinct line names and linecolors to use
lines <- londontube_edgelist |>
  dplyr::distinct(line, linecolor)

# create graph object
tubegraph <- igraph::graph_from_data_frame(
  d = londontube_edgelist,
  vertices = londontube_vertices,
  directed = FALSE
)

# visualize tube graph using linecolors for edge color
set.seed(123)
ggraph(tubegraph) +
  geom_node_point(color = "black", size = 1) +
  geom_edge_link(aes(color = line), width = 1) +
  scale_edge_color_manual(name = "Line",
                          values = lines$linecolor) +
  theme_void()
```

While it's great that we can do this so easily, it's a pretty confusing visualization for anyone who knows London. The Circle Line doesn't look very circular, the Picadilly Line seems to he heading southeast instead of northeast. In the west, the Metropolitan and Picadilly Lines seem to have swapped places. Of course, this graph is not using geographical coordinates to plot its vertices.

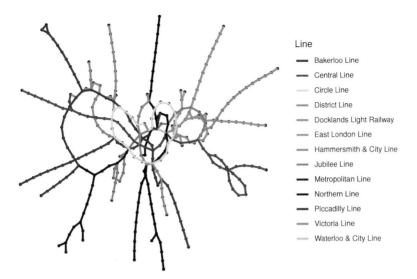

Line
— Bakerloo Line
— Central Line
— Circle Line
— District Line
— Docklands Light Railway
— East London Line
— Hammersmith & City Line
— Jubilee Line
— Metropolitan Line
— Northern Line
— Piccadilly Line
— Victoria Line
— Waterloo & City Line

FIGURE 3.18: Random graph visualization of the London Tube network graph with the edges colored by the different lines

We can change this by expanding our edgelist to include the latitudes and longitudes of the `from` and `to` stations in each edge, and then we can layer a map on this graph. First, let's create those new longitude and latitude columns in the edgelist, and check that it works.

```r
# reorganize to include longitude and latitude for start and end
new_edgelist <- londontube_edgelist |>
  dplyr::inner_join(londontube_vertices |>
                      dplyr::select(id, latitude, longitude),
                    by = c("from" = "id")) |>
  dplyr::rename(lat_from = latitude, lon_from = longitude) |>
  dplyr::inner_join(londontube_vertices |>
                      dplyr::select(id, latitude, longitude),
                    by = c("to" = "id")) |>
  dplyr::rename(lat_to = latitude, lon_to = longitude)

# view
head(new_edgelist)
```

```
##    from  to           line linecolor lat_from lon_from  lat_to   lon_to
## 1    11 163 Bakerloo Line    #AE6017  51.5226  -0.1571 51.5225 -0.1631
## 2    11 212 Bakerloo Line    #AE6017  51.5226  -0.1571 51.5234 -0.1466
## 3    49  87 Bakerloo Line    #AE6017  51.5080  -0.1247 51.5074 -0.1223
```

```
## 4   49 197 Bakerloo Line    #AE6017  51.5080  -0.1247 51.5098 -0.1342
## 5   82 163 Bakerloo Line    #AE6017  51.5199  -0.1679 51.5225 -0.1631
## 6   82 193 Bakerloo Line    #AE6017  51.5199  -0.1679 51.5154 -0.1755
```

That looks like it worked. Now we can use the `ggmap` package in R to layer
a map of London on top of the base `ggraph` layer, and then use the various
latitude and longitude columns to make our network geographically accurate,
as in Figure 3.19[12].

```
# recreate graph object to capture additional edge data
tubegraph <- igraph::graph_from_data_frame(
  d = new_edgelist,
  vertices = londontube_vertices,
  directed = FALSE
)

# layer a London map (requires Google Maps API key)
library(ggmap)
londonmap <- get_map(location = "London, UK", source = "google")

# visualize using geolocation
ggmap(londonmap, base_layer = ggraph(tubegraph)) +
  geom_node_point(aes(x = longitude, y = latitude),
                  color = "black", size = 1) +
  geom_edge_link(aes(x = lon_from, y = lat_from,
                     xend = lon_to, yend = lat_to,
                     color = line), width = 1) +
  scale_edge_color_manual(name = "Line",
                          values = lines$linecolor)
```

In Figure 3.19, it looks like everything is in the right place. This kind of graph-
ical layering can be extremely important when there is an inherent coordinate
system lying behind the vertices of your graph and where none of the existing
layout algorithms can recreate that coordinate system.

3.1.4   Interactive graph visualization using `visNetwork`

We have seen earlier how many large networks are too complicated to make
sense of visually using static approaches like those we have already reviewed
in `igraph` or `ggraph`. Nevertheless, interactive visualizations of networks can
be useful where there is an interest in visual exploration of particular vertices

---

[12]A Google Maps API key is needed to use ggmap - see https://github.com/dkahle/ggmap
for more information.

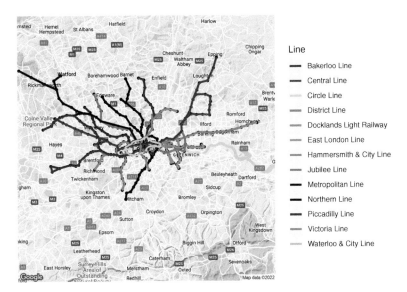

FIGURE 3.19: Geographically accurate London Tube network

or small subnetworks, even when the overall network is visually complex. We will touch upon a couple of commonly used interactive graph visualization packages here, all of which use Javascript libraries behind the scenes to create the interactive visualizations.

visNetwork is a simple but effective package which uses the vis.js API to create HTML widgets containing interactive graph visualizations. It is fairly easy to use, with its main function visNetwork() taking a dataframe of node information and a dataframe of edge information, as well as a few other optional arguments. The columns in these dataframes are expected to have certain default column names. Vertices/nodes are expected to at least have an id column but can also contain:

- label: the label of the vertex
- group: the group of the vertex if there are groups
- value: used to determine the size of the vertex
- title: used as a tooltip on mouseover
- Other columns can be included to be passed to specific values/properties in the visualization, such as color or shape.

The edge dataframe must contain a from and to column, and can also contain label, value and title to customize the edges as with the vertices, as well as other properties such as arrows or dashes.

Figure 3.20 is a very simple statically rendered example of the visNetwork function at work using our G_{work} graph from Section 2.1.1. Note that the visLayout() function can be used for various customizations, including passing a random seed variable to vis.js to ensure reproducibility.

```
library(visNetwork)

nodes <- data.frame(
id = 1:4,
label = c("David", "Zubin", "Suraya", "Jane")
)

edges <- data.frame(
  from = c(1, 1, 1, 4, 4),
  to = c(2, 3, 4, 2, 3)
)

visNetwork(nodes, edges) |>
  visLayout(randomSeed = 123)
```

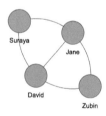

FIGURE 3.20: Static image of visNetwork rendering of the G_work graph

In fact, assuming that we are working with igraph objects, the easiest way to deploy visNetwork is to use the visIgraph() function, which takes an igraph object and restructures it behind the scenes to use the vis.js API, even inheriting whatever igraph layout you prefer. Let's recreate our karate graph in visNetwork, as in Figure 3.21[13].

```
library(igraph)
library(ggraph)
```

---

[13]Note that if you are passing an igraph layout to visNetwork, you will need to use the randomSeed argument directly in the visIgraph() function.

```
# get karate edgelist
karate_edgelist <- read.csv("https://ona-book.org/data/karate.csv")

# create graph object
karate <- igraph::graph_from_data_frame(karate_edgelist,
                                        directed = FALSE)

# different colors and shapes for Mr Hi and and John A
V(karate)$color <- ifelse(V(karate)$name %in% c("Mr Hi", "John A"),
                          "lightblue",
                          "pink")

V(karate)$shape <- ifelse(V(karate)$name %in% c("Mr Hi", "John A"),
                          "square",
                          "circle")

# more visible edges
E(karate)$color = "grey"
E(karate)$width <- 3

# visualize from igraph
visNetwork::visIgraph(karate, layout = "layout_with_fr",
                      randomSeed = 123)
```

> **Playing around:** The `visNetwork` package allows you to take advantage of a ton of features in the `vis.js` API, including a wide range of graph customization, and the ability to make your graph editable or to add selector menus to search for specific nodes or groups of nodes. It's worth experimenting with all its different capabilities. A thorough manual can be found at `https://datastorm-open.github.io/visNetwork/`. Why don't you try to recreate the workfrance graph from this chapter in `visNetwork`?

3.1.5 Interactive graph visualization using `networkD3`

The `networkD3` package creates responsive and interactive network visualizations using the `D3` javascript library, which has some beautiful options for common network layouts like force-directed or chord diagrams.

To create a simple force-directed visualization based on an edgelist, use the `simpleNetwork()` function. All this needs is a simple dataframe where by

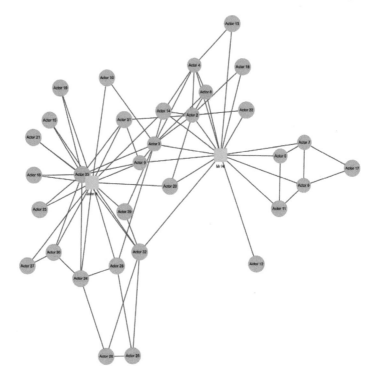

FIGURE 3.21: Static image of `visNetwork` rendering of the basic Karate graph using a force-directed layout

default the first two columns represent the edgelist[14]. Here is an example for the `karate` network, with a static image of the result shown in Figure 3.22. Note that it is not possible to set a random seed with `networkD3`.

```
library(networkD3)

# get karate edgelist
karate_edgelist <- read.csv("https://ona-book.org/data/karate.csv")

# visualize
networkD3::simpleNetwork(karate_edgelist)
```

The `forceNetwork()` function allows greater levels of customization of the visualization. This function requires an edgelist and a vertex set in a specific format. However, we can use the function `igraph_to_networkD3()` to easily

---

[14]You can use the arguments in the `simpleNetwork()` function to define the Source and Target columns if they are not the first two columns

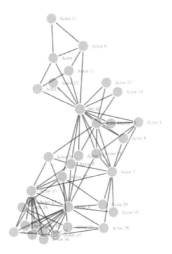

FIGURE 3.22: Static image of `networkD3` rendering of the Karate graph

create a list containing what we need from an `igraph` object. In the next example, we recreate the graph in Figure 3.22, but we put Mr Hi and John A into a different group, with a static image of the result shown in Figure 3.23. Note that node names only appear when nodes are clicked.

```r
# get karate edgelist
karate_edgelist <- read.csv("https://ona-book.org/data/karate.csv")

# create igraph object
karate <- igraph::graph_from_data_frame(karate_edgelist,
                                         directed = FALSE)

# give Mr Hi and John A a different group
V(karate)$group <- ifelse(
  V(karate)$name %in% c("Mr Hi", "John A"), 1, 2
)

# translate to networkD3 - creates a list with links and nodes dfs
# links have a source and target column and group if requested
netd3_list <- networkD3::igraph_to_networkD3(karate,
                                             group = V(karate)$group)

# visualize
```

```
networkD3::forceNetwork(
  Links = netd3_list$links,
  Nodes = netd3_list$nodes,
  NodeID = "name",
  Source = "source",
  Target = "target",
  Group = "group"
)
```

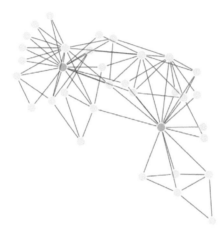

FIGURE 3.23: Static image of force-directed `networkD3` rendering of the Karate graph

Other types of `D3` network visualizations are also available such as `chordNetwork()`, and `sankeyNetwork()`, with many of these more appropriate for data visualization purposes than for the exploration and analysis of networks. As a quick example of using `sankeyNetwork()` to visualize data flows, load the `eu_referendum` data set from the `onadata` package or download it from the internet[15]. This shows statistics on voting by region and area in the United Kingdom's 2016 referendum on membership of the European Union. In this example, we will calculate the 'Leave' and 'Remain' votes by region and visualize them using `sankeyNetwork()`, with a static image of the result shown in Figure 3.24. It is worth taking a look at the intermediate objects created by this code so you can better understand how to construct the `Nodes` and `Links` dataframes that are commonly expected by `networkD3` functions.

---

[15]https://ona-book.org/data/eu_referendum.csv

```r
library(dplyr)
library(networkD3)
library(tidyr)

# get data
eu_referendum <- read.csv(
  "https://ona-book.org/data/eu_referendum.csv"
)

# aggregate by region
results <- eu_referendum |>
  dplyr::group_by(Region) |>
  dplyr::summarise(Remain = sum(Remain), Leave = sum(Leave)) |>
  tidyr::pivot_longer(-Region, names_to = "result",
                      values_to = "votes")

# create unique regions, "Leave" and "Remain" for nodes dataframe
regions <- unique(results$Region)
nodes <- data.frame(node = c(0:13),
                    name = c(regions, "Leave", "Remain"))

# create edges/links dataframe
results <- results |>
  dplyr::inner_join(nodes, by = c("Region" = "name")) |>
  dplyr::inner_join(nodes, by = c("result" = "name"))

links <- results[ , c("node.x", "node.y", "votes")]
colnames(links) <- c("source", "target", "value")

# visualize using sankeyNetwork
networkD3::sankeyNetwork(
  Links = links, Nodes = nodes, Source = 'source', Target = 'target',
  Value = 'value', NodeID = 'name', units = 'votes', fontSize = 12
)
```

> **Thinking ahead:** As we have shown in the examples in this section, the `networkD3` package offers useful, convenient ways for non-Javascript programmers to make use of many of the great capabilities of the D3 visualization library. See `https://christophergandrud.g ithub.io/networkD3/` for more examples. However, the package's customization potential is limited. For those who can program in D3, the scope exists to create amazing interactive graph visualizations, with limitless customization potential.

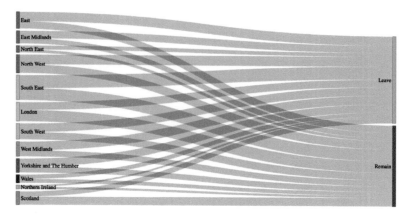

FIGURE 3.24: Static image of visualization of regional vote flows in the UK's European Union Referendum in 2016 using `sankeyNetwork()`

3.2 Visualizing graphs in Python

We will look at two approaches to graph visualization in Python. First, we will look at static graph plotting via the `networkx` and `matplotlib` packages. Then we will look at interactive plotting via the `pyvis` package. As in the previous section, we will work with Zachary's Karate Club to demonstrate most of the visualization options. Let's load and create that graph object now.

```
import pandas as pd
import networkx as nx

# get edgelist as Pandas DataFrame
karate_edgelist = pd.read_csv("https://ona-book.org/data/karate.csv")

# create graph from Pandas DataFrame
karate = nx.from_pandas_edgelist(karate_edgelist,
source = 'from', target = 'to')
```

3.2.1 Static plotting using `networkx` and `matplotlib`

The `draw()` function in `networkx` provides a basic visualization of a graph in `matplotlib` using a force-directed "spring" layout, as can be seen in Figure 3.25. Remember also to set a seed to ensure reproducibility of the visualization.

```
import numpy as np
from matplotlib import pyplot as plt

# set seed for reproducibility
np.random.seed(123)

fig = nx.draw(karate)
plt.show()
```

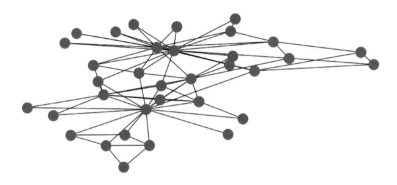

FIGURE 3.25: Basic static visualization of Karate network

The draw_networkx() function has a much wider range of options for customizing the appearance of graphs. For example, we can change the color of all or specific nodes or edges, or label specific nodes but not others, such as in Figure 3.26.

```
# set seed for reproducibility
np.random.seed(123)

# create dict with labels only for Mr Hi and John A
node = list(karate.nodes)
labels = [i if i == "Mr Hi" or i == "John A" else ""
for i in karate.nodes]
nodelabels = dict(zip(node, labels))

# create color list
colors = ["lightblue" if i == "Mr Hi" or i == "John A" else "pink"
for i in karate.nodes]

nx.draw_networkx(karate, labels = nodelabels, node_color = colors,
edge_color = "grey")
plt.show()
```

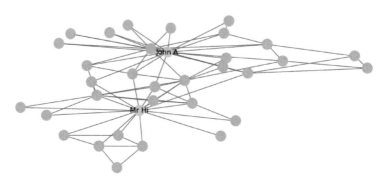

FIGURE 3.26: Static visualization of Karate network with adjustments to color and labeling

A limited selection of layouts is available and can be applied to the static visualization. For example, this is how to apply a circular layout, with the output in Figure 3.27.

```
# set seed for reproducibility
np.random.seed(123)

# circular layout
nx.draw_circular(karate, labels = nodelabels, node_color = colors,
edge_color = "grey")
plt.show()
```

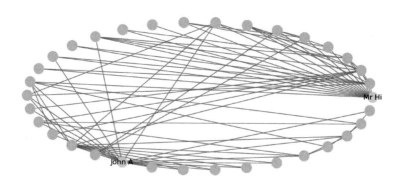

FIGURE 3.27: Static visualization of Karate network with circular layout

This is how to apply a Kamada-Kawai force-directed layout, with the output in Figure 3.28. Note that some layout algorithms like Kamada-Kawai make use of the `scipy` package and therefore this will need to be installed in your Python environment.

```
# set seed for reproducibility
np.random.seed(123)
```

```
# circular layout
nx.draw_kamada_kawai(karate, labels = nodelabels, node_color = colors,
edge_color = "grey")
plt.show()
```

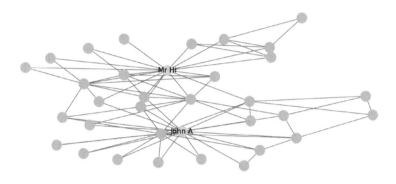

FIGURE 3.28: Static visualization of Karate network with Kamada-Kawai force-directed layout

Playing around: The visual capabilities of `networkx` in Python are more limited than `igraph` or `ggraph` in R, but there still are a range of ways to customize your visualization. Try making further changes to the visualizations shown in this section by trying different layouts or by looking at the range of arguments that can be adjusted in the `draw_networkx()` function. You can look up more details on all this at `https://networkx.org/documentation/stable/reference/drawing.html`.

3.2.2 Interactive visualization using **networkx** and **pyvis**

Similar to the `visNetwork` package in R, the `pyvis` package provides an API allowing the creation of interactive graphs using the `vis.js` Javascript library. As you will mostly be creating graph objects using `networkx`, the easiest way to use `pyvis` is to take advantage of its `networkx` integration.

To visualize a `networkx` graph using `pyvis`, start by creating a `Network()` class and then use the `from_nx()` method to import the `networkx` object. The `show()` method will render an interactive plot. Figure 3.29 shows a static image of the output.

```
from pyvis.network import Network

# create pyvis Network object
net = Network(height = "500px", width = "600px", notebook = True)

# import karate graph
net.from_nx(karate)
net.show('out1.html')
```

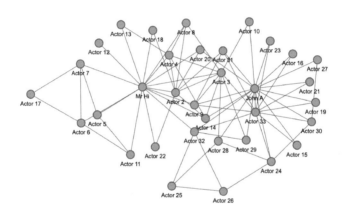

FIGURE 3.29: Static image of visualization of Karate graph using pyvis and networkx

pyvis expects specific names for the visual properties of nodes and edges, for example color and size. If these named properties are added to the nodes and edges dicts of the networkx object, they will be passed to pyvis. Figure 3.30 shows a static image of the output.

```
# adjust colors
for i in karate.nodes:
  karate.nodes[i]['size'] = 20 if i == "Mr Hi" or i == "John A" \
  else 10

  karate.nodes[i]['color'] = "lightblue" if i == "Mr Hi" \
```

```
  or i == "John A" else "pink"

# create edge color
for i in karate.edges:
  karate.edges[i]['color'] = "grey"

# create pyvis Network object
net = Network(height = "500px", width = "600px", notebook = True)

# import from networkx to pyvis and display
net.from_nx(karate)
net.show('out2.html')
```

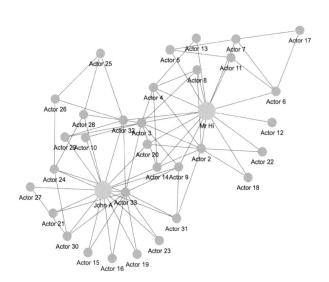

FIGURE 3.30: Static image of adjusted visualization of Karate graph using `pyvis` and `networkx`

> **Playing around:** Different user interface controls can be added directly onto your pyvis visualizations using the show_buttons() method allowing you to experiment directly with the graph's look and feel. For example, you can add buttons to experiment with the physics of the force-directed layout, or the node or edge properties. This can be useful when you are experimenting with options. You can learn more at the tutorial pages at https://pyvis.readthedocs.io/en/latest/.

3.3   Learning exercises

3.3.1   Discussion questions

1. Why is visualization an important consideration when studying graphs?
2. Describe some ways a graph visualization can be adjusted to reflect different characteristics of the vertices. For example, how might we represent more 'important' vertices visually?
3. Describe some similar adjustments that could be made to the edges.
4. Describe some likely challenges with large graph visualizations which may make it harder to draw conclusions from them.
5. What is the difference between a static and an iteractive visualization? In what ways might interactive visualizations overcome some of the challenges associated with large static graph visualizations?
6. Choose your favorite programming language and list out some package options for how to visualize graphs in that language.
7. For each package option you listed, describe what kinds of graphs each package would be best suited for.
8. Describe what is meant by a graph layout.
9. List some layout options which are available in the packages you selected for Questions 6 and 7.
10. If you visualize the same graph twice using the same layout, the outputs may look different. Why is this the case and what can be done to control it?

3.3.2 Data exercises

Load the `madmen_vertices` and `madmen_edges` data sets from the `onadata` package or download them from the internet[16]. This represents a network of characters from the TV show *Mad Men* with two characters connected by an edge if they were involved in a romantic relationship together.

1. Create a graph object from these data sets.
2. Create a basic visualization of the network using one of the methods from this chapter.
3. Adjust your visualization to distinguish between Male and Female characters.
4. Adjust your visualization to highlight the six main characters.
5. Adjust your visualization to differentiate between relationships where the characters were married or not married.
6. Experiment with different layouts. Which one do you prefer and why?

Now load the `schoolfriends_vertices` and `schoolfriends_edgelist` data sets from the `onadata` package or download them from the internet[17]. This data set represents friendships reported between schoolchildren in a high school in Marseille, France in 2013. The vertex set provides the ID, class and gender of each child, and the edgelist has two types of relationships. The first type is a reported friendship where the `from` ID reported the `to` ID as a friend. The second type is a known Facebook friendship between the two IDs.

7. Create two different graph objects—one for the reported friendship and the other for the Facebook friendship. Why is one graph object different from the other?
8. Create a basic visualization of both graphs using a method of your choice. Try to create versions of the graphs that contain isolates (nodes not connected to others) and do not contain isolates.
9. Experiment with different layouts for your visualization. Which one do you prefer and why? Do you see any potential communities in these graphs? Which type of friendship appears to be more 'selective' in your opinion?
10. Adjust both visualizations to differentiate the vertices by gender. Which type of relationship is more likely to be gender-agnostic in your opinion? Try the same question for class differentiation.

---

[16]https://ona-book.org/data/madmen_vertices.csv and https://ona-book.org/data/madmen_edges.csv
[17]https://ona-book.org/data/schoolfriends_vertices.csv and https://ona-book.org/data/schoolfriends_edgelist.csv

4

Restructuring Data for Use in Graphs

So far we have learned how to define and visualize graphs to allow us to work with them and to gain some basic insights from them. But we have made a really big assumption in doing so. We have assumed that the data we need to create our graph is always available in exactly the form in which we will need it. Usually this is an edgelist or a set of dataframes of edges and vertices. In reality, only certain types of data exist in this form by default. Typically, electronic communication data will often—though not always—have a 'from' and 'to' structure, because that is how communication works and because many of the underlying systems like email, calendar or other communication networks are already built on databases that have a graph-like structure.

However, there are a lot of problems where we may want to apply graph theory, but where the data does not exist in a way that makes it easy to create a graph. In these situations, we will need to *transform* the data from its existing shape to a graph-friendly shape—a set of vertices and edges.

There are two important considerations in transforming data into a graph-friendly structure. Both of these considerations depend on the problem you are trying to solve with the graph, as follows:

1. What entities am I interested in connecting? These will be the vertices of your graph. This could be a single entity type like a set of people, or it could be multiple entity types, such as connecting people to organizational units. Complex graphs will usually involve multiple entity types.

2. How do I define the relationship between the vertices? These will be the edges of your graph. Again, there can be multiple relationship types, such as 'reports to' or 'works with,' depending on how complex your graph needs to be.

In addition to these fundamental considerations, there are also questions of design in how you construct your graph. This is because there is often more than one option for how you can model the entities and relationships you are interested in. For example, imagine that you have two types of relationships where 'works with' means that two people have worked together on the same project and 'located with' means that two people are based in the same

DOI: 10.1201/9781003266815-4

location. One option for modeling these in a single graph is to have a single entity type (person) connected with edges that have a 'relationship type' property ('works with' or 'located with'). Another option is to have several entity types—person, project and location—as vertices, and to connect people to projects and locations using a single edge type that means 'is a member of.' In the first option, the relationships are modeled directly, but in the second they are modeled indirectly. Both may work equally well for the problem that is being solved by the graph, but one choice may be more useful or efficient than another.

To be able to go about these sorts of transformations requires technical and data design skills and judgment. There is no 'one size fits all' solution. The transformations required and how you go about them depends a great deal on the context and the purpose of the work. Nevertheless, in this chapter we will demonstrate two examples which reflect common situations where data needs to be transformed from a graph-unfriendly to a graph-friendly structure. Working through these examples should illustrate a simple design process to follow and help demonstrate typical data transformation methods that could be applied in other common situations.

In the first example, we will study a situation where data exists in traditional rectangular tables, but where we need to transform it in order to understand connections that we cannot understand directly from the tables themselves. This is extremely common in practice and many organizations perform these sorts of transformations in order to populate graph databases from more traditional data sources. In the second example, we will study how to extract information from documents in a way that helps us understand connections between entities in those documents. This is another common situation that has strong applications in general, but has particular potential in the fields of law and crime investigation. Both these examples will be demonstrated in detail using R, and the last section of the chapter will provide examples of how to perform similar transformations using Python.

4.1 Transforming data in rectangular tables for use in graphs

In this example we are going to use some simplified tables from the *Chinook* database[1], an open-source database which contains records of the customers, employees and transactions of a music sales company. We will be working with

---

[1]You can find and download the full version of the *Chinook* open-source SQLite database at https://www.sqlitetutorial.net/sqlite-sample-database/

four simplified tables from this database which you can load from the `onadata` package now or download from the internet as follows:

```
# download chinook database tables
chinook_employees <- read.csv(
  "https://ona-book.org/data/chinook_employees.csv"
)
chinook_customers <- read.csv(
  "https://ona-book.org/data/chinook_customers.csv"
)
chinook_invoices <- read.csv(
  "https://ona-book.org/data/chinook_invoices.csv"
)
chinook_items <- read.csv(
  "https://ona-book.org/data/chinook_items.csv"
)
```

4.1.1 Creating a simple graph of a management hierarchy

First, let's take a look at a simple example of a graph that already exists explicitly in one of these data tables. Let's take a look at a few rows of the `chinook_employees` data set.

```
head(chinook_employees)
```

```
##    EmployeeId FirstName LastName ReportsTo
## 1           1    Andrew    Adams        NA
## 2           2     Nancy  Edwards         1
## 3           3      Jane  Peacock         2
## 4           4  Margaret     Park         2
## 5           5     Steve  Johnson         2
## 6           6   Michael Mitchell         1
```

We can easily create a graph of the management relationships using this table. In such a graph, we would have a single entity type (the employee) as the vertices and the management relationship ('is a manager of') as the edges. For simplicity, let's use first names as vertex names. By joining our data on itself, using `EmployeeId = ReportsTo`, we can create two columns with the first names of those in each management relationship.

```
# load dplyr for tidy manipulation in this chapter
library(dplyr)
```

```
# create edgelist
(orgchart_edgelist1 <- chinook_employees |>
  dplyr::inner_join(chinook_employees,
                    by = c("EmployeeId" = "ReportsTo")))
```

```
##    EmployeeId FirstName.x LastName.x ReportsTo EmployeeId.y FirstName.y LastName.y
## 1           1      Andrew      Adams        NA            2       Nancy    Edwards
## 2           1      Andrew      Adams        NA            6     Michael   Mitchell
## 3           2       Nancy    Edwards         1            3        Jane    Peacock
## 4           2       Nancy    Edwards         1            4    Margaret       Park
## 5           2       Nancy    Edwards         1            5       Steve    Johnson
## 6           6     Michael   Mitchell         1            7      Robert       King
## 7           6     Michael   Mitchell         1            8       Laura   Callahan
```

We can see that the `FirstName.x` column is the manager and so should be the `from` column and the `Firstname.y` column should be the `to` column in our edgelist. We should also remove rows where there is no edge.

```
(orgchart_edgelist2 <- orgchart_edgelist1 |>
  dplyr::select(from = FirstName.x, to = FirstName.y)) |>
  dplyr::filter(!is.na(from) & !is.na(to))
```

```
##        from       to
## 1    Andrew    Nancy
## 2    Andrew  Michael
## 3     Nancy     Jane
## 4     Nancy Margaret
## 5     Nancy    Steve
## 6   Michael   Robert
## 7   Michael    Laura
```

Now we can create a directed `igraph` object using the 'is a manager of' relationship.

```
library(igraph)
```

```
# create orgchart graph
(orgchart <- igraph::graph_from_data_frame(
  d = orgchart_edgelist2
))
```

```
## IGRAPH c026bf4 DN-- 8 7 --
## + attr: name (v/c)
## + edges from c026bf4 (vertex names):
## [1] Andrew ->Nancy    Andrew ->Michael  Nancy ->Jane    Nancy ->Margaret Nancy ->Steve
```

```
## [6] Michael->Robert    Michael->Laura
```

We now have a directed graph with named vertices, so this should be easy to plot. Let's use ggplot with a dendrogram (tree) layout, as in Figure 4.1.

```
library(ggraph)
```

```
# create management structure as dendrogram (tree)
set.seed(123)
ggraph(orgchart, layout = 'dendrogram') +
  geom_edge_elbow() +
  geom_node_label(aes(label = name), fill = "lightblue") +
  theme_void()
```

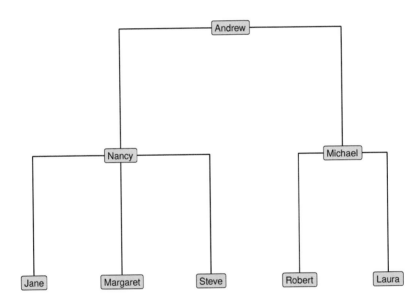

FIGURE 4.1: Management hierarchy of Chinook as a tree (dendrogram)

4.1.2   Connecting customers through sales reps

Now let's try to build a graph based an a slightly more complex definition of connection. We are going to connect Chinook's customers based on whether or not they share the same support rep. First, let's take a look at the customers table.

```
head(chinook_customers)
```

```
##   CustomerId FirstName     LastName SupportRepId
## 1          1     Luís     Gonçalves            3
## 2          2    Leonie       Köhler            5
## 3          3  François     Tremblay            3
## 4          4     Bjørn       Hansen            4
## 5          5 František Wichterlová            4
## 6          6    Helena         Holý            5
```

We see a `SupportRepId` field which corresponds to the `EmployeeId` field in the `chinook_employees` table. We can join these tables to get an edgelist of customers to support reps. Let's also create full names for better reference.

```
# create customer to support rep edgelist
cust_reps <- chinook_customers |>
  dplyr::inner_join(chinook_employees,
                    by = c("SupportRepId" = "EmployeeId")) |>
  dplyr::mutate(
    CustomerName = paste(FirstName.x, LastName.x),
    RepName = paste(FirstName.y, LastName.y)
  ) |>
  dplyr::select(RepName, CustomerName, SupportRepId)

# view head
head(cust_reps)
```

```
##            RepName          CustomerName SupportRepId
## 1   Jane Peacock          Luís Gonçalves            3
## 2  Steve Johnson          Leonie Köhler            5
## 3   Jane Peacock       François Tremblay            3
## 4 Margaret Park           Bjørn Hansen            4
## 5 Margaret Park František Wichterlová            4
## 6  Steve Johnson           Helena Holý            5
```

Now we have an option of creating two types of graphs. First we could create a graph from the data as is, using the `CustomerName` and `RepName` as the edgelist, and where the relationship is 'is a customer of.' Let's create that graph, and view it in Figure 4.2. We see a graph with three distinct connected components, each with a hub-and-spoke shape.

```
# create igraph
cust_rep_graph <- igraph::graph_from_data_frame(
  d = cust_reps
)
```

```
# create customer and rep property for vertices
V(cust_rep_graph)$Type <- ifelse(
  V(cust_rep_graph)$name %in% cust_reps$RepName,
  "Rep",
  "Customer"
)

# visualize with color and name aesthetic
set.seed(123)
ggraph(cust_rep_graph, layout = "fr") +
  geom_edge_link(color = "grey", alpha = 0.7) +
  geom_node_label(aes(color = Type, label = name), size = 2) +
  theme_void()
```

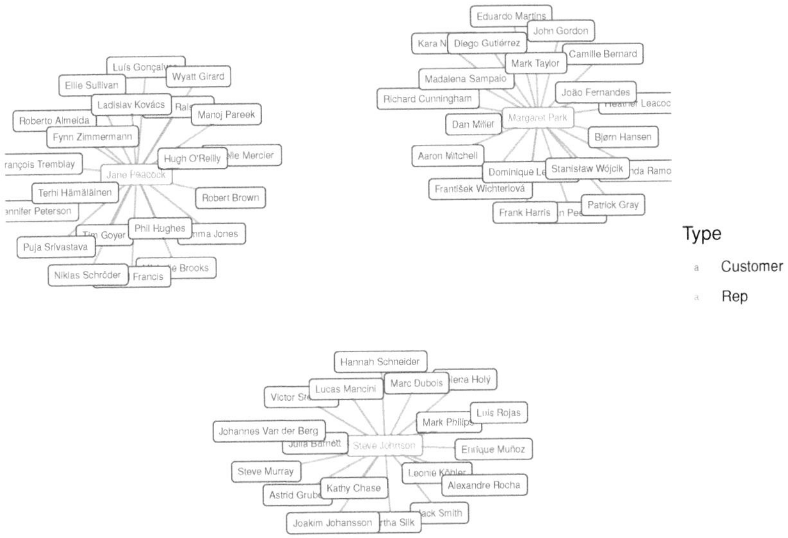

FIGURE 4.2: Graph of Chinook customers connected to their sales reps

Recall our original objective is to connect customers if they have the same
support rep. It is possible to use this graph to do this indirectly, applying the
logic that customers are connected if there is a path between them in this
graph. However, we may wish to ignore the support reps completely in our
graph and make direct connections between customers if they share the same
support rep. To do this, we need to do some further joining to our previous
cust_reps dataframe.

If we join this dataframe back to our chinook_customers dataframe, we can
get customer-to-customer connections via a common support rep as follows:

```
# connect customers via common support rep
cust_cust <- cust_reps |>
  dplyr::inner_join(chinook_customers, by = "SupportRepId") |>
  dplyr::mutate(Customer1 = CustomerName,
                Customer2 = paste(FirstName, LastName)) |>
  dplyr::select(Customer1, Customer2, RepName)
```

```
# view head
head(cust_cust)
```

```
##          Customer1         Customer2      RepName
## 1 Luís Gonçalves     Luís Gonçalves Jane Peacock
## 2 Luís Gonçalves François Tremblay Jane Peacock
## 3 Luís Gonçalves   Roberto Almeida Jane Peacock
## 4 Luís Gonçalves Jennifer Peterson Jane Peacock
## 5 Luís Gonçalves   Michelle Brooks Jane Peacock
## 6 Luís Gonçalves         Tim Goyer Jane Peacock
```

Now we are not interested in creating a pseudograph where customers are connected to themselves, so we should remove any rows where Customer1 and Customer2 are the same.

```
# remove loop edges
customer_network_edgelist <- cust_cust |>
  dplyr::filter(
    Customer1 != Customer2
  )
```

```
# view head
head(customer_network_edgelist)
```

```
##          Customer1         Customer2      RepName
## 1 Luís Gonçalves François Tremblay Jane Peacock
## 2 Luís Gonçalves   Roberto Almeida Jane Peacock
## 3 Luís Gonçalves Jennifer Peterson Jane Peacock
## 4 Luís Gonçalves   Michelle Brooks Jane Peacock
## 5 Luís Gonçalves         Tim Goyer Jane Peacock
## 6 Luís Gonçalves     Frank Ralston Jane Peacock
```

Now we have a network edgelist we can work with, and we have RepName available to use as an edge property. Note that relationships will appear in both directions in this data set, but we can take care of that by choosing to represent them in an undirected graph. Let's build and visualize the graph, as in Figure 4.3. We see a graph consisting of three complete subgraphs with the edges color coded by the support rep.

```
# create igraph object
customer_network <- igraph::graph_from_data_frame(
  d = customer_network_edgelist,
  directed = FALSE
)

# visualize
set.seed(123)
ggraph(customer_network) +
  geom_edge_link(aes(color = RepName), alpha = 0.3) +
  geom_node_point(color = "lightblue", size = 6) +
  theme_void()
```

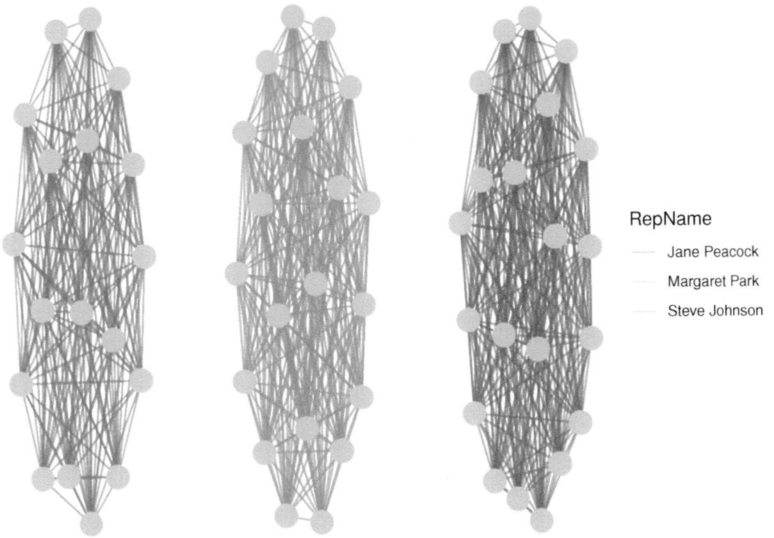

FIGURE 4.3: Customer-to-customer network for Chinook based on customers sharing the same sales rep

Thinking ahead: Recall from Section 2.1.2 that a complete graph is a graph where every pair of vertices are connected by an edge. Can you see how it follows from the shape of the graph in Figure 4.2 that when we transform the data to produce Figure 4.3, we expect to produce complete subgraphs? Can you also see how visually dense those complete subgraphs are? We will look at the measurement of density in graphs later, but a complete graph will always have a density of 1.

4.1.3   Connecting customers through common purchases

To illustrate a further layer of complexity in reshaping data for use in graphs, let's imagine that we want to connect customers on the basis of their purchases of common products. We may wish to set some parameters to this relationship; for example, a connection might be based on a minimum number of common products purchased, to give us flexibility around the definition of connection.

To do this we will need to use three tables: chinook_customers, chinook_invoices and chinook_items. To associate a given customer with a purchased item, we will need to join all three of these tables together. Let's take a quick look at the latter two.

```
# view some invoices
head(chinook_invoices, 3)
```

```
##   InvoiceId CustomerId
## 1         1          2
## 2         2          4
## 3         3          8
```

```
# view some items
head(chinook_items, 3)
```

```
##   InvoiceId TrackId
## 1         1       2
## 2         1       4
## 3         2       6
```

We can regard the TrackId as an item, and using a couple of joins we can quickly match customers with items. It is possible that customers may have purchased the same item numerous times, but we are not interested in that for this work and so we just need the distinct customer and track pairings.

```
# generate distinct customer-item pairs
cust_item <- chinook_customers |>
  dplyr::inner_join(chinook_invoices) |>
  dplyr::inner_join(chinook_items) |>
  dplyr::mutate(CustName = paste(FirstName, LastName)) |>
  dplyr::select(CustName, TrackId) |>
  dplyr::distinct()

# view head
head(cust_item, 3)

##          CustName TrackId
## 1 Luís Gonçalves    3247
## 2 Luís Gonçalves    3248
## 3 Luís Gonçalves     447
```

Similar to our previous example, we can now use this to create an undirected network with two vertex entities: customer and item.

```
# initiate graph object
customer_item_network <- igraph::graph_from_data_frame(
  d = cust_item,
  directed = FALSE
)

# create vertex type
V(customer_item_network)$Type <- ifelse(
  V(customer_item_network)$name %in% cust_item$TrackId,
  "Item",
  "Customer"
)
```

This is a big network. Let's visualize it simply, as in Figure 4.4.

```
set.seed(123)
ggraph(customer_item_network, layout = "fr") +
  geom_edge_link(color = "grey", alpha = 0.7) +
  geom_node_point(aes(color = Type), size = 2) +
  theme_void()
```

We can see from looking at this graph that there are a large number of items that only one customer has purchased. Therefore, the items themselves seem to be extraneous information for this particular use case. If we are not interested in the items themselves, we can instead create the connections between

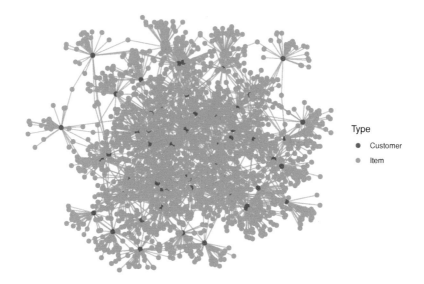

FIGURE 4.4: Network connecting customers via items purchased

customers directly. In a similar way to the previous problem, we can join
the cust_item table on itself to connect customers based on common item
purchases, and we should remove links between the same customer.

```
# join customers to customers via common items
cust_cust_itemjoin <- cust_item |>
  dplyr::inner_join(cust_item, by = "TrackId") |>
  dplyr::select(CustName1 = CustName.x,
                CustName2 = CustName.y, TrackId) |>
  dplyr::filter(CustName1 != CustName2)

# view head
head(cust_cust_itemjoin)
```

```
##         CustName1              CustName2 TrackId
## 1 Luís Gonçalves       Edward Francis       449
## 2 Luís Gonçalves Richard Cunningham      1157
## 3 Luís Gonçalves Richard Cunningham      1169
## 4 Luís Gonçalves        Astrid Gruber      2991
## 5 Luís Gonçalves          Emma Jones       280
## 6 Luís Gonçalves          Emma Jones       298
```

The issue with this data set is that it will count every instance of a common item purchase twice, with the customers in opposite orders, and this is double counting. So, we need to group the pairs of customers irrelevant of their order and ensure we don't double up on items.

```
# avoid double counting
cust_item_network <- cust_cust_itemjoin |>
  dplyr::group_by(Cust1 = pmin(CustName1, CustName2),
                  Cust2 = pmax(CustName1, CustName2)) |>
  dplyr::summarise(TrackId = unique(TrackId), .groups = 'drop')


# view head
head(cust_item_network)
```

```
## # A tibble: 6 x 3
##   Cust1          Cust2            TrackId
##   <chr>          <chr>              <int>
## 1 Aaron Mitchell Alexandre Rocha     2054
## 2 Aaron Mitchell Bjørn Hansen        1626
## 3 Aaron Mitchell Enrique Muñoz       2027
## 4 Aaron Mitchell Hugh O'Reilly       2018
## 5 Aaron Mitchell Niklas Schröder      857
## 6 Aaron Mitchell Phil Hughes         1822
```

If that worked, we should see that the table `cust_cust_itemjoin` has twice as many rows as `cust_item_network`.

```
# check double size
nrow(cust_cust_itemjoin)/nrow(cust_item_network)
```

```
## [1] 2
```

This looks good. So we now can count up how many common items each pair of customers purchased.

```
# count common items
cust_item_network <- cust_item_network |>
  dplyr::count(Cust1, Cust2, name = "Items")


# view head
head(cust_item_network)
```

```
## # A tibble: 6 x 3
##    Cust1           Cust2             Items
##    <chr>           <chr>             <int>
## 1 Aaron Mitchell Alexandre Rocha        1
## 2 Aaron Mitchell Bjørn Hansen           1
## 3 Aaron Mitchell Enrique Muñoz          1
## 4 Aaron Mitchell Hugh O'Reilly          1
## 5 Aaron Mitchell Niklas Schröder        1
## 6 Aaron Mitchell Phil Hughes            1
```

We are now ready to construct our customer-to-customer graph, with `Items` as an edge property. We can visualize it with an edge color code indicating how many common items were purchased, as in Figure 4.5.

```
# create undirected graph
custtocust_network <- igraph::graph_from_data_frame(
  d = cust_item_network,
  directed = FALSE
)

# visualize with edges color coded by no of items
set.seed(123)
ggraph(custtocust_network) +
  geom_edge_link(aes(color = ordered(Items)), alpha = 0.5) +
  geom_node_point(color = "lightblue", size = 6) +
  labs(edge_color = "# of Common Items") +
  theme_void()
```

If we wish, we can restrict the definition of connection. For example, we may define it as 'purchased at least two items in common,' as in Figure 4.6. We can use the `subgraph()` function in `igraph` for this, and the result reveals a graph with two connected components, indicating that there are two independent groups of customers who are related according to some commonality in music purchasing.

```
# select edges that have Item value of at least 2
edges <- E(custtocust_network)[E(custtocust_network)$Items >= 2]

# create subgraph using these edges
two_item_graph <- igraph::subgraph.edges(custtocust_network,
                                          eids = edges)

# visualise
set.seed(123)
```

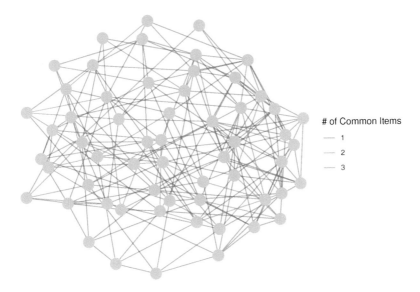

FIGURE 4.5: Chinook customer-to-customer network based on common item purchases

```
ggraph(two_item_graph, layout = "fr") +
  geom_edge_link(color = "grey", alpha = 0.7) +
  geom_node_point(color = "lightblue", size = 6) +
  theme_void()
```

4.1.4 Approaches using Python

To illustrate similar approaches in Python, we will redo the work in Section 4.1.3. First, we will download the various data sets.

```
import pandas as pd
import numpy as np

# download chinook database tables
chinook_customers = pd.read_csv(
  "https://ona-book.org/data/chinook_customers.csv"
)
chinook_invoices = pd.read_csv(
  "https://ona-book.org/data/chinook_invoices.csv"
)
chinook_items = pd.read_csv(
```

FIGURE 4.6: Chinook customer-to-customer network based on at least two common items purchased

```
   "https://ona-book.org/data/chinook_items.csv"
)
```

Now we join the three tables together, create the `FullName` variable and ensure that we don't have any duplicate relationships:

```
# join customers to invoices
joined_tables = pd.merge(
  chinook_customers,
  chinook_invoices
)

# join result to items
joined_tables = pd.merge(joined_tables, chinook_items)

# create FullName
joined_tables['FullName'] = joined_tables['FirstName'] + ' ' + \
joined_tables['LastName']

# drop duplicates and view head
cust_item_table = joined_tables[['FullName', 'TrackId']]\
.drop_duplicates()
cust_item_table.head()
```

```
##          FullName  TrackId
## 0  Luís Gonçalves     3247
## 1  Luís Gonçalves     3248
## 2  Luís Gonçalves      447
## 3  Luís Gonçalves      449
## 4  Luís Gonçalves      451
```

Now we can create a graph of connections between customers and items and visualize it as in Figure 4.7.

```python
import networkx as nx
from matplotlib import pyplot as plt

# create networkx object
cust_item_network = nx.from_pandas_edgelist(cust_item_table,
source = "FullName", target = "TrackId")

# color items differently to customers
colors = ["red" if i in cust_item_table['FullName'].values else "green"
for i in cust_item_network.nodes]

# visualize
np.random.seed(123)
nx.draw_networkx(cust_item_network, node_color = colors, node_size = 2,
edge_color = "grey", with_labels = False)
plt.show()
```

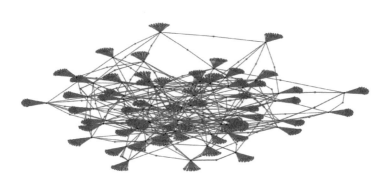

FIGURE 4.7: Visualization of the Chinook customer-to-item network with customers as red vertices and items as green vertices

Now to create the customer-to-customer network based on common item purchases, we do further joins on the data sets and remove connections between the same customers.

```
# merge customers on common track IDs
cust_cust_table = pd.merge(cust_item_table, cust_item_table,
on = "TrackId")

# rename columns
cust_cust_table.rename(
  columns={'FullName_x' :'CustName1', 'FullName_y' :'CustName2'},
  inplace=True
)

# remove loop edges
cust_cust_table = cust_cust_table[
  ~(cust_cust_table['CustName1'] == cust_cust_table['CustName2'])
]

# view head
cust_cust_table.head()
```

```
##                 CustName1   TrackId            CustName2
## 4          Luís Gonçalves       449        Edward Francis
## 5          Edward Francis       449        Luís Gonçalves
## 11         Luís Gonçalves      1157   Richard Cunningham
## 12     Richard Cunningham      1157        Luís Gonçalves
## 17         Luís Gonçalves      1169   Richard Cunningham
```

Now we can drop duplicates based on the `TrackId`, count the items by pair of customers, and we will have our final edgelist:

```
# drop duplicates
cust_cust_table = cust_cust_table.drop_duplicates('TrackId')

# count common items
cust_cust_table = cust_cust_table.groupby(['CustName1', 'CustName2'],
as_index = False).TrackId.nunique()
cust_cust_table.rename(columns = {'TrackId': 'Items'}, inplace = True)

# view head
cust_cust_table.head()
```

```
##              CustName1          CustName2   Items
## 0       Aaron Mitchell      Enrique Muñoz       1
## 1       Aaron Mitchell      Hugh O'Reilly       1
## 2       Aaron Mitchell    Niklas Schröder       1
## 3       Aaron Mitchell        Phil Hughes       1
## 4      Alexandre Rocha     Aaron Mitchell       1
```

Now we are ready to create and visualize our customer-to-customer network, as in Figure 4.8.

```
# create networkx object
cust_cust_network = nx.from_pandas_edgelist(cust_cust_table,
source = "CustName1", target = "CustName2", edge_attr = True)
```

```
# visualize
np.random.seed(123)
nx.draw_networkx(cust_cust_network, node_color = "lightblue",
edge_color = "grey", with_labels = False)
plt.show()
```

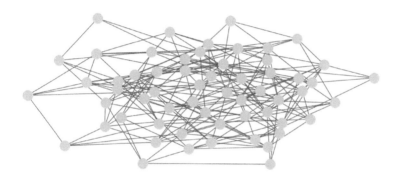

FIGURE 4.8: Visualization of the Chinook customer-to-customer network based on any common item purchase

And if we wish to restrict connections to two or more common item purchases, we can create a subgraph based on the number of items, as in Figure 4.9. Some experimentation with the parameter k in networkx's spring layout (which determines the optimal distance between vertices) is needed to appropriately visualize the two distinct connected components in this graph.

```
# get edges with items >= 2
twoitem_edges = [i for i in list(cust_cust_network.edges) if
cust_cust_network.edges[i]['Items'] >= 2]
```

```
# create subgraph
twoitem_network = cust_cust_network.edge_subgraph(twoitem_edges)
```

```
# visualize in FR (spring) layout
np.random.seed(123)
layout = nx.spring_layout(twoitem_network, k = 0.05)
```

```
nx.draw_networkx(twoitem_network, node_color = "lightblue",
edge_color = "grey", with_labels = False, pos = layout)
plt.show()
```

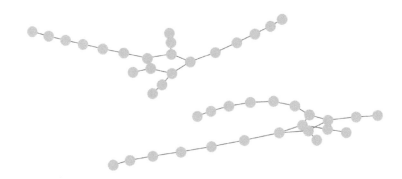

FIGURE 4.9: Visualization of the Chinook customer-to-customer network based on at least two common item purchases

4.2 Transforming data from documents for use in graphs

In our second example, we will look at how to extract information that sits in semi-structured documents and how to convert that information to a graph-like shape to allow us to understand relationships that interest us. Semi-structured documents are documents which have a certain expected format through which we can reliably identify important actors or entities. These could be legal contracts, financial statements or other types of structured forms. Through extracting entities from these documents, we can identify important relationships between them, such as co-publishing, financial transactions or contractual obligations.

To illustrate this, we will show how to extract information from a TV script in a way where we can determine which characters have spoken in the same scene together, and then use this information to create a network of TV characters. We will use an episode script from the hit TV comedy show *Friends*. A full set of scripts from all episodes of *Friends* can be found online at https://fangj.github.io/friends/. For this learning example, we will focus on the character network from the first episode of *Friends*. The script of the first episode can be found at https://fangj.github.io/friends/season/0101.html. Once we have learned the basic methods using the first episode, some of the end-of-chapter exercises will encourage the extension of these methods to further episodes.

4.2.1 Scraping data from semi-structured documents

First, we will look at how to obtain a list of numbered scenes and the characters in each scene, through 'scraping' these details from the online script. To help us with this, we will use the `rvest` R package, which is designed for scraping information from webpages.

Let's take a look at the web code for Season 1, Episode 1. You can do this by opening the script webpage in Google Chrome and then pressing Cmd+Option+C (or Ctrl+Shift+C in Windows) to open the Elements Console where you can view the HTML code of the page side-by-side with the page itself. This should look like Figure 4.10.

FIGURE 4.10: Viewing the script of Season 1, Episode 1 of *Friends* with the Elements console open in Google Chrome

One of the things we can see immediately is that most of the words that precede a colon are of interest to us. In fact, most of them are character names that say something in a scene. We also see that lines that contain the string "Scene:" are pretty reliable indicators of scene boundaries.

The first thing we should do is get this HTML code in a list or vector of HTML nodes which represent the different pieces of formatting and text in the document. Since this will contain the separated lines spoken by each character, this will be really helpful for us to work from. So let's download the HTML code and break it into HTML nodes so that we have a nice, tidy vector of script content.

```r
# loading rvest also loads the xml2 package
library(rvest)

url_string <- "https://fangj.github.io/friends/season/0101.html"

# get script as vector of HTML nodes
nodes <- xml2::read_html(url_string) %>%
    xml2::as_list() %>%
    unlist()

# view head
head(nodes)
```

```
##                                              html.head.title
##  "The One Where Monica Gets a New Roomate (The Pilot-The Uncut Version)"
##                                                    html.body1
##                                                        "\n\n"
##                                                  html.body.h1
## "The One Where Monica Gets a New Roommate (The Pilot-The Uncut Version)"
##                                                    html.body3
##                                                        "\n\n"
##                                               html.body.font
##                                                        "\n\n"
##                                             html.body.font.p
##                          "Written by: Marta Kauffman & David Crane"
```

This has generated a named character vector that contains a lot of different splitout parts of the script, but most importantly it contains the lines from the script, for example:

```r
nodes[16]
```

```
##                                             html.body.font.p
## "[Scene: Central Perk, Chandler, Joey, Phoebe, and Monica are there.]"
```

Now, to generate something useful for our task, we need to create a vector that contains the word 'New Scene' if the line represents the beginning of a scene, and the name of the character if the line represents something spoken by a character. This will be the best format for what we want to do.

The first thing we will need to do is swap any text string containing "Scene:" to the string "New Scene." We can do this quite simply using an ifelse() on the nodes vector, where we use grepl() to identify which entries are in nodes that contain the string "Scene:"

```
# swap lines containing the string 'Scene:' with 'New Scene'
nodes_newscene <- ifelse(grepl("Scene:", nodes), "New Scene", nodes)

# check that there are at least a few 'New Scene' entries now
sum(nodes_newscene == "New Scene")
```

```
## [1] 15
```

That worked nicely. Now, you might also have noticed that, for dialogue purposes, character names precede a colon at the beginning of a line. So that might be a nice way to extract the names of characters with speaking parts in a scene (although it might give us a few other things that have preceded colons in the script which we do not want, but we can deal with that later).

So what we will do is use regular expression syntax (regex) to tell R that we are looking for anything at the beginning of a line preceding a colon. We will use a lookahead regex string as follows: ^[A-Za-z]+(?=:).

Let's look at that string and make sure we know what it means. The ^[A-Za-z]+ component means 'find any substring of alphabetic text of any length including spaces at the beginning of a string.' The part in parentheses (?=:) is known as a lookahead—it means look ahead of that substring of text and find situations where a colon is the next character. This is therefore instructing R to find any string of alphabetic text at the start of a line that precedes a colon and return it. If we use the R package stringr and its function str_extract() with this regex syntax, it will go through every entry of the nodes vector and transform it to just the first string of text found before a colon. If no such string is found, it will return an NA value. This is great for us because we know that, for the purpose of dialogue, characters' names are always at the start of nodes, so we certainly won't miss any if we just take the first instance in each line. We should also, for safety, not mess with the scene breaks we have put into our vector.

```
library(stringr)

# outside of 'New Scene' tags extract anything before : in every line
nodes_char <- ifelse(nodes_newscene != "New Scene",
                     stringr::str_extract(nodes_newscene,
                                          "^[A-Za-z ]+(?=:)"),
                     nodes_newscene)

# check a sample
set.seed(123)
nodes_char[sample(30)]
```

```
## [1] NA        NA        NA        NA        NA        "Monica"     NA
## [8] NA        NA        NA        NA        "Chandler"  NA          NA
## [15] NA       NA        NA        NA        NA        NA           NA
## [22] NA       NA        "Joey"    "Phoebe"  NA        "New Scene"  NA
## [29] NA       "Written by"
```

So this is working, but we have more cleaning to do. For example, we will want to get rid of the NA values. We will also see if we take a look that there is a character called 'All' which probably should not be in our network. We can also see phrases like 'Written by' which are not dialogue characters, and strings containing 'and' which involve combinations of characters. So we can create special commands to remove any instances of these phrases[2].

```r
# remove NAs
nodes_char_clean1 <- nodes_char[!is.na(nodes_char)]

# remove entries with "all", " and " or "by" irrelevant of the case
nodes_char_clean2 <- nodes_char_clean1[
  !grepl("all| and |by", tolower(nodes_char_clean1))
]

# check
nodes_char_clean2[sample(20)]
```

```
## [1] "Chandler" "Monica"   "Chandler" "Monica"   "Phoebe"    "Joey"   "Phoebe"  "Joey"
## [9] "Monica"   "Monica"   "Chandler" "Chandler" "New Scene" "Ross"   "Joey"    "Chandler"
## [17] "Joey"     "Chandler" "Phoebe"   "Chandler"
```

Let's assume our cleaning is done, and we have a nice vector that contains either the names of characters that are speaking lines in the episode or "New Scene" to indicate that we are crossing a scene boundary. We now just need to convert this vector into a simple dataframe with two columns for scene and character. We already have our character lists, so we really just need to iterate through our nodes vector and, for each entry, count the number of previous occurrences of "New Scene" and add one.

```r
# number scene by counting previous "New Scene" entries and adding 1
scene_count <- c()

for (i in 1:length(nodes_char_clean2)) {
  scene_count[i] <- sum(grepl("New Scene", nodes_char_clean2[1:i])) + 1
}
```

---

[2]The limited cleaning commands here work for this specific episode, but they would need to be expanded to be used on more episodes to take into account any unpredictable formatting in the scripts. The reality of most scraping exercises is that some code has to be written to deal with exceptions.

Then we can finalize our dataframe by putting our two vectors together and removing any repeated characters in the same scene. We can also correct for situations where the script starts with a New Scene and we can consistently format our character names to title case, to account for different case typing.

```
library(dplyr)

results <- data.frame(scene = scene_count,
                      character = nodes_char_clean2) |>
   dplyr::filter(character != "New Scene") |>
   dplyr::distinct(scene, character) |>
   dplyr::mutate(
     scene = scene - min(scene) + 1, # set first scene number to 1
     character = character |>
       tolower() |>
       tools::toTitleCase() # title case
   )

# check the first ten rows
head(results, 10)
```

```
##      scene character
## 1        1    Monica
## 2        1      Joey
## 3        1  Chandler
## 4        1    Phoebe
## 5        1      Ross
## 6        1    Rachel
## 7        1  Waitress
## 8        2    Monica
## 9        2  Chandler
## 10       2      Ross
```

4.2.2   Creating an edgelist from the scraped data

Now that we have scraped the data of characters who have spoken in each numbered scene, we can try to build an edgelist between characters based on whether they have both spoken in the same scene. We can also consider adding a weight to each edge based on the number of scenes in which both characters have spoken.

To do this, we will need to generate a set of unique pairs from the list of characters in each scene. To illustrate, let's look at the characters in Scene 11:

```
(scene11_chars <- results |>
  dplyr::filter(scene == 11) |>
  dplyr::pull(character))
```

```
## [1] "Rachel"   "Chandler" "Joey"        "Monica"   "Paul"
```

The unique pairs from this scene are formed by starting with the first character
in the list and pairing with each of those that follow, then starting with the
second and pairing with each that follows, and so on until the final pair is
formed from the second-to-last and last elements of the list. So for Scene 11
our unique pairs would be:

- **Rachel pairs:** Rachel-Chandler, Rachel-Joey, Rachel-Monica, Rachel-Paul
- **Chandler pairs:** Chandler-Joey, Chandler-Monica, Chandler-Paul
- **Joey pairs:** Joey-Monica, Joey-Paul
- **Monica pairs**: Monica-Paul

So we should write a function called unique_pairs() which accepts a character
vector of arbitrary length and forms pairs progressively in this way. Then we
can apply this function to every scene.

```
unique_pairs <- function(char_vector = NULL) {
  # ensure unique entries
  vector <- as.character(unique(char_vector))
  # create from-to column dataframe
  df <- data.frame(char1 = character(),
                   char2 = character(),
                   stringsAsFactors = FALSE)
  # iterate over each entry to form pairs
  if (length(vector) > 1) {
    for (i in 1:(length(vector) - 1)) {
      char1 <- rep(vector[i], length(vector) - i)
      char2 <- vector[(i + 1): length(vector)]

      df <- df %>%
        dplyr::bind_rows(
          data.frame(char1 = char1,
                     char2 = char2,
                     stringsAsFactors = FALSE)
        )
    }
  }
  #return result
  df
}
```

Now let's test our new function on the Scene 11 characters:

```
unique_pairs(scene11_chars)
```

```
##           char1     char2
## 1      Rachel  Chandler
## 2      Rachel      Joey
## 3      Rachel    Monica
## 4      Rachel      Paul
## 5    Chandler      Joey
## 6    Chandler    Monica
## 7    Chandler      Paul
## 8        Joey    Monica
## 9        Joey      Paul
## 10     Monica      Paul
```

That looks right. Now we can easily generate our edgelist from this episode by applying our new function to each scene.

```
# run unique_pairs by scene
friends_ep101 <- results |>
  dplyr::group_by(scene) |>
  dplyr::summarise(unique_pairs(character)) |>
  dplyr::ungroup()

# check
head(friends_ep101)
```

```
## # A tibble: 6 x 3
##    scene char1   char2
##    <dbl> <chr>   <chr>
## 1      1 Monica  Joey
## 2      1 Monica  Chandler
## 3      1 Monica  Phoebe
## 4      1 Monica  Ross
## 5      1 Monica  Rachel
## 6      1 Monica  Waitress
```

This looks like it worked. Now we can just count the number of times each distinct pair occurs in order to get our edge weights (making sure to ignore the order of the characters).

```r
# create weight as count of scenes
friends_ep101_edgelist <- friends_ep101 |>
  dplyr::select(-scene) |>
  dplyr::mutate(from = pmin(char1, char2), to = pmax(char1, char2)) |>
  dplyr::count(from, to, name = "weight")

# check
head(friends_ep101_edgelist)
```

```
## # A tibble: 6 x 3
##   from     to         weight
##   <chr>    <chr>       <int>
## 1 Chandler Customer        1
## 2 Chandler Joey            8
## 3 Chandler Monica          6
## 4 Chandler Paul            2
## 5 Chandler Phoebe          5
## 6 Chandler Rachel          6
```

We can now use this edgelist to create an undirected network graph for the first episode of *Friends*. First, we will create an igraph object and then we will visualize it using edge thickness based on weights, as in Figure 4.11.

```r
# create igraph object
friends_ep1_network <- igraph::graph_from_data_frame(
  d = friends_ep101_edgelist,
  directed = FALSE
)

# visualize
set.seed(123)
ggraph(friends_ep1_network) +
  geom_edge_link(aes(edge_width = weight), color = "grey", alpha = 0.5,
                 show.legend = FALSE) +
  geom_node_label(aes(label = name), color = "blue") +
  scale_x_continuous(expand = expansion(mult = 0.1)) +
  theme_void()
```

4.2.3   Approaches in Python

To repeat the work in the previous sections in Python, we will use the BeautifulSoup package to scrape our web script of the first episode of *Friends*.

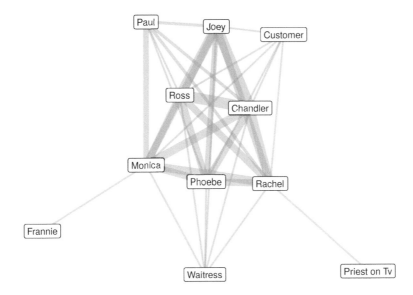

FIGURE 4.11: Visualization of the network of characters in Episode 1 of *Friends*, based on characters speaking in the same scene together

```
import requests
from bs4 import BeautifulSoup

url = "https://fangj.github.io/friends/season/0101.html"
script = requests.get(url)

# parse the html of the page
friends_ep1 = BeautifulSoup(script.text, "html.parser")
```

The object `friends_ep1` contains all the HTML code of the script webpage. Now we need to look for the string `Scene:` and replace it with the string `<b>New Scene:</b>`. It should be clear soon why we should put the replacement string in bold HTML tags.

```
originalString = "Scene:"
replaceString = "<b>New Scene:</b>"
friends_ep1_replace = BeautifulSoup(str(friends_ep1)\
.replace(originalString, replaceString))
```

Now we know from viewing the webpage or inspecting the HTML code that the characters' names who are speaking in scenes will be inside bold or strong HTML tags. So, first let's get everything that is in bold or strong tags in the document, and then let's match for any alphabetic string (including spaces) prior to a colon using regular expression syntax. This should include the New Scene tags that we created in the last step.

```
# use re (regular expressions) package
import re

# find everything in bold tags with alpha preceding a colon
searchstring = re.compile("^[A-Za-z ]+(?=:)")
friends_ep1_bold = friends_ep1_replace.find_all(['b', 'strong'],
text = searchstring)

# extract the text and remove colons
friends_ep1_list = [friends_ep1_bold[i].text.replace(':', '')
for i in range(0, len(friends_ep1_bold) - 1)]

# check first few unique values returned
sorted(set(friends_ep1_list))[0:7]
```

```
## ['All', 'Chandler', 'Chandler ', 'Customer', 'Frannie', 'Joey', 'Monica']
```

This looks promising; now we need to get rid of the 'All' entries and any entries containing 'and.'

```
friends_ep1_list2=[entry.strip() for entry in friends_ep1_list
if "All" not in entry and " and " not in entry]

# check first few entries
sorted(set(friends_ep1_list2))[0:7]
```

```
## ['Chandler', 'Customer', 'Frannie', 'Joey', 'Monica', 'New Scene', 'Paul']
```

Now we are ready to organize our characters by scene. First, we do a scene count, then we create a dataframe and obtain unique character lists by scene.

```
import pandas as pd

# number scene by counting previous "New Scene" entries and adding 1
scene_count = []

for i in range(0,len(friends_ep1_list2)):
  scene_count.append(friends_ep1_list2[0:i+1].count("New Scene"))
```

```
# create a pandas dataframe
df = {'scene': scene_count, 'character': friends_ep1_list2}
scenes_df = pd.DataFrame(df)

# remove New Scene rows
scenes_df = scenes_df[scenes_df.character != "New Scene"]

# get unique characters by scene
scenes = scenes_df.groupby('scene')['character'].unique()

# check
scenes.head()


## scene
## 1     [Monica, Joey, Chandler, Phoebe, Ross, Rachel,...
## 2     [Monica, Chandler, Ross, Rachel, Phoebe, Joey,...
## 3                                              [Phoebe]
## 4                             [Ross, Joey, Chandler]
## 5                                       [Monica, Paul]
## Name: character, dtype: object
```

Now we need to create a function to find all unique pairs inside a scene character list. Here's one way to do it:

```
import numpy as np

# define function
def unique_pairs(chars: object) -> pd.DataFrame:
  # start with uniques
  characters = np.unique(chars)
  # create from-to list dataframe
  char1 = []
  char2 = []
  df = pd.DataFrame({'char1': char1, 'char2': char2})
  # iterate over each entry to form pairs
  if len(characters) > 1:
    for i in range(0, len(characters) - 1):
      char1 = [characters[i]] * (len(characters) - i - 1)
      char2 = [characters[i] for i in range(i + 1, len(characters))]
      # append to dataframe
      df2 = pd.DataFrame({'char1': char1, 'char2': char2})
      df = df.append(df2, ignore_index = True)
    return df
```

```
# test on scene 11
unique_pairs(scenes[11])
```

```
##          char1    char2
## 0    Chandler     Joey
## 1    Chandler   Monica
## 2    Chandler     Paul
## 3    Chandler   Rachel
## 4        Joey   Monica
## 5        Joey     Paul
## 6        Joey   Rachel
## 7      Monica     Paul
## 8      Monica   Rachel
## 9        Paul   Rachel
```

This looks right. Now we need to apply this to every scene and gather the results into one DataFrame.

```
# start DataFrame
char1 = []
char2 = []

edgelist_df = pd.DataFrame({'char1': char1, 'char2': char2})

for scene in scenes:
  df = unique_pairs(scene)
  edgelist_df = edgelist_df.append(df, ignore_index = True)
```

Now we can order across the rows alphabetically and count the occurrences of each unique character pair to get our edge weights.

```
# sort each row alphabetically
edgelist_df = edgelist_df.sort_values(by = ['char1', 'char2'])

# count by unique pair
edgelist = edgelist_df.groupby(['char1', 'char2']).\
apply(len).to_frame("weight").reset_index()

# check
edgelist.head()
```

```
##          char1      char2   weight
## 0    Chandler   Customer        1
```

```
## 1   Chandler      Joey        8
## 2   Chandler    Monica        6
## 3   Chandler      Paul        2
## 4   Chandler    Phoebe        5
```

This is what we need to create and visualize our graph of Episode 1 of *Friends*, which can be seen in Figure 4.12 with the edge thickness determined by edge weight.

```
import networkx as nx
from matplotlib import pyplot as plt

# create networkx object
friends_ep1_network = nx.from_pandas_edgelist(edgelist,
source = "char1", target = "char2", edge_attr=True)

# visualize with edge weight as edge width
np.random.seed(123)
weights = list(
  nx.get_edge_attributes(friends_ep1_network, 'weight').values()
)
nx.draw_networkx(
  friends_ep1_network, node_color = "lightblue", node_size = 60,
  edge_color = "grey", with_labels = True, width = np.array(weights)
)
plt.show()
```

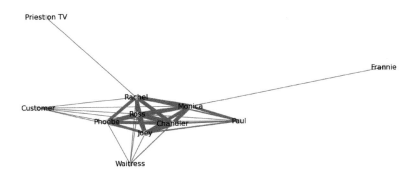

FIGURE 4.12: Graph of *Friends* character network from Episode 1 with edge width indicating the number of shared scenes

4.3   Learning exercises

4.3.1   Discussion questions

1. What kinds of data sources are most likely to already exist in a graph-friendly form? Why?
2. What are the two most important things to define when you intend to transform data into a graph-friendly structure?
3. Imagine that you are working in a global law firm with a database that has three tables. One table lists employee location details including office and home address. A second table includes details on which clients each employee has been working for and what specialty areas they focus on with each client. A third table lists the education history of each employee including school and major/subject area. List out or sketch all the different ways you can think to turn this data into a graph.
4. Pick one or two of your answers from Question 3 and write down two options for how to structure a graph for each of them. For one option, consider a graph where employees are the only vertices. Then consider a graph where there are at least two different entity types as vertices.
5. Considering your answers to Question 4, how might your edges be defined in each of your options? Would the edges have any properties?

For the examples in Questions 6-10, discuss ways that information could be extracted, reshaped and loaded into a graph in order to serve a useful analytic purpose.

6. Loyalty card data for a retail company showing detailed information on customer visits and purchases.

7. Data from the calendars of a large number of company employees.

8. Data from automatic number plate scanning from police cameras on major roads in a large city.

9. Data on addresses of deliveries made by a courier company.

10. Electronic files of legal contracts between different organizations to deliver specified services at specified prices.

4.3.2 Data exercises

Load the park_reviews data set from the onadata package or download it from the internet[3]. This data contains the reviews of a collection of Yelp users on dog parks in the Phoenix, Arizona area.

1. Create an edgelist and vertex set that allows you to build a graph showing both the parks and the users as entity types. Include the stars rating as an edge property and ensure that entity types are distinguishable in your data.
2. Use your edgelist and vertex set to create a graph object that has edge and vertex properties.
3. Visualize your graph in a way that differentiates between users and parks. Use your visualization to point out users that have reviewed numerous dog parks.
4. Generate a subgraph consisting only of edges where the stars rating was 5. Repeat your visualization for this subgraph. Use it to identify a frequently 5-star rated park. Has any user reviewed more than one park as 5-star rated?

Go to the webpage containing the script for Season 1, Episode 2 of *Friends* at https://fangj.github.io/friends/season/0102.html.

5. Repeat the steps in Section 4.2 to scrape this webpage to obtain a list of scenes and characters speaking in each scene. Watch out for any additional cleaning that might be necessary for this script compared to the Episode 1 script.
6. Use the methods in Section 4.2, including the unique_pairs() function, to create an edgelist for the character network for Episode 2 with the same edge weight based on the number of scenes in which the characters both spoke.
7. Create a graph for Episode 2 and visualize the graph.
8. Combine the edgelist for both Episodes 1 and 2 by adding the weights for each character pair, and then create and visualize a new graph that combines both episodes.
9. **Extension:** Try to wrap the previous methods in a function that creates an edgelist for any arbitrary *Friends* episode found at https://fangj.github.io/friends/. Add more cleaning commands for unexpected formatting that you might see in different scripts.
10. **Extension:** Try to run your function on all Season 1 episodes of *Friends* and use the results to create and visualize a graph of the character network of the entire first season.

---

[3]https://ona-book.org/data/park_reviews.csv

5

Paths and Distance

Over the course of the earlier chapters, as we learned how to transform data into graph-friendly structures and how to create and visualize graphs, we started to see some concepts emerge informally which we will now start to formally describe and support by means of some mathematical definition and measurement. For example, we have seen that vertices can be connected directly or indirectly to other vertices by means of a single edge or a series of edges. We have observed visually that there can be greater 'distance' between some vertices in graphs compared to others, and in some cases it is simply not possible to get from one vertex to another along any edges in a graph.

The process of moving from vertex to vertex along edges in a graph is known as *graph traversal*. Graph traversal is an extremely important topic that underlies any sort of graph search algorithm. Graph search algorithms, in turn, are foundational in determining the optimal or shortest paths between pairs of vertices, or the set of shortest paths from a given vertex to all other vertices. Shortest paths are themselves important in the definition of distance and diameter in networks. Distance and diameter are useful and intuitive measurements that are frequently used in understanding 'closeness' or 'familiarity' between vertices or in the overall network, and in determining different degrees of influence between vertices.

In this chapter we will progressively look at each of these concepts, so that the reader has a good understanding of their meaning and how they are derived, before we delve into the convenient functions in R and Python which can calculate paths, distance and diameter. Then, toward the end of the chapter, we will look at some short case studies which put these concepts to use in the analysis of a network of office workers.

The early work in this chapter will use a graph which we will call G_{14}, and which is shown in Figure 5.1. This graph contains 14 vertices labelled 1 through 14, where a path of edges exists between any pair of vertices. This is known as a *connected graph*.

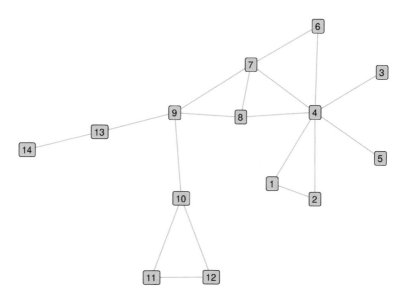

FIGURE 5.1: The G_{14} graph

5.1 Theory of graph traversal, paths and distance

5.1.1 Paths and graph traversal

Given any two vertices A and B in a graph G, a **path** between A and B is any series of edges in G that begin at A and end at B. For example, in our G_{14} graph, the following are examples of paths between Vertex 9 and Vertex 4:

- $9 \longleftrightarrow 8 \longleftrightarrow 4$
- $9 \longleftrightarrow 7 \longleftrightarrow 4$
- $9 \longleftrightarrow 7 \longleftrightarrow 8 \longleftrightarrow 4$
- $9 \longleftrightarrow 8 \longleftrightarrow 7 \longleftrightarrow 4$
- $9 \longleftrightarrow 7 \longleftrightarrow 6 \longleftrightarrow 4$
- $9 \longleftrightarrow 8 \longleftrightarrow 7 \longleftrightarrow 6 \longleftrightarrow 4$
- $9 \longleftrightarrow 7 \longleftrightarrow 8 \longleftrightarrow 7 \longleftrightarrow 4$

A **simple path** or **acyclic path** is a path where no vertex is repeated. All except the last path above are simple paths between Vertex 9 and Vertex 4 in G_{14}. In general, because we are interested in efficient paths between vertices, we are only interested in simple paths in a graph. While the number of general paths between two vertices in a graph can be infinite due to possible repeated cycles, the number of simple paths between any two vertices in a graph is always finite. When we refer to a path from now on, we will always mean a simple path unless we say otherwise.

> **Playing around:** Let's reminisce about Chapter 1 where we studied the *Bridges of Königsberg* problem. You may recall that an *Eulerian path* or *Euler walk* is a path that visits every vertex in a graph at least once and that uses every edge in a graph exactly once. Consider subgraphs of G_{14} by taking subsets of vertices and the edges that connect them. How many vertices are in the largest subgraph you can form from G_{14} that contains an Eulerian Path? If you are an R user, you could consider using the `eulerian` package to verify your answer.

In order to determine whether a path exists between two vertices A and B in a graph, we need to be able to search or traverse the graph for possible routes across its edges, starting at Vertex A and ending at Vertex B, and passing through other vertices as necessary. Let's take an example from our G_{14} graph. Let's say we want to determine if a path exists between Vertex 9 and Vertex 5. When a human looks at a simple graph like this, it is visually obvious that such a path exists. However, as we have mentioned in earlier chapters, most complex graphs cannot be visualized as simply as this one, and computer programs are not human. So we are going to need a more systematic and programmable way of searching the graph for a path from Vertex 9 to Vertex 5.

One option is to traverse the graph using a *breadth-first approach*. This means that we search all of the immediate neighbors of Vertex 9, then we search the immediate neighbors of the immediate neighbors, and so on until we either eventually find Vertex 5 or until we have covered all vertices and concluded that there is no possible path to Vertex 5. Here is a simple breadth-first algorithm which would achieve this:

1. The immediate neighbors of Vertex 9 are Vertices 7, 8, 10 and 13. We have not found Vertex 5, but we mark Vertex 9 and these neighbor vertices as having been searched.
2. The unsearched immediate neighbors of Vertices 7, 8, 10 and 13 are Vertices 4, 6, 11, 12 and 14. We still have not found Vertex 5, but we add these vertices to the list of vertices which have been searched.
3. The unsearched immediate neighbors of Vertices 4, 6, 11, 12 and 14 are Vertices 1, 2, 3 and 5. We have found Vertex 5 and therefore a path exists between Vertex 9 and Vertex 5.

Alternatively, we could traverse the graph using a *depth-first approach*. This means that we choose a neighboring vertex of Vertex 9, then find a neighboring vertex of that neighboring vertex, and keep going until we cannot find any more unsearched neighboring vertices. When this happens, we move back a

vertex and look for an unsearched neighboring vertex. If we find one, we repeat
our process. If not, we move back another vertex and so on until we either find
Vertex 5 or we have searched all vertices and conclude that a path to Vertex
5 does not exist. Here is a simple depth-first algorithm which would achieve
this:

1. We select Vertex 10 as an immediate neighbor of Vertex 9 and mark
   both Vertices 9 and 10 as searched.

2. We select Vertex 11 as an unsearched immediate neighbor of Vertex
   10 and mark it as searched.

3. We select Vertex 12 as an unsearched immediate neighbor of Vertex
   11 and mark it as searched.

4. We cannot find an unsearched immediate neighbor of Vertex 12. So
   we move back to Vertex 11.

5. We cannot find an unsearched immediate neighbor of Vertex 11. So
   we move back to Vertex 10.

6. We cannot find an unsearched immediate neighbor of Vertex 10. So
   we move back to Vertex 9.

7. We select Vertex 8 as an unsearched immediate neighbor of Vertex
   9.

8. We select Vertex 4 as an unsearched immediate neighbor of Vertex
   8.

9. We select Vertex 3 as an unsearched immediate neighbor of Vertex
   4.

10. We cannot find an unsearched immediate neighbor of Vertex 3. So
    we move back to Vertex 4.

11. We select Vertex 5 as an unsearched immediate neighbor of Vertex 4.
    We have found Vertex 5 and therefore a path exists between Vertex
    9 and Vertex 5.

It appears that the breadth-first approach is quicker and more computationally
efficient than the depth-first approach, but this really depends on the specifics
of the search. Breadth-first searches like to stay close to the starting node, and
gradually increase their search radius. Depth-first searches like to 'run away
and come back.' In our G_{14} example above, because the network is very small
and all nodes are within a short path from Vertex 9, a breadth-first search
will usually find the target vertex quickly compared to a depth-first search,
whose speed will depend on the route it takes. However, when target nodes are
very 'far away' in the network, depth-first approaches can be more efficient.
On average, however, computation time complexity for both search types is
similar[1].

---

[1]The computation time complexity for both search types is proportional to the square
of the number of vertices in the graph when an adjacency matrix is used.

Thinking ahead: Consider the *smallest number of edges* that need to be traversed to get from Vertex 9 to Vertex 5 in our G_{14} graph. Work out what you think that is, and then try to use a depth-first search to move from Vertex 9 to Vertex 5 in different ways. Will the depth-first search always return a path with the smallest number of edges? Why or why not? What about the breadth-first search?

5.1.2 Path length and distance

For a path from vertex A to vertex B in a graph, the **length** of the path is the sum of the weights of the edges traversed in the path. If a graph does not have an edge weight property, then the weight of every edge is assumed to be equal to 1. Therefore, in an unweighted graph, the length of the path is the number of edges traversed on that path.

Looking at the (simple) paths from Vertex 9 to Vertex 4 in G_{14} as enumerated in Section 5.1.1, we can see that two of the paths have length 2, three of them have length 3, and one has length 4. Now let's look at a new graph G_{14W} which has weighted edges as in Figure 5.2.

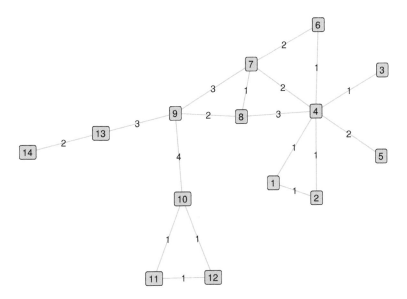

FIGURE 5.2: The G_{14W} weighted graph

The list of all simple paths from Vertex 9 to Vertex 4 in G_{14W} and their lengths are as follows:

- $9 \leftrightarrow 8 \leftrightarrow 4$ (Length 5)
- $9 \leftrightarrow 7 \leftrightarrow 4$ (Length 5)
- $9 \leftrightarrow 7 \leftrightarrow 8 \leftrightarrow 4$ (Length 7)
- $9 \leftrightarrow 8 \leftrightarrow 7 \leftrightarrow 4$ (Length 5)
- $9 \leftrightarrow 7 \leftrightarrow 6 \leftrightarrow 4$ (Length 6)
- $9 \leftrightarrow 8 \leftrightarrow 7 \leftrightarrow 6 \leftrightarrow 4$ (Length 6)

The **distance** between vertices A and B—sometimes notated as $d(A, B)$—is the length of the shortest path between A and B. Note that there is no requirement for a unique shortest path, and the shortest path could be traversed in more than one way in a graph. In our unweighted graph G_{14} the distance between Vertex 9 and Vertex 4 is 2. In the weighted graph G_{14W} the distance between Vertex 9 and Vertex 4 is 5. If no path exists between A and B, then the distance is called 'infinite' or denoted as ∞ by convention. If A and B are vertices of an undirected graph, then $d(A, B) = d(B, A)$. However, this may not be true for a directed graph.

Distance is an extremely important concept in graphs and has many practical applications. In physical networks like road or rail networks, distance is meant quite literally with greater distances between vertices usually translating to greater time taken or more resources used to traverse between those vertices. In social networks, distance can relate to the 'familiarity' or 'commonality' between two individuals. Greater distance between individuals in a network usually implies lower likelihood that those individuals know each other in real life, or lower likelihood that information given to one individual will find its way to other individuals. In graphs that represent the knowledge or interests of individuals (such as 'likes' in social networks or in knowledge graphs), greater distance between an individual and a topic, event or product usually implies that the individual is less likely to be interested in that topic, event or product. The utility of graph distance measures in fields like transport, communications, marketing, sociology and psychology should therefore be quite obvious.

Distance in weighted graphs needs to be treated with care, particularly in sociological and psychological contexts. Often unweighted distance will be more relevant than weighted distance. For example, if edges are weighted according to the 'strength' of a connection between individuals, then the weighted distance between two individuals might be the result of a sequence of multiple edges with low weights, even if those individuals are directly connected by an edge with a higher weight. A simple example of this is in Figure 5.3, where the weighted distance from A to B is 2, which arises via the path $A \leftrightarrow C \leftrightarrow B$, despite the fact that A and B are adjacent vertices. It is important to understand the meaning of 'weight' in your research context before determining if weighted or unweighted distance is appropriate.

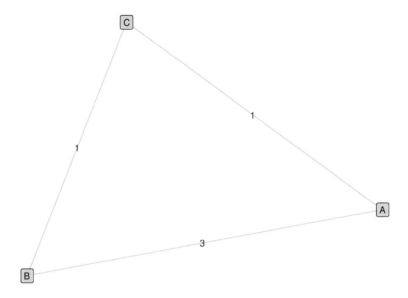

FIGURE 5.3: Distance needs to be treated with care in weighted graphs. In this case, the weighted distance from A to B arises from a path of two edges, even though A and B are adjacent in the graph.

5.1.3 Shortest path algorithms

Due to the importance of distance in graphs, various algorithms have been developed to calculate shortest paths. Some of these algorithms—such as Dijkstra's algorithm or the Bellman-Ford algorithm—focus on a *single source* shortest path, which calculates the shortest path between a given vertex and all other vertices in the graph. Others—such as Johnson's algorithm or the Floyd-Warshall algorithm— focus on the *all pairs* shortest path problem and calculate the shortest path between any pair of vertices in the graph. Special algorithms have also been developed to facilitate fast calculation of shortest path between a specific pair of vertices, such as the A* algorithm.

Dijkstra's algorithm is perhaps the most well-known (and most established) shortest path algorithm, and the easiest to explain. Let's take a look at how this algorithm works by using our unweighted G_{14} graph as an illustrative example. Dijkstra's algorithm accepts a single initial vertex and calculates the distance between that vertex and all other vertices in the graph. Let's use Vertex 9 as our initial vertex. Dijkstra's algorithm operates in a series of iterative steps as follows:

1. We assign a tentative distance between Vertex 9 and itself as zero, and between Vertex 9 and all other vertices as ∞. We then mark Vertex 9 as searched.

2. Move to each of the neighbors of Vertex 9, and calculate the length of the path from Vertex 9 to each of those neighbors and update the tentative distance to this length. In this case, we give a tentative distance of 1 to Vertices 7, 8, 10 and 13. We then mark these vertices as searched.

3. We next go to each of Vertices 7, 8, 10 and 13 in turn, marking each one as current as we proceed. For each current vertex, we calculate the length of the shortest path from Vertex 9 to each of the unsearched neighbors of the current vertex which *pass through the current vertex*. If that length is smaller than the existing tentative distance, update the tentative distance with this length. If we move to Vertex 7 first, we see two unsearched neighbors: Vertices 4 and 6. The distance from Vertex 9 to both these vertices passing through Vertex 7 is 2, which is less than ∞, and so we update the tentative distances from Vertex 9 to Vertices 4 and 6 to 2.

4. In a similar fashion we update the tentative distances from Vertex 9 to Vertices 11, 12 and 14 to 2.

5. We mark Vertices 4, 6, 11, 12 and 14 as searched and move to these vertices as current vertices and repeat the process for their neighbors. In this way, we update the tentative distance from Vertex 9 to Vertices 1, 2, 3 and 5 to 3. We mark Vertices 1, 2, 3 and 5 as searched.

6. We have now searched all vertices in the graph, and the tentative distances between Vertex 9 and all other vertices are now assigned as the final distances.

> **Playing around:** Try to repeat the process of Dijkstra's algorithm for the weighted graph G_{14W}. Which vertex has the shortest distance from Vertex 9 and which vertex has the longest distance?

Single source shortest path algorithms like Dijkstra's algorithm can be used to solve the all pairs distance problem by simply repeating the algorithm for each vertex in the graph. For large graphs, however, this can be inefficient, which explains why alternative algorithms have been developed for the all pairs problem[2].

---

[2]Basic time complexity for Dijkstra's algorithm for a single source vertex is proportional to the square of the number of vertices in the graph. As a comparison, basic time complexity for the all pairs Floyd-Warshall algorithm is proportional to the cube of the number of vertices in the graph. Based on this, you would expect both algorithms to calculate all pairs distance in approximately the same computation time, but numerous modern computational methods have been able to cut these computation times significantly for different varieties of large graphs. Johnson's algorithm, for example, is known to perform particularly well on sparse graphs.

5.1.4   Graph diameter and density

The *diameter* of a graph G is the maximum distance between any pair of
vertices in G. Alternatively stated, it is the longest shortest path between
vertices in G. If a graph is not a connected graph, then by definition its
diameter is infinite. Diameter is usually only a useful measure in connected
graphs, or in studying connected subgraphs of larger graphs.

The diameter of a social network is an intuitive measure of the overall 'closeness' of the individuals in that network. Networks with smaller diameters can
often be considered as more 'close-knit' communities. However, care needs to
be taken in interpreting the diameter of a network, particularly given that
other measures may be more representative of how close-knit a community is.
Common alternative metrics used to assess overall network 'closeness' include:

- Average distance between all pairs of vertices
- The **density** of the network, which is defined as the number of edges divided
  by the total possible number of edges in a graph[3]. A complete graph, for
  example, would have a density of 1. Graphs with lower density are called
  sparse graphs.

Consider the two graphs in Figure 5.4. In the first graph, the diameter is 5,
and in the second the diameter is 4. However, the average distance between
vertices in the first graph is 2.38, and in the second graph it is 2.49. Both
graphs have the same density of 0.2. Therefore, one measure would regard the
first graph as 'closer,' another would regard the second graph as closer, and
the third measure would regard them as the same.

---

[3]If $|V|$ is the number of vertices in a directed graph, then the number of possible edges
is $|V|(|V| - 1)$, and in an undirected graph it is $\frac{|V|(|V|-1)}{2}$. Therefore, if $|E|$ is the number
of edges, we can derive the formula for density D as $\frac{|E|}{|V|(|V|-1)}$ for a directed graph and
$\frac{2|E|}{|V|(|V|-1)}$ for an undirected graph.

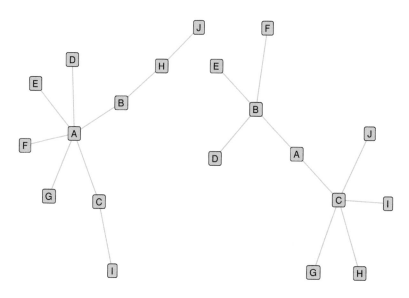

FIGURE 5.4: Two graphs illustrating how closeness can be measured in different ways

Playing around: Graph distance and diameter is of great interest in everyday life. You may know the theory of the *six degrees of separation*, which suggests that the entire world is a connected graph where the distance between any two people is at most 6. Alternatively stated, the world is a connected graph with a diameter of no more than 6. Several industry-specific case studies of this have arisen for research and just for fun. The first was a 1969 paper by two psychologists (Travers & Milgram (1969)), which used an experiment of chain letters to determine that the average distance between people in a population in Nebraska and Massachusetts was 6.2. A 2011 study of the Facebook graph (Ugander et al. (2011)) determined that the Facebook member network was almost fully connected with 99.91% of vertices in a connected subgraph, and that the average distance between vertices was 4.7. In the entertainment industry, the *Bacon number* is used to denote the distance between an individual and the actor Kevin Bacon, based on participation in the same movie or TV production. In academia, the *Erdös number* is used to denote the distance between an individual and the mathematician Paul Erdös. Both Bacon and Erdös have arisen as central points because they were highly active in their disciplines and as a result have high centrality in their network. We will look at centrality in the next chapter, but if you are interested you can find the Bacon number of any actor by visiting https://oracleofbacon.org/.

5.2 Calculating paths, distance, diameter and density

5.2.1 Calculating in R

Thanks to packages like igraph in R, it is much easier to calculate path, distance and density metrics than to understand the theory behind them. In this section we will illustrate various functions that can be used to easily calculate these metrics. Before we begin, let's create the graphs G_{14} and G_{14W} from the previous section by loading the g14_edgelist data set from the onadata package or by downloading it from the internet[4].

```
# download the edgelist
g14_edgelist <- read.csv("https://ona-book.org/data/g14_edgelist.csv")

# view head
head(g14_edgelist)
```

```
##    from to weight
## 1     9 10      4
## 2    10 11      1
## 3    11 12      1
## 4    10 12      1
## 5     9 13      3
## 6    13 14      2
```

Let's start by creating the weighted G_{14W} graph from the previous section.

```
# create weighted graph
(g14w <- igraph::graph_from_data_frame(g14_edgelist, directed = FALSE))
```

```
## IGRAPH 7ee58a1 UNW- 14 18 --
## + attr: name (v/c), weight (e/n)
## + edges from 7ee58a1 (vertex names):
##  [1] 9 --10 10--11 11--12 10--12 9 --13 13--14 9 --8  9 --7  8 --7  4 --6  4 --7  8 --4  6 --7
## [14] 4 --1  4 --2  4 --3  4 --5  1 --2
```

The all_simple_paths() function in igraph returns all paths from a specified vertex, and expects at least an igraph object and a vertex name for the from vertex as arguments. If the to argument specifies a vertex, then the function will return only paths between the from and to vertices. Otherwise, it will return a list containing all paths from the specified vertex to all other vertices. Note that these functions expect the vertex name as a character string.

---

[4]https://ona-book.org/data/g14_edgelist.csv

```
igraph::all_simple_paths(g14w, from = "9", to = "4")
```

```
## [[1]]
## + 3/14 vertices, named, from 7ee58a1:
## [1] 9 8 4
##
## [[2]]
## + 4/14 vertices, named, from 7ee58a1:
## [1] 9 8 7 4
##
## [[3]]
## + 5/14 vertices, named, from 7ee58a1:
## [1] 9 8 7 6 4
##
## [[4]]
## + 4/14 vertices, named, from 7ee58a1:
## [1] 9 7 8 4
##
## [[5]]
## + 3/14 vertices, named, from 7ee58a1:
## [1] 9 7 4
##
## [[6]]
## + 4/14 vertices, named, from 7ee58a1:
## [1] 9 7 6 4
```

We see that this agrees with our manual calculations in Section 5.1.1 and is the same whether or not the edges are weighted. This function is easy to use in the case of undirected graphs. When using with digraphs, there is an additional argument called mode, specifying the direction of the paths you are seeking. out, in, all or total are the accepted values for this argument.

The all_shortest_paths() function performs the same task as the previous function but restricts the output to paths of the shortest length. This function returns a list of objects, but the paths can be found in the res element of the list.

```
shortest_9to4 <- igraph::all_shortest_paths(g14w, from = "9", to = "4")
shortest_9to4$res
```

```
## [[1]]
## + 3/14 vertices, named, from 7ee58a1:
## [1] 9 8 4
##
```

```
## [[2]]
## + 3/14 vertices, named, from 7ee58a1:
## [1] 9 7 4
##
## [[3]]
## + 4/14 vertices, named, from 7ee58a1:
## [1] 9 8 7 4
```

Note that the function has returned the shortest path according to edge weights. To ignore edge weights, simply set `weights = NA`. This is equivalent to calculating shortest paths in our unweighted G_{14} graph.

```
shortest_9to4_uw <- igraph::all_shortest_paths(g14w,
                                               from = "9", to = "4",
                                               weights = NA)

shortest_9to4_uw$res
```

```
## [[1]]
## + 3/14 vertices, named, from 7ee58a1:
## [1] 9 7 4
##
## [[2]]
## + 3/14 vertices, named, from 7ee58a1:
## [1] 9 8 4
```

The `distances()` function calculates distance in a graph. By default, it calculates the distance between all pairs of vertices and returns the results as a distance matrix.

```
distances(g14w)
```

```
##      9 10 11 13 8  4  6  1 12 14  7  2  3  5
## 9    0  4  5  3 2  5  5  6  5  5  3  6  6  7
## 10   4  0  1  7 6  9  9 10  1  9  7 10 10 11
## 11   5  1  0  8 7 10 10 11  1 10  8 11 11 12
## 13   3  7  8  0 5  8  8  9  8  2  6  9  9 10
## 8    2  6  7  5 0  3  3  4  7  7  1  4  4  5
## 4    5  9 10  8 3  0  1  1 10 10  2  1  1  2
## 6    5  9 10  8 3  1  0  2 10 10  2  2  2  3
## 1    6 10 11  9 4  1  2  0 11 11  3  1  2  3
## 12   5  1  1  8 7 10 10 11  0 10  8 11 11 12
## 14   5  9 10  2 7 10 10 11 10  0  8 11 11 12
## 7    3  7  8  6 1  2  2  3  8  8  0  3  3  4
```

```
## 2  6 10 11  9 4  1  2  1 11 11 3  0  2  3
## 3  6 10 11  9 4  1  2  2 11 11 3  2  0  3
## 5  7 11 12 10 5  2  3  3 12 12 4  3  3  0
```

Again, specific subsets of vertices can be selected and the function will return a matrix for just those subsets, and the same mode argument can be used for digraphs. Weights can be ignored by setting weights = NA. The algorithm used to calculate the shortest path is automatically selected, but can be specified using the algorithm argument.

```
distances(g14w, v = "9", to = "4", weights = NA,
          algorithm = "bellman-ford")
```

```
##    4
## 9 2
```

The mean_distance() function calculates the average distance between all pairs of vertices. Note that this function does not consider edge weights.

```
mean_distance(g14w)
```

```
## [1] 2.736264
```

To consider edge weights in calculating average distance, you should take the mean of the off-diagonal elements of the distance matrix. This is most easily done by extracting the lower and upper triangles of the distance matrix.

```
# get lower and upper triangles of weighted distance matrix
dist <- distances(g14w)
off_diag_dist <- dist[upper.tri(dist) | lower.tri(dist)]

# calcuate mean
mean(off_diag_dist)
```

```
## [1] 6.208791
```

Graph diameter can be calculated using the diameter() function and is equal to the maximal element of the distance matrix. Again, weights can be ignored by setting weights = NA.

```
diameter(g14w)
```

```
## [1] 12
```

If a graph is not connected, the `diameter()` function will return the diameter of the largest connected component by default. The function `farthest_vertices()` will return a pair vertices at either end of a diameter path, and the function `get_diameter()` will return a full diameter path.

```
farthest_vertices(g14w, weights = NA)
```

```
## $vertices
## + 2/14 vertices, named, from 7ee58a1:
## [1] 11 1
##
## $distance
## [1] 5
```

```
get_diameter(g14w, weights = NA)
```

```
## + 6/14 vertices, named, from 7ee58a1:
## [1] 11 10 9  8  4  1
```

Finally, the `edge_density()` function will calculate the density of the graph. You can find the formula for edge density in an earlier footnote in this chapter and, if you like, you can verify this manually for our G_{14W} graph.

```
edge_density(g14w)
```

```
## [1] 0.1978022
```

> **Playing around:** The `distance()` function in `igraph` allows you to select from three algorithms to use: Dijkstra, Bellman-Ford and Johnson. If you are interested in computation speed, you could try an experiment on a large graph to see which one is faster. The `microbenchmark` package in R is useful for running a computation many times and benchmarking its average speed. You could try creating a directed graph from the `wikivote` data set in the `onadata` package or via the internet[5], calculating the distance matrix using each of the three algorithms and benchmarking the speed. I found the Johnson algorithm to be about four times faster than the others. Don't try this, however, if you are on a low memory or slow CPU computer.

---

[5]`https://ona-book.org/wikivote.csv`

5.2.2 Calculating in Python

The functions for path, distance, density and diameter in the `networkx` package in Python are very similar to those in `igraph` in R. First, let's load our weighted graph G_{14W}.

```
import networkx as nx
import pandas as pd


g14w_edges = pd.read_csv("https://ona-book.org/data/g14_edgelist.csv")


g14w = nx.from_pandas_edgelist(g14w_edges, source = "from",
target = "to", edge_attr = True)
```

To calculate all simple paths between two specified nodes, use the `all_simple_paths()` function.

```
simple_paths = nx.all_simple_paths(G = g14w, source = 9, target = 4)
[path for path in simple_paths]
```

```
## [[9, 8, 7, 4], [9, 8, 7, 6, 4], [9, 8, 4], [9, 7, 8, 4], [9, 7, 4], [9, 7, 6, 4]]
```

To calculate all shortest paths between two specified nodes, use the `all_shortest_paths()` function. By default, this will ignore edge weights.

```
shortest_paths_uw = nx.all_shortest_paths(G = g14w, source = 9,
target = 4)
[path for path in shortest_paths_uw]
```

```
## [[9, 8, 4], [9, 7, 4]]
```

To consider edge weights, use the name of the weight attribute as the value of the `weight` argument.

```
shortest_paths_w = nx.all_shortest_paths(G = g14w, source = 9,
target = 4, weight = 'weight')
[path for path in shortest_paths_w]
```

```
## [[9, 8, 4], [9, 7, 4], [9, 8, 7, 4]]
```

For undirected graphs, the `shortest_path()` function will calculate a single shortest path for every pair of vertices in the graph, returning the paths in a dict. You can also specify source and target node subsets.

```
shortest_paths_from9 = nx.shortest_path(g14w, source = 9,
weight = 'weight')

# view one path to vertex 11
shortest_paths_from9.get(11)
```

```
## [9, 10, 11]
```

For directed graphs, various algorithm-specific functions are available, such as `dijkstra_path()`, `bellman_ford_path()` and many others.

Distances can be calculated using the `shortest_path_length()` function, either to produce all distances or to focus on a specific source and/or target. This will return a dict if a single source or target is provided, or a tuple otherwise.

```
distances_from9 = nx.shortest_path_length(g14w, source = 9,
weight = 'weight')
distances_from9
```

```
## {9: 0, 8: 2, 13: 3, 7: 3, 10: 4, 4: 5, 14: 5, 6: 5, 11: 5, 12: 5, 1: 6, 2: 6, 3: 6, 5: 7}
```

Average distance can be calculated using the `average_shortest_path_length()` function. Include weights as an argument to get the average weighted distance.

```
nx.average_shortest_path_length(g14w, weight = 'weight')
```

```
## 6.208791208791209
```

Diameter can be calculated using the `diameter()` function, but this will only compute the unweighted diameter.

```
nx.diameter(g14w)
```

```
## 5
```

To calculate the weighted diameter, simply take the maximum value of the weighted distances across all pairs.

```
distances = nx.shortest_path_length(g14w, weight = 'weight')
max([max(distance[1].values()) for distance in distances])
```

```
## 12
```

Finally, edge density can be calculated using the `density()` function.

```
nx.density(g14w)
```

```
## 0.1978021978021978
```

5.3 Examples of uses

To illustrate uses of paths and distance in organizational settings, we will go through a couple of examples. We will look at real data from the `workfrance` graph which we introduced earlier in Section 3.1.3. The `workfrance` data set contains information captured in an experimental study in an office building in France. Vertices in this data set represent individual employees, and edges exist between employees if they have spent a minimum amount of time together in the same place in the building. Let's download the data and create the graph in R.

```
set.seed(123)
```

```
# download workfrance data sets
workfrance_edges <- read.csv(
    "https://ona-book.org/data/workfrance_edgelist.csv"
)
workfrance_vertices <- read.csv(
    "https://ona-book.org/data/workfrance_vertices.csv"
)
```

```
# create graph
(workfrance <- igraph::graph_from_data_frame(
    d = workfrance_edges,
    vertices = workfrance_vertices,
    directed = FALSE
))
```

```
## IGRAPH 07cbale UN-- 211 932 --
## + attr: name (v/c), dept (v/c), mins (e/n)
## + edges from 07cbale (vertex names):
##  [1] 3 --159  253--3    3 --447  3 --498  3 --694  3 --751  3 --859  3 --908  14 --18
## [10] 99 --14  14 --441  520--14  14 --544  14 --653  14 --998  15 --120  15 --160  15 --162
## [19] 15 --178  15 --259  15 --261  15 --295  15 --353  15 --372  15 --464  15 --491  15 --498
## [28] 15 --909  15 --1090 39 --18  99 --18   429--18   488--18   527--18   18 --621  18 --650
## [37] 753--18   18 --797  18 --845  99 --27   160--27   259--27   295--27   27 --346  27 --1392
```

```
## [46] 34 --156  34 --250  34 --259  34 --489  34 --615  34 --694  34 --884  34 --959  219--38
## [55] 38 --435  39 --71   39 --72   39 --99   118--39   39 --219  39 --339  39 --407  39 --468
## [64] 39 --871  39 --939  43 --285  43 --339  43 --809  43 --866  43 --985  118--47   47 --366
## + ... omitted several edges
```

We have built a graph with 211 vertices and 932 edges. The vertices have a dept property which indicates the department the person works in, and the edges have a mins property which indicates the number of minutes spent together in the same place. The mins property could be considered a measure of how strong the connection between two individuals is, so let's make it a weight in the graph.

```
E(workfrance)$weight <- E(workfrance)$mins
```

5.3.1 Facilitating introductions in a workplace

A simple use case of shortest paths is to help connect individuals via common connections or intermediaries. Let's take two vertices from our workfrance graph who are from different departments. Let's select Vertices 3 and 55. Let's see what departments they are in.

```
V(workfrance)$dept[V(workfrance)$name %in% c("3", "55")]
```

```
## [1] "DMI" "SSI"
```

Now let's determine the unweighted distance between these two employees in the network.

```
distances(workfrance, v = "3", to = "55", weights = NA)
```

```
##    55
## 3  2
```

These two individuals have an unweighted distance of 2 in the network, meaning they can connect through one intermediary. Now we can use our all_shortest_paths() function to determine who the common intermediary is.

```
all_shortest_paths(workfrance, from = "3", to = "55", weight = NA)$res
```

```
## [[1]]
## + 3/211 vertices, named, from 07cba1e:
## [1] 3    447 55
```

There is one common intermediary: employee 447. Therefore, if employees 3 and 55 do not know each other, employee 447 may be able to introduce them. Note that there may be more than one suggestion for intermediaries. For example:

```
(paths <- all_shortest_paths(workfrance, from = "3", to = "290",
                             weight = NA)$res)
```

```
## [[1]]
## + 3/211 vertices, named, from 07cba1e:
## [1] 3    859 290
##
## [[2]]
## + 3/211 vertices, named, from 07cba1e:
## [1] 3    694 290
```

In this case, we could consider using the edge weights to rank the intermediary options, on the basis that higher weights may indicate stronger connections. Let's visualize these two options by looking at the subgraph with edge weights in Figure 5.5.

```
subgraph <- induced_subgraph(workfrance,
                             vids = c("3", "290", "694", "859"))

ggraph(subgraph) +
    geom_edge_link(aes(edge_width = weight, label = weight),
                   color = "grey", alpha = 0.7,
                   show.legend = FALSE) +
    geom_node_label(size = 3, fill = "lightblue", aes(label = name)) +
    theme_void()
```

Here we may recommend employee 859 first on the basis of higher edge weights and therefore possibly greater familiarity with employees 3 and 290.

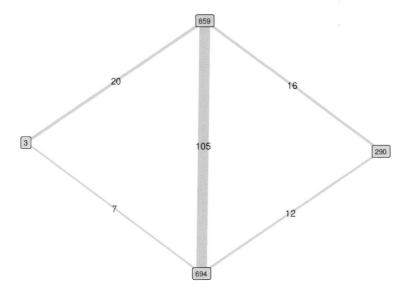

FIGURE 5.5: Selecting an intermediary according to higher edge weights

> **Playing around:** You may have seen this kind of 'introduction' system at work through social networks such as *LinkedIn*, which can suggest how to be introduced to another member via a common connection. You may also have seen the distance of an individual from you in the network, with direct connections (distance of 1) labelled as 1st, connections of connections (distance of 2) labelled as 2nd, and so on. These huge networks rarely calculate distances of greater than 3 or suggest connection paths with more than one intermediary because of the massive computational cost of doing so. If you have a *LinkedIn* profile, you may want to go and explore your second order connections and view the intermediaries who can connect you. This is the equivalent of looking at all the shortest paths between you and that individual in the network.

5.3.2 Finding distant colleagues in a workplace

Now, imagine that a professional event is being organized in the office building in France, where employees will be assigned to one of 21 tables of ten people[6]. You have been asked to try to help ensure that the tables contain a good mix of individuals and to avoid tables where everyone knows each other very well.

---

[6]We can assume the 211th person is hosting the event.

Before we start, we should check whether this graph has any disconnected components.

```
is.connected(workfrance)
```

```
## [1] TRUE
```

So there are no disconnected components in this graph. Let's also look at the diameter of this graph to get a sense of the maximum possible distance between any pair of individuals.

```
diameter(workfrance, weights = NA)
```

```
## [1] 6
```

As a first step, we can pick 21 people who have an unweighted distance of 1 from each other and sit them all at a different table. That would certainly be a good starting point. We can use the neighbors() function in igraph and look for a vertex that has the most neighbors[7].

```
# create vectors to capture name and no of neighbors
v_name <- c()
n_neighbors <- c()

# capture name and no of neighbors for every vertex
for (v in V(workfrance)$name) {
    v_name <- append(v_name, v)
    n_neighbors <- append(n_neighbors,
                          length(neighbors(workfrance, v)))
}

# find the max
v_name[which.max(n_neighbors)]
```

```
## [1] "603"
```

It looks like employee 603 has the most neighbors. Let's find out how many.

```
n_neighbors[which.max(n_neighbors)]
```

```
## [1] 28
```

---

[7]You can also use the degree() function for this—more in the next chapter.

We could pick any 20 from the neighbors of employee 603 and that would be a great starting point for our 21 tables. Let's pick those with the highest mins property (assuming that this represents a closer relationship). We can use the inc() function to get all edges containing employee 603 and then select those that have the highest mins property.

```
edges603 <- E(workfrance)[inc("603")]
sort603_mins <- sort(edges603$mins, decreasing = TRUE)
(top_edges603 <- edges603[order(sort603_mins)][1:20])
```

```
## + 20/932 edges from 07cba1e (vertex names):
##  [1] 603--1392 603--1323 603--1362 859--603  603--954  603--1245 603--779  603--649  691--603
## [10] 694--603  706--603  603--725  487--603  420--603  428--603  387--603  401--603  603--272
## [19] 290--603  346--603
```

Now we have the 'closest' 20 people to employee 603. Let's create an edge subgraph and extract the vertices.

```
subgraph603 <- igraph::subgraph.edges(workfrance, eid = top_edges603)
V(subgraph603)$name
```

```
##  [1] "290"  "420"  "428"  "691"  "706"  "694"  "859"  "346"  "387"  "401"  "487"  "603"  "649"
## [14] "725"  "779"  "954"  "1245" "1323" "1362" "1392" "272"
```

We can also look at the departments of these individuals:

```
V(subgraph603)$dept
```

```
##  [1] "DG"   "DISQ" "DISQ" "DISQ" "DMCT" "DMI"  "DMI"  "DST"  "DST"  "DST"  "DST"  "DST"  "DST"
## [14] "DST"  "DST"  "DST"  "DST"  "DST"  "DST"  "DST"  "SRH"
```

We see some considerable department similarity, which makes sense. Now that we have found the first person for each table, we will want to try to make sure that we sit that person with nine other people who have some distance from them, and to minimize neighbors sitting at the same table. Let's start with our first employee 603, and call this Table 1. Because there are only 21 tables but employee 603 has 28 neighbors, we might be willing to allow one neighbor to sit at Table 1. Let's sit them with the neighbor with whom they spent the least minutes.

```
edges603[which.min(edges603$mins)]
```

```
## + 1/932 edge from 07cba1e (vertex names):
## [1] 77--603
```

So we will sit employee 603 with employee 77. Now we can select a third individual who has a reasonable distance in the network from both employee 603 and employee 77. Let's look at all these distances.

```
(distance603_77 <- distances(workfrance, v = c("603", "77"),
                             weights = NA))
```

```
##  89 97 118 220 378 656 720 741 886 1204 1209 1492 290 502 47 119 198 213 253 267 270 343 366 420
## 603  3  2   2   2   3   3   3   2   3    2    3    4   1   4  2   2   2   2   2   1   2   2   2   1
## 77   2  1   2   1   2   2   2   2   2    1    2    3   2   4  3   3   3   3   3   2   3   3   3   2
##  428 445 478 520 525 660 691 836 39 43 59 63 72 80 122 211 219 246 257 285 339 407 466 468 533
## 603   1   2   2   2   2   2   1  2  2  3  3  3  2  2   2   3   3   2   2   3   2   2   3   2   4
## 77    2   3   3   3   2   3   2  3  3  3  3  2  2  3   1   3   3   3   3   3   3   2   3   3   3
##  702 706 753 784 790 793 809 866 871 889 894 923 939 3 15 34 54 74 79 99 120 131 134 141 156 158
## 603   3   1   2   2   3   3   3   3   3   2   2   2   3 2  3  2  3  2  3  1   2   3   3   2   2   3
## 77    4   2   2   3   3   3   3   3   3   2   3   3   2 2  2  2  2  1  2  2   2   3   3   2   2   2
##  159 160 162 165 178 183 193 205 236 242 250 259 261 295 333 353 372 425 447 453 460 464 489 491
## 603   2   2   2   4   3   2   3   3   2   4   3   2   2   2   2   3   2   4   3   2   3   3   3   3
## 77    1   2   1   3   3   2   2   3   3   3   2   1   2   2   2   2   3   3   2   3   2   2   2
##  498 574 615 642 677 694 751 763 859 880 884 909 959 1067 1090 1164 1238 1342 38 172 184 210 222
## 603   3   3   3   3   3   1   3   3   1   3   3   2   3    2    3    2    3    2  4   3   3   1   3
## 77    2   2   2   2   4   2   2   2   2   2   2   3   2    3    3    2    3    2  1   3   4   2   4
##  248 252 269 275 322 374 424 465 477 486 504 510 513 527 577 634 638 674 743 771 867 882 893 908
## 603   3   2   3   2   3   3   2   3   3   3   3   3   3   3   3   2   3   3   2   3   3   2   3   2
## 77    4   3   4   3   3   4   3   4   4   3   4   4   4   3   4   3   4   4   3   4   4   3   4   3
##  921 1485 27 71 77 147 215 346 387 401 426 429 487 488 580 582 603 649 725 779 954 1245 1323
## 603   3    2  2  1  1   1   1   1   1   1   2   2   1   2   2   2   0   1   1   1   1    1    1
## 77    3    3  2  2  0   2   1   1   2   2   2   1   2   2   2   2   1   1   2   2   2    2    2
##  1362 1392 14 181 441 544 778 998 1260 106 245 435 440 117 197 200 413 432 461 475 496 626 653
## 603    1    1  2   2   3   3   3   3    3   3   3   3   2   1   3   2   2   3   2   2   3   3   2
## 77     2    2  3   3   4   4   3   4    4   3   3   2   2   2   3   3   3   3   3   3   4   4   2
##  874 977 1414 18 232 272 531 621 650 744 797 845 55 110 164 173 628 970 985
## 603   2   3    2  2   2   1   2   3   2   2   2   2  3   3   3   2   4   3
## 77    3   4    3  2   3   2   3   3   3   3   3   3  4   3   3   2   4   2
```

We could use the mean of the distances to decide on the person with the furthest distance from those already selected.

```
which.max(colMeans(distance603_77))
```

```
## 502
##  14
```

We can select employee 502 for the third seat, and we iterate to find the remainder of the people at the table. In this iteration, we make sure that the same person does not arise twice in the calculations.

```
table1 <- c("603", "77", "502")

# complete remainder of table
for (i in 4:10) {
    # get distances from already chosen table members
    dists <- distances(workfrance, v = table1, weights = NA)
    # get vertices with maximum mean distance excluding already chosen
    new <- dists |>
        as.data.frame() |>
        subset(select = !(colnames(dists) %in% table1)) |>
        colMeans() |>
        which.max() |>
        names()
    # add first of these to table
    table1[i] <- new[1]
}

# view complete table 1
table1
```

```
##  [1] "603" "77"  "502" "533" "496" "970" "165" "677" "977" "38"
```

Now let's assign a `table` property to the `workfrance` graph and take a look at where our members of Table 1 appear, as in Figure 5.6.

```
# add a table property to workfrance graph
V(workfrance)$table <- ifelse(
    V(workfrance)$name %in% table1, "1", "2-21"
)

# visualize
set.seed(123)
ggraph(workfrance, layout = "fr") +
    geom_edge_link(color = "grey", alpha = 0.7) +
    geom_node_point(size = 4, aes(color = as.factor(table))) +
    labs(color = "Table") +
    theme_void()
```

It looks as if we have done a good job of maximizing for distance in the network in our Table 1 selection. Let's check the average distance among the employees at Table 1.

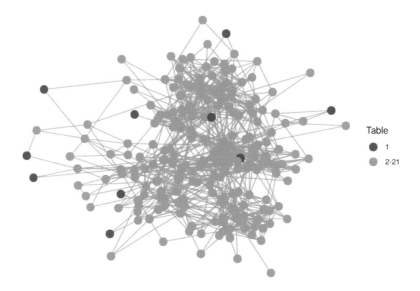

FIGURE 5.6: Individuals selected for Table 1 based on optimizing for distance

```
mean(distances(workfrance, v = table1, to = table1, weights = NA))
```

```
## [1] 3.96
```

Given that the diameter of the graph is 6, and that we decided to include a pair of individuals with a distance of 1 on this table, a mean distance of 3.96 seems pretty good. Let's look at the department mix of our ten people at Table 1.

```
V(workfrance)$dept[V(workfrance)$name %in% table1]
```

```
## [1] "DG"   "DMCT" "DMI"  "DMI"  "DSE"  "DST"  "DST"  "SFLE" "SFLE" "SSI"
```

We have seven departments represented at a table of ten, which seems another good indication of a diverse table. This gives you a sense of how you can use paths and distance as a mathematical model for familiarity in a network. If you are interested in continuing this process to fill further tables, see the exercises at the end of this chapter.

5.4 Learning exercises

5.4.1 Discussion questions

1. Define what is meant by graph traversal and describe why it is an important topic in network analysis.
2. Describe what is meant by a path, a simple path and a shortest path. Provide examples of each using the G_{14} and the G_{14W} graph.
3. Describe the difference between a breadth-first and a depth-first graph search algorithm. Name an example of each.
4. Define the distance between two vertices in a graph. Using G_{14} or G_{14W}, give an example of vertices which have a distance of 3, and list all shortest paths between those vertices.
5. Define the diameter of a connected graph. List a path whose distance is equal to the diameter of G_{14}.
6. Define the density of a graph. What does it mean for a graph to be sparse?
7. If a graph G has four vertices A, B, C, and D, and its only edges are from A to all other vertices, calculate the density of G.
8. Write down a procedure to describe how Dijkstra's algorithm would calculate all shortest paths from Vertex 7 in G_{14}.
9. Manually determine all simple paths and all shortest paths between Vertices 1 and 13 in G_{14}.
10. Manually determine all shortest weighted paths between Vertices 1 and 13 in G_{14W}.

5.4.2 Data exercises

1. Use appropriate functions to determine all simple paths and all shortest paths between Vertices 1 and 13 in G_{14} and check that the output agrees with your manual calculation in Discussion Question 9.
2. Use appropriate functions to determine all shortest weighted paths between Vertices 1 and 13 in G_{14W} and check that the output agrees with your manual calculation in Discussion Question 10.
3. Create a subgraph of G_{14W} consisting only of vertices 6 through 14. Use an appropriate procedure to calculate the unweighted and weighted distances between all pairs of vertices in this subgraph.
4. Calculate the unweighted and weighted diameter of the subgraph from the previous exercise, and calculate its density.

For Exercises 5 to 7, load the `friends_tv_edgelist` data set from the `onadata` package or download it from the internet[8]. This is a full network of all characters appearing in every season of the *Friends* TV series based on characters speaking in the same scene together. Each edge has a weight according to the number of scenes those characters both spoke in together, but ignore this for this set of exercises and simply create an unweighted, undirected graph from this edgelist.

5. Check whether the *Friends* network is connected and calculate the diameter of the network. Find a path with length equal to the diameter. The diameter is surprisingly small for a network of this size. Why might this be?

6. Find all *simple* paths from Billy Crystal to Mr Bing and from Janice to Mrs Bing. Try to calculate what proportion of the connections have distance 2 in this graph. The results may help with the answer to the previous question.

7. Calculate the density of the network. Create a subgraph consisting of the six main characters: Monica, Chandler, Phoebe, Ross, Rachel and Joey. Calculate the density of this subgraph. What term would you use to describe this subgraph?

8. A 'clique' in a graph is a subgraph which is complete (that is, all vertices are connected to each other and the density is 1). Can you find a clique in the *Friends* graph that does not contain any of the main characters[9]?

9. Create a new subgraph by removing the six main characters from the original graph. Check whether this subgraph is connected. What can you conclude from this?

10. Calculate the largest diameter of connected components of this new graph. Find the pair of characters associated with this diameter path. Find the largest clique in this graph.

11. **Extension:** Extend the example in Section 5.3.2 by creating a second table for the event. Remember that this second table cannot include anyone selected for Table 1. Explore your results by visualizing them and analyzing the average distance for Table 2 and the mix of departments for Table 2.

12. **Extension:** Repeat the process in Question 11 to try to fill all 21 tables at the event. Visualize your results with the vertices color coded by table number. Calculate the mean distances for each table. Do you notice anything interesting? Can you think of ways to improve this method?

---

[8] https://ona-book.org/data/friends_tv_edgelist.csv

[9] We are getting a little ahead of ourselves with cliques, and we will look at these more in a later chapter, but you might want to try to find some functions in your software of choice for finding cliques.

6

Vertex Importance and Centrality

It follows from much of the earlier work we have been doing in this book that the vertices of a graph can provide rich information about a network, its structure and its dynamics. In sociology and psychology contexts, this is particularly true, because more often than not vertices represent people. The fact that people play different roles and have different influences inside groups and communities has motivated centuries of sociological and psychological research, so it is unsurprising that the concept of vertex importance and influence is of great interest in the study of people or organizational networks.

But importance and influence are not precisely defined concepts, and to make them real within the context of graphs and networks we need to find some sort of mathematical definition for them. In many visual graph layouts, more important or influential vertices that have stronger roles in overall connectivity will usually be positioned toward the center of a group of other vertices[1]. Intuitively therefore, we use the term 'centrality' to describe the importance or influence of a vertex in the connected structure of a graph.

In this chapter we will go through the most common types of centrality that can be measured for vertices in graphs, and discuss how they can be interpreted in the context of people or organizational networks. We will show how to calculate different types of centrality in R or Python and how to illustrate centrality in graph visualizations. We will then reprise our example of the French office building network from the previous chapter to illustrate the utility of centrality in network analysis.

In this chapter we will use the G_{14} graph which we introduced in the previous chapter, which is an undirected and unweighted graph. Most centrality measures are valid and easily calculated for directed graphs, and will depend on defining the direction of the edges to consider. Figure 6.1 shows the G_{14} graph with four vertices of interest colored differently from other vertices.

---

[1]If you want to see an earlier example of this, take a look at Figure 3.8 for Zachary's Karate Club network and note the positions of the influential actors, Mr Hi and John A.

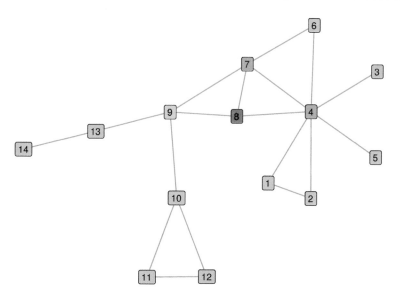

FIGURE 6.1: The G_{14} graph with four vertices of interest colored differently

6.1   Vertex centrality measures in graphs

As we look at the G_{14} graph in Figure 6.1, we see that the colored nodes seem to occupy prominent roles in the connective structure of the graph. If we removed Vertex 9, for example, we would split our graph into three disconnected components. Vertex 4 seems to be connected to a lot of immediate neighbors, and we would also split the graph if we removed it, leaving behind some isolates[2]. Vertex 7 seems to occupy a stealthy position from which to efficiently reach other vertices, while Vertex 8 seems to sit in between those other three and probably can't be ignored for that reason alone.

What if these vertices represented people in an organization? Would the departure of Vertex 4 mean that Vertices 1, 2, 3 and 5 lose their entire connection to the remainder of the organization? Would the departure of Vertex 9 split the organization in terms of the flow of work? If we wanted to distribute important information across the organization by means of these connections, which vertex would be a good place to start? By understanding centrality we can start to appreciate the possible impact of changes to the network, or identify important or influential actors in the network.

---

[2]Recall that isolates are vertices that are not connected to any other vertices.

6.1.1 Degree centrality

The **degree centrality** or **valence** of a vertex v is the number of edges connected to v. Alternatively stated, in an unweighted and undirected graph it is simply the number of neighbors of v or the number of vertices of distance 1 from v. For example, the degree centrality of Vertex 8 in G_{14} is 3, and for Vertex 4 it is 7. It should not be difficult to see that Vertex 4 has the highest degree centrality in G_{14}.

Degree centrality is a measure of immediate connection in a network. It could be interpreted as immediate reach in a social network. Its precise interpretation depends strongly on the nature of the connection. In a network of academic co-authoring, someone with high degree centrality has collaborated directly with a larger number of other academics. In our French office building network from Section 5.3, someone of high degree centrality is likely to be well-known socially to a greater number of colleagues.

Related to degree centrality is *ego size*. The n-th order ego network of a given vertex v is a set including v itself and all vertices of distance at most n from v. The n-th order ego size is the number of vertices in the n-th order ego network. In G_{14}, Vertex 8 has a 1st order ego size of 4, a 2nd order ego size of 11, and a third order ego size of 14 (the entire graph). It easily follows that the 1st order ego size of a vertex is one greater than the degree centrality of the vertex.

6.1.2 Closeness centrality

The **closeness centrality** of a vertex v in a connected graph is the inverse of the sum of the distances from v to all other vertices. Let's take a moment to understand this better by looking at an example. We will calculate the closeness centrality of Vertex 8 from G_{14}. Vertex 8 has the following distances to other vertices:

- Distance 1 to vertices 4, 7 and 9
- Distance 2 to vertices 1, 2, 3, 5, 6, 10 and 13
- Distance 3 to vertices 11, 12 and 14

The sum of these distances is 26, and the inverse of 26 is 0.038. Inverting this distance means that lower total distances will generate higher closeness centrality. Therefore, the vertex with the highest closeness centrality will be the most efficient in reaching all the other vertices in the graph. While Vertex 8 has one of the highest closeness centralities in G_{14}, Vertex 7 has a slightly higher closeness centrality, because its additional direct edge to Vertex 6 gives it a slightly lower total distance of 25 to the other vertices, and therefore a slightly higher closeness centrality of 0.04.

Closeness centrality is a measure of how efficiently the entire graph can be traversed from a given vertex. This is particularly valuable in the study of information flow. In social networks, information shared by those with high closeness centrality will likely reach the entire network more efficiently. In our French office building network from Section 5.3, those with high closeness centrality may be better choices for efficiently spreading a message through social interactions or word-of-mouth.

6.1.3 Betweenness centrality

The **betweenness centrality** of a vertex v is calculated by taking each pair of other vertices x and y, calculating the number of shortest paths between x and y that go through v, dividing by the total number of shortest paths between x and y, then summing over all such pairs of vertices in the graph. We can use the following process to manually calculate this for Vertex 8 in G_{14}:

- If we look at all pairs of Vertices 9 through 14, we conclude that Vertex 8 is not on any shortest paths between these vertices (betweenness centrality: 0).
- Similarly for Vertices 1 through 7 we conclude that Vertex 8 is not on any of these shortest paths either (betweenness centrality: 0).
- Now we look at all paths between Vertex 7 and Vertices 9 through 14, and conclude that Vertex 8 is not on any shortest paths for these pairs because Vertices 7 and 9 are adjacent (betweenness centrality: 0).
- Now we look at all paths between Vertex 6 and Vertices 9 through 14, and conclude that Vertex 8 is not on any of these shortest paths, because a shorter route is through Vertex 7 (betweenness centrality: 0).
- Finally, we look at all pairs between Vertices 1 through 5 and Vertices 9 through 14, and conclude that for each of the 30 such pairs there are two shortest paths, one of which goes through Vertex 7 and the other through Vertex 8 (betweenness centrality: $0.5 \times 30 = 15$).
- Summing over these, we conclude that the betweenness centrality of Vertex 8 in G_{14} is 15.

Using similar logic, it is not too difficult to reason that Vertex 9 has the highest betweenness centrality in G_{14}. If we split the graph on either side of Vertex 9, we have betweenness centralities of zero in the sets of vertices on each side, but any path between vertices on either side of Vertex 9 *must* pass through Vertex 9. There are 46 such paths between Vertices 1 through 8 and Vertices 10 through 14, and so the total betweenness centrality of Vertex 9 is 46.

Betweenness centrality is a measure of how important a given vertex is in connecting other pairs of vertices in the graph. It makes intuitive sense that Vertex 9 should have the highest betweenness centrality because its removal would have the largest destructive effect on overall connectivity in G_{14}, splitting it into a disconnected graph with three connected components. In people networks, individuals with higher betweenness centrality can be regarded as playing important roles in ensuring overall connectivity of the network, and if they are removed from the network the risks of overall disconnection are higher. This has strong applications in studying the effects of departures from organizations.

> **Playing around:** It's worth thinking about some of the things we did in the previous chapter based on our new understanding of degree, closeness and betweenness centrality. For example, how do certain types of central vertices influence the overall 'closeness' of a network? What would happen to average distance or edge density if we remove certain central vertices? Try playing around with removing Vertices 4 (highest degree centrality), 7 (highest closeness centrality) and 9 (highest betweenness centrality) from G_{14} and determining the impact of these removals on diameter, mean distance and density.

6.1.4 Eigenvector centrality

The **Eigenvector centrality** or **relative centrality** or **prestige** of a vertex is a measure of how connected the vertex is to other influential vertices. It is impossible to define this without a little linear algebra.

Recall from Section 2.1.4 that the adjacency matrix $A = (a_{ij})$ for an unweighted graph G containing p vertices is defined as $a_{ij} = 1$ if i and j are adjacent vertices in G and 0 otherwise. A vector $x = (x_1, x_2, ..., x_p)$ and scalar value λ are considered an eigenvector and eigenvalue of A if they satisfy the equation

$$Ax = \lambda x$$

If we require that x can only have positive entries, then a unique solution exists to this equation which has maximum eigenvalue λ. We take x and λ for this solution and define the eigenvector centrality for vertex v as

$$\frac{1}{\lambda} \sum_{w \in G} a_{vw} x_w$$

Because this is solving for a system of linear equations with coefficients that relate to the connectedness of neighboring vertices, its solution is a measure of the relative influence of a vertex as a function of the influences of the vertices it is connected to. Vertices can have high influence through being connected to a lot of other vertices with low influence, or through being connected to a small number of highly influential vertices. Vertex 10 in G_{14} has an eigenvector centrality of 0.12, and Vertex 2 has an eigenvector centrality of 0.23. This makes sense because Vertex 2 is connected to Vertex 4, which we already know has the highest degree centrality in the network. Intuitively, it shouldn't be too hard to appreciate that Vertex 4 has the highest eigenvector centrality in G_{14}.

In directed graphs, eigenvector centrality gives rise to interesting measures of different types of influence. For example, imagine a citation network where certain authors are regularly citing a lot of influential articles. These authors are known as *hubs*, and their *outgoing* eigenvector centrality will be high. *Hub score* is the outgoing eigenvector centrality of a vertex. Meanwhile, authors who have high incoming eigenvector centrality will be frequently referenced by hubs, and these authors are known as *authorities*. *Authority score* is the *incoming* eigenvector centrality of a vertex. These types of measures are becoming increasingly adopted in fields such as bibliometrics. Note that in undirected graphs the hub score, authority score and eigenvector centrality of vertices are identical.

Playing around: We have not looked at the impact of edge weights on centrality in this chapter. This is because it is unusual to consider edge weights in centrality measures. Nonetheless, most centrality measures do have approaches to consider edge weights, and this is a topic of ongoing research. Usually in these situations, edge weights are transformed to be cost functions—for example by inverting them—so that edges with higher weights are considered 'preferable' in graph traversal. To see what I mean, go back and have a look at the G_{14W} weighted graph from the previous chapter. Pick pairs of vertices and see what the shortest path between them would be using the sum of weights of edges, and what it would be using the sum of the inverse weights of edges.

6.2   Calculating and illustrating vertex centrality

6.2.1   Calculating in R

Degree centrality can be calculated for a specific set of vertices using the degree() function in igraph. By default, the degree centrality will be calculated for all vertices. Let's load up our G_{14} graph to demonstrate as we did in the previous chapter.

```
library(igraph)
library(dplyr)

# get g14 edgelist and ignore weights
g14_edgelist <- read.csv("https://ona-book.org/data/g14_edgelist.csv")
g14_unweighted <- g14_edgelist |>
  dplyr::select(-weight)

# create g14 graph
g14 <- igraph::graph_from_data_frame(g14_unweighted, directed = FALSE)

# calculate degree centrality for all vertices
igraph::degree(g14)
```

```
##   9 10 11 13  8  4  6  1 12 14  7  2  3  5
##   4  3  2  2  3  7  2  2  2  1  4  2  1  1
```

We can see that Vertex 4 has a degree centrality of 7, which agrees with our earlier manual calculations. Ego networks and ego sizes can be determined using the ego() and ego_size() functions.

```
# 2nd order ego network of Vertex 4
igraph::ego(g14, order = 2, nodes = "4")
```

```
## [[1]]
## + 9/14 vertices, named, from 7fe5d00:
## [1] 4 8 6 1 7 2 3 5 9
```

```
# size of ego network
igraph::ego_size(g14, order = 2, nodes = "4")
```

```
## [1] 9
```

Closeness centrality is calculated using the closeness() function for all or a subset of vertices. Let's verify that this function returns the same results for Vertices 7 and 8 that we manually calculated earlier.

```
igraph::closeness(g14, vids = c("7", "8"))
```

```
##          7          8
## 0.04000000 0.03846154
```

Betweenness centrality is calculated using the `betweenness()` function in a similar way. Let's verify our previous manual calculations for Vertices 8 and 9.

```
igraph::betweenness(g14, v = c("8", "9"))
```

```
##  8  9
## 15 46
```

Finally, eigenvector centrality can be calculated using the `eigen_centrality()` function. Note that this returns a list including various details about the computation[3]. To see the actual centralities, you should call the `vector` element of the output list. Note also that this function scales the values by default so that the maximum eigenvector centrality is 1. To avoid this, set `scale = FALSE`.

```
eigens <- igraph::eigen_centrality(g14, scale = FALSE)
eigens$vector
```

```
##          9         10         11         13          8          4          6          1         12
## 0.30157876 0.11585270 0.04773223 0.09618665 0.37800315 0.55038069 0.29000589 0.22676118
 0.04773223
##         14          7          2          3          5
## 0.02806617 0.44350955 0.22676118 0.16059484 0.16059484
```

We can see confirmation here that Vertex 4 has the highest eigenvector centrality.

> **Playing around:** There are a few other centrality-like measures available in `igraph` which you could explore and try to understand. Examples include `page_rank()` for Google's measure of importance of a webpage, and `hub_score()` and `authority_score()` for directed networks. Consider testing these out on some data sets, like the `wikivote` data set from the `onadata` package or downloaded from the internet[4].

6.2.2 Calculating in Python

Again, as in the work in the previous chapter, centrality functions in `networkx` are very similar to those in `igraph`. The `degree()` function calculates degree centrality for all vertices by default, or you can specify a list of vertices.

---

[3]For example, if you are curious to know the eigenvalue, you can look at the `value` element of the list

[4]https://ona-book.org/data/wikivote.csv

```
import networkx as nx
import pandas as pd

# download edgelist and remove weights
g14_edgelist = pd.read_csv(
  "https://ona-book.org/data/g14_edgelist.csv"
)
g14_undirected = g14_edgelist.drop('weight', axis = 1)

# create undirected g14 graph
g14 = nx.from_pandas_edgelist(g14_undirected, source = 'from',
target = 'to')

# calculate degree centrality of Vertices 4 and 9
nx.degree(g14, [4, 9])
```

```
## DegreeView({4: 7, 9: 4})
```

There are also methods called `degree()` for a `Graph()` object as well as `in_degree()` and `out_degree()` for `DiGraph()` objects in networkx.

```
g14.degree(4)
```

```
## 7
```

The ego network of a vertex can be obtained using the `ego_graph()` function. To obtain the 2nd order ego network of Node 4:

```
ego_4_2 = nx.ego_graph(g14, n = 4, radius = 2)
ego_4_2.nodes
```

```
## NodeView((9, 8, 7, 4, 6, 1, 2, 3, 5))
```

Closeness centrality is calculated using the `closeness_centrality()` function. However, in networkx this is normalized by multiplying the result by $n - 1$ where n is the number of vertices in the graph. To obtain non-normalized closeness centrality, it will be necessary to divide the output of this function by $n - 1$.[5]

---

[5]You may wonder why $n - 1$? This is simply the total number of other vertices that we are calculating the paths to. Strangely, there is no option to non-normalize in the arguments of this function as of recent versions of networkx. In any case, for the purposes of comparing vertices, it doesn't matter a great deal whether you normalize or not.

```
# get non-normalized closeness centrality for Vertex 7
norm_closeness = nx.closeness_centrality(g14, 7)
norm_closeness/(len(g14.nodes) - 1)
```

```
## 0.04
```

Betweenness centrality is calculated using the `betweenness_centrality()` function. Again this is normalized by default but this can be set to `False` in the arguments[6]. This function calculates values for all nodes and returns them in a dict.

```
# get non-normalized betweenness centrality for Vertex 9
between = nx.betweenness_centrality(g14, normalized = False)
between.get(9)
```

```
## 46.0
```

Finally, eigenvector centrality is calculated using the `eigenvector_centrality()` function, with a dict returned similar to `betweenness_centrality()`.

```
eigen = nx.eigenvector_centrality(g14)
eigen.get(4)
```

```
## 0.5503779695532801
```

Closeness, betweenness and eigenvector centrality are calculated using *incoming* edges in `networkx` digraphs. To calculate the outgoing equivalent, simply use the `reverse()` method on the digraph to make all outgoing edges incoming and vice versa.

> **Playing around**: `networkx` has a very wide range of centrality measures available. Visit the Centrality section of its documentation[7] and have a look at the options. Many of these are very specific to graph use cases in different industries and disciplines, but see if you can understand them and even give them a try with a data set.

---

[6]The normalization here divides the result by the number of vertex pairs in a graph with $n - 1$ vertices, which is $(n - 1)(n - 2)$ for directed graphs and $\frac{(n-1)(n-2)}{2}$ for undirected graphs.

[7]https://networkx.org

6.2.3 Illustrating centrality in graph visualizations

As we reviewed in Chapter 3, we will often make adjustments when visualizing graphs to illustrate certain aspects of the graph's structure. For example, we highlight certain vertices with color or adjust the thickness of certain edges. When we want to visually illustrate the importance or influence of vertices in graphs, we will often do so using centrality measures. The two most common methods are to adjust vertex size according to centrality or to use a centrality-related color scale. We will illustrate a couple of examples using ggraph in R to show some of the options available.

For greatest efficiency, it's always a good idea to add centralities as vertex properties in graphs. Let's add a few of these now in our G_{14} graph.

```
V(g14)$degree <- degree(g14)
V(g14)$betweenness <- betweenness(g14)
V(g14)$eigen <- eigen_centrality(g14)$vector
```

Now we can create a visualization where we map the size of vertices to the degree vertex property, as in Figure 6.2. Note the scale_size() function which is useful for setting a scale to suit your visualization.

```
set.seed(123)
ggraph(g14, layout = "lgl") +
  geom_edge_link(color = "grey", alpha = 0.7) +
  geom_node_point(aes(size = degree), color = "lightblue",
                  show.legend = FALSE) +
  scale_size(range = c(5,15)) +
  geom_node_text(aes(label = name)) +
  theme_void()
```

Alternatively, Figure 6.3 shows the same graph with the vertex colors scaled according to normalized eigenvector centrality. This helps us see that the vertices to the left of Vertex 9 in G_{14} do not have particularly influential connections compared to those to the right.

```
set.seed(123)
ggraph(g14, layout = "lgl") +
  geom_edge_link(color = "grey", alpha = 0.7) +
  geom_node_point(size = 6, aes(color = eigen)) +
  scale_color_gradient(low = "lightblue", high = "red") +
  geom_node_text(aes(label = name)) +
  theme_void()
```

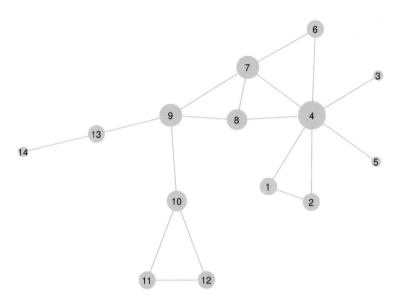

FIGURE 6.2: G_{14} with vertex size scaled according to degree centrality

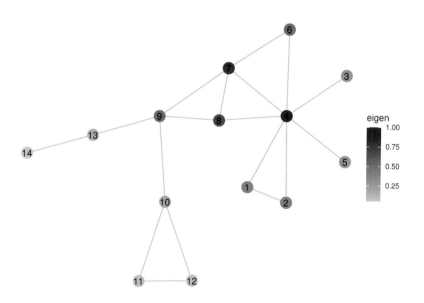

FIGURE 6.3: G_{14} with vertex size scaled according to normalized eigenvector centrality

> **Playing around:.** Play around with different ways of visualizing the centralities of vertices in G_{14}. Try using color, size or both. And also try the different types of centrality to see if the look of the graph changes substantially between them.

6.3 Examples of uses

In this section we will reprise the workfrance unweighted graph from the previous chapter and will use it to illustrate some common uses for centrality measures. First, we will look at how to find network-wide and department level 'superconnectors,' then we will look at how to find potential socially influential actors in a network. Let's load up the workfrance graph again.

```
set.seed(123)

# download workfrance data sets
workfrance_edges <- read.csv(
  "https://ona-book.org/data/workfrance_edgelist.csv"
)
workfrance_vertices <- read.csv(
  "https://ona-book.org/data/workfrance_vertices.csv"
)

# create graph
workfrance <- igraph::graph_from_data_frame(
    d = workfrance_edges,
    vertices = workfrance_vertices,
    directed = FALSE
)
```

6.3.1 Finding 'superconnectors'

Individuals with high betweenness centrality in people networks could be regarded as 'superconnectors.' Superconnectors can play very valuable roles in the social integration of new entrants to the network, and they can also present greater risk of connective disruption if they leave the network. Imagine a new hire is about to join the DMI department in our workfrance network. We want to assign two 'buddies' to this individual to help them socially integrate into the workplace more effectively. Given that it is important for the individual to assimilate into their own department and into the workplace as a whole, we want to select the best two current employees to assist with both goals. Let's start with the DMI department first.

In order to study the DMI department as a self-contained network, we will create an induced subgraph which contains only those in that department and the connections between them, and visualize this network, labeling the employee IDs, as in Figure 6.4.

```
# create DMI subgraph
DMI_vertices <- V(workfrance)[V(workfrance)$dept == "DMI"]
DMI_graph <- igraph::induced.subgraph(workfrance, vids = DMI_vertices)

# visualize
set.seed(123)
ggraph(DMI_graph) +
  geom_edge_link(color = "grey", alpha = 0.7) +
  geom_node_point(color = "lightblue", size = 4) +
  geom_node_text(aes(label = name), size = 2) +
  theme_void()
```

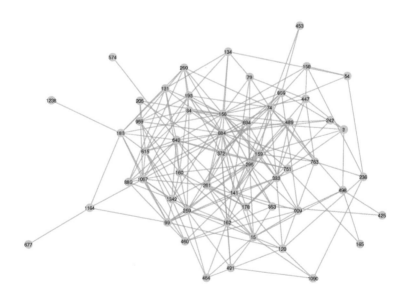

FIGURE 6.4: The induced subgraph of the DMI department in our French workplace

Now we are interested in those who have the strongest role in connecting others in this network. Let's find the top three individuals in terms of betweenness centrality.

```r
# get IDs of top 3 betweenness centralities
ranked_betweenness_DMI <- DMI_graph |>
  betweenness() |>
  sort(decreasing = TRUE)

(top3_DMI <- names(ranked_betweenness_DMI[1:3]))
```

```
## [1] "156" "74"  "884"
```

These are the IDs of the top three superconnectors in the DMI department. Now we can visualize the graph again, but let's adjust vertex size by betweenness and color the top 3 superconnectors, as in Figure 6.5.

```r
# add betweenness vertex property
V(DMI_graph)$betweenness <- betweenness(DMI_graph)

# add top three superconnectors property
V(DMI_graph)$top3 <- ifelse(V(DMI_graph)$name %in% top3_DMI, 1, 0)

# visualize
set.seed(123)
ggraph(DMI_graph) +
  geom_edge_link(color = "grey", alpha = 0.7) +
  geom_node_point(aes(color = as.factor(top3), size = betweenness),
                  show.legend = FALSE) +
  scale_color_manual(values = c("lightblue", "pink")) +
  geom_node_text(aes(label = name), size = 2) +
  theme_void()
```

In a similar way, we can find the superconnectors of the overall `workfrance` network.

```r
# get IDs of top 3 betweenness centralities
ranked_betweenness_workfrance <- workfrance |>
  betweenness() |>
  sort(decreasing = TRUE)

#get top 3
(top3_workfrance <- names(ranked_betweenness_workfrance[1:3]))
```

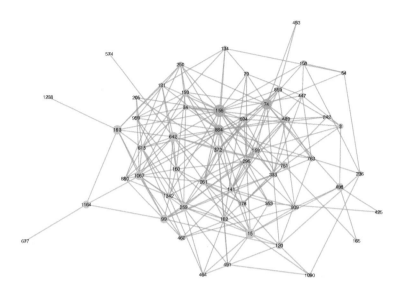

FIGURE 6.5: DMI subgraph with the top 3 superconnectors identified

```
## [1] "603" "99"  "322"
```

In Figure 6.6, we create a graph of the `workfrance` network with vertex size
scaled by betweenness centrality. We color by department so we can easily see
which departments our superconnectors are in.

```
# add betweenness property
V(workfrance)$betweenness <- betweenness(workfrance)

# label only if a top 3 superconnector
V(workfrance)$btwn_label <- ifelse(
  V(workfrance)$name %in% top3_workfrance,
  V(workfrance)$name,
  ""
)

# visualize
set.seed(123)
ggraph(workfrance) +
  geom_edge_link(color = "grey", alpha = 0.7) +
  geom_node_point(aes(color = dept, size = betweenness),
                  show.legend = FALSE) +
  geom_node_text(aes(label = btwn_label), size = 4) +
  theme_void()
```

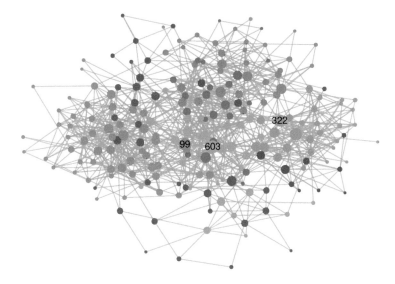

FIGURE 6.6: French workplace graph with the top 3 superconnectors identified

We can see upon examination that our top 3 organization-wide superconnectors are all in different departments. Putting all this together, it would seem that a good choice of buddies for the new hire would be employee 156 for departmental integration and employee 603 for office-wide integration, although any combination of the six individuals identified through this analysis would probably be decent choices.

6.3.2 Identifying influential employees

Influential actors in a network can be very useful to identify. In organizational contexts, working with more influential employees can make a difference to how certain initiatives or changes can be perceived by other employees. Influential employees can also be useful in efficiently tapping into prevalent opinions across the entire employee population. Imagine that we want to identify individuals from across the organization to participate in important workshops to problem solve some critical operational initiatives. These initiatives will affect employees at both an overall and a department level; therefore, it would be ideal to have individuals who are influential within each department as well as across the entire organization.

Again, let's look at a single department—the DMI department—as an example. Because we are interested in overall influence, this could mean we are equally interested in employees with a lot of connections or employees who are

'stealthily' influential in being connected to a smaller number of other highly
connected employees. The best measure for this is eigenvector centrality.

First we identify the top three most influential individuals in the DMI department as measured by eigenvector centrality by working on the DMI subgraph.

```
# working with lists so use purrr package
library(purrr)

# get IDs of top 3 eigen centrality
ranked_eigen_DMI <- DMI_graph |>
  eigen_centrality() |>
  pluck("vector") |>
  sort(decreasing = TRUE)

#get top 3
(top3_DMI_eigen <- names(ranked_eigen_DMI[1:3]))
```

```
## [1] "884" "156" "642"
```

We see two employee IDs that are in common with our top 3 superconnectors. We can also identify the top 3 most influential individuals across the
workfrance graph according to their eigenvector centrality.

```
# get IDs of top 3 eigen centrality
ranked_eigen_workfrance <- workfrance |>
  eigen_centrality() |>
  pluck("vector") |>
  sort(decreasing = TRUE)

#get top 3
(top3_workfrance_eigen <- names(ranked_eigen_workfrance[1:3]))
```

```
## [1] "603" "649" "147"
```

We see one individual in common with our top 3 superconnectors. Let's visualize this network so we can identify the department mix of our top 3 most
influential individuals, as in Figure 6.7.

```
# add betweenness property
V(workfrance)$eigen <- eigen_centrality(workfrance)$vector

# label only if a top3 superconnector
V(workfrance)$eigen_label <- ifelse(
```

```
  V(workfrance)$name %in% top3_workfrance_eigen,
  V(workfrance)$name, "")
)

# visualize
ggraph(workfrance) +
  geom_edge_link(color = "grey", alpha = 0.7) +
  geom_node_point(aes(color = dept, size = eigen),
                  show.legend = FALSE) +
  geom_node_text(aes(label = eigen_label), size = 4) +
  theme_void()
```

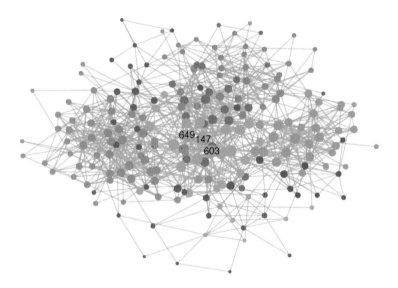

FIGURE 6.7: French workplace graph with the top 3 most influential vertices identified

This time we see that our three most influential individuals are all in the same department, suggesting that this department may be a strategically important one to involve in any planned change initiatives.

6.4   Learning exercises

6.4.1   Discussion questions

1. Describe the general concept of vertex centrality in networks and why it is important.
2. Define the degree centrality of a vertex v in an undirected graph G in at least two different ways. How would you interpret the degree centrality of v in an organizational network? Manually calculate the degree centrality of Vertices 9, 10 and 11 in G_{14}.
3. Draw the 2nd order ego network of Vertex 8 in G_{14}. What is the 2nd order ego size of Vertex 8?
4. Define closeness centrality and describe how it can be interpreted. Manually calculate the closeness centrality of Vertex 10 in G_{14} (feel free to express your answer as a fraction).
5. Define betweenness centrality and describe how it can be interpreted. Manually calculate the betweenness centrality of Vertex 4 in G_{14}.
6. Describe how you would interpret the eigenvector centrality of a vertex in an undirected graph G.
7. For each of the four main centrality measures—degree, closeness, betweenness and eigenvector—write down some potential benefits from knowing which individuals rank highest in a people network.
8. When visualizing graphs, name some ways to illustrate vertex centrality.
9. Why might some centrality functions in R or Python not actually output the raw centrality measure? Give an example of this. Do you think it matters? What would you do to correct it if you need to?
10. Describe some additional considerations in the calculation of vertex centrality in the case of directed graphs and in the case of weighted graphs.

6.4.2   Data exercises

1. Use an appropriate function to calculate the degree centrality of Vertices 9, 10 and 11 in G_{14} and verify that the output matches your manual calculations from the earlier questions.
2. Create and visualize the 2nd order ego network of Vertex 8 in G_{14}.
3. Use an appropriate function to calculate the closeness centrality of Vertex 10 in G_{14} and verify that it agrees with your manual calculation from the earlier questions.

4. Use an appropriate function to calculate the betweenness centrality of Vertex 4 in G_{14} and verify that it agrees with your manual calculation from the earlier questions.
5. Find the mean eigenvector centrality of all vertices in G_{14}. Do this twice, raw and normalized.
6. Visualize G_{14} with the size of the vertices scaled to their eigenvector centrality and the color scaled to their closeness centrality.

For questions 6 to 10, create an undirected graph from the Facebook friendships in the `schoolfriends_edgelist` and `schoolfriends_vertices` data sets in the onadata package or downloaded from the internet[8]. Recall from the exercises in Chapter 3 that this data contains information on friendships between students in a French high school. Make sure not to include the reported friendships in this graph. There are a lot of isolates in this graph because it only represents 'known' Facebook friendships, and you should remove isolates before proceeding[9].

6. Identify the top 3 individuals with the most Facebook connections.
7. Determine 1st order and 2nd order ego sizes of the individual with the most Facebook connections. What proportion of the total connected population is included in these ego networks?
8. Plot the distribution of the degree centrality of all vertices using a histogram or density plot.
9. Identify which individuals have the maximum closeness centrality, betweenness centrality and eigenvector centrality in the graph. Visualize the network color coded by class and identify where these individuals are. What do you notice?
10. If you were the principal of this high school and were deciding class placements for next year, how might this information be useful to you?

Extension: For these questions, create a *directed* graph from the *reported* friendships in the same data set, and remove the isolates as before.

11. Identify the individuals with the maximum in-degree centrality and the maximum out-degree centrality in this network. How would you describe these two individuals in the friendship dynamics of the high school? Do you see anything in common with the Facebook friendships?

---

[8] https://ona-book.org/data/schoolfriends_edgelist.csv and https://ona-book.org/data/schoolfriends_vertices.csv

[9] One easy way to identify isolates in a graph object G in R is to identify them using `isolates <- which(degree(G) == 0)`, and then remove them using `G_new <- remove.vertices(G, isolates)`.

12. Calculate the hub scores and authority scores of the vertices. How would you interpret these?

13. Determine the 1st order ego network of the individual with the highest authority score. Visualize this as a *directed* network with vertices color coded by class. Do the same for the individual with the highest hub score. Can you use these visualizations to describe why these individuals have high authority/hub scores?

7

Components, Communities and Cliques

The study of group dynamics would be pretty ineffective if we were not able to identify and study important subgroups. Networks of people are often made up of subsets that interact more intensely among each other than they do with the rest of the network, and it is often very important in research and analysis to identify or approximate these subsets as best as possible so that they can be studied more closely. In complex networks, this is not an easy task. Most of the computational methods we have available to us for finding densely connected subsets of vertices (usually called *communities*) are iterative approximations which make use of heuristics[1] and are rarely 100% accurate[2]. However, in the study of networks in the organizational sciences, we do not need high levels of precision to be able to draw valuable insights, and therefore these modern approximation techniques are very powerful tools for us to have at our disposal.

In the work we have done thus far in the book, we have already been exposed to subgraphs—we have used induced vertex subgraphs containing a specified set of vertices and all edges between them. However, in these situations we were able to specify the precise subset of vertices that we were interested in. In this chapter we will look at methods to identify or 'detect' subsets of vertices based on certain properties of the induced subgraphs of those vertices. We will start with simpler problems such as identifying subsets of vertices which are completely disconnected from others, and then we will proceed to look at graph partitioning and the identification of cliques and communities of vertices which, though not disconnected from other parts of the graph, have higher levels of density between each other than with the rest of the network.

---

[1]Heuristics are methodological 'shortcuts' which can vastly reduce the complexity of a problem but usually sacrifice some element of accuracy in doing so.

[2]Many problems of graph 'clustering'—that is, finding partitions of a graph that maximize intra-group density but minimize between-group density—have already been shown to be NP-hard.

DOI: 10.1201/9781003266815-7

7.1 Theory of components, partitions and clusters

7.1.1 Connected components of graphs

We learned earlier that a graph G is **connected** if a path exists between any pair of vertices u and v in G. If G is a directed graph, we say G is **weakly connected** if it would be connected when viewed as an undirected graph. We say that G is **strongly connected** if a path exists *from u to v* for any pair of vertices u and v in G. We say G is **unilaterally connected** if a path exists *either* from u and v *or* from v to u for any pair of vertices u and v in G.

A **connected component** of a graph is a connected subset of vertices, none of which are connected to any other vertex in the graph. As an example, the undirected graph in Figure 7.1 consists of three connected components, each with three vertices. In the directed graph in Figure 7.2, one component is strongly connected ($A \longrightarrow B \longrightarrow C \longrightarrow A$), one is unilaterally connected ($D \longrightarrow E \longrightarrow F$) and the third is weakly connected ($G \longrightarrow I \longleftarrow H$).

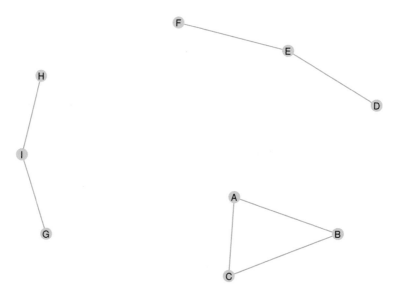

FIGURE 7.1: A graph with three connected components, each containing three vertices

Connected components of disconnected graphs are important to identify because many of the measures we have learned so far break down for disconnected graphs. For example, the diameter of a disconnected graph is theoretically defined as infinite by mathematical convention, but this is not a useful

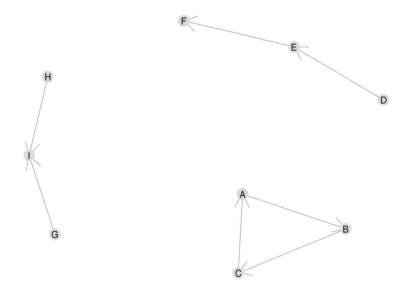

FIGURE 7.2: A directed graph with three connected components, one strongly connected, one weakly connected and one unilaterally connected

practical measure. Usually when we want to know the diameter of a graph, we want to understand the largest *finite* distance between any two vertices, which translates to the diameter of the largest connected component in the graph. Therefore, most calculations of diameter in disconnected graphs require us to be able to identify the largest connected component.

It is not too difficult to think of an algorithm that can determine all the connected components of a graph. If you are interested in this, see the exercises at the end of this chapter.

> **Playing around**: Go back and try to find some examples in earlier chapters of graphs that are disconnected, and calculate the diameter that is returned by the functions in R or Python packages. For example, you could try the Random Acts of Pizza graph from the exercises at the end of Chapter 3 or the graph of reported friendships from the schoolfriends data set at the end of the previous chapter. What do diameter functions return for these graphs?

7.1.2   Vertex partitioning

Often graphs will be connected, but we still want to divide the vertices up into mutually exclusive subgroups of interest. Such a division is called a **partition** of a graph. In a partition, all vertices must be in one and only one subgroup. Partitions are created through making cuts in a graph.

A **cut** in a graph G is a set of edges that divide the vertices of G into two disjoint subsets. The number of edges is known as the *size* of the cut. In Figure 7.3, edges e3, e4 and e5 divide the graph into two disjoint connected sets and represents a cut of size 3.

A **minimum cut** is a cut where no other cut exists in G with a smaller number of edges. In Figure 7.3, it should not be difficult to see that mimimum cuts have size 1 and can be achieved with either e1 or e2. In both cases, these minimum cuts divide the graph into a connected component and an isolate[3].

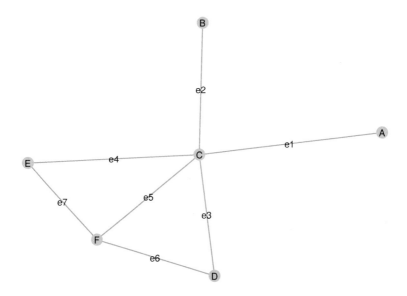

FIGURE 7.3: Cuts are defined by edges that split the vertices of a graph into disjoint subsets

A partition of a graph G is obtained through a series of cuts. For example, if we make a cut using e3, e5 and e7 in Figure 7.3, we split the graph into two disjoint connected graphs. If we then make a further cut using e1, we split the graph into three disjoint sets: two disjoint connected sets and an isolate.

---

[3]Maximum cuts are cuts where no other cuts exist with a greater number of edges. Maximum cuts in graphs are extremely challenging to determine. Luckily, we rarely need them in organizational network analysis.

In directed graphs, cuts can be defined according to the direction of edges, and in weighted graphs, minimum cuts can be determined through the weights of edges. The most popular algorithm for determining the minimum cut of a graph is the Stoer-Wagner algorithm (Stoer & Wagner (1997)).

7.1.3 Vertex clustering and community detection

Vertex **clustering** refers to the process of partitioning a graph in order to satisfy a certain objective. Most commonly in organizational network analysis, that objective is to achieve a high edge density between the vertices inside a cluster, and a low edge density between vertices that are in different clusters. Such highly connected clusters are usually referred to as **communities** and the process of determining optimal communities in a graph is known as **community detection** or **community discovery**[4]. Community detection is an unsupervised process. When we perform community detection on a graph, we do not know in advance how many communities we seek to find or the size of those communities.

The most commonly used (and fastest) community detection algorithm is the Louvain algorithm. The Louvain algorithm partitions a graph into subsets of vertices by trying to maximize the *modularity* of the graph. Modularity measures how dense the connections are within subsets of vertices in a graph by comparing the density to that which would be expected from a random graph. In an unweighted and undirected graph, modularity takes a value between -0.5 and $+1$. Any value above zero means that the vertices inside the subgroups are more densely connected than would be expected by chance. The higher the modularity of a graph, the more connected the vertices are inside the subgroups compared to between the subgroups, and therefore the more certain we can be that the subgroups represent genuine communities of more intense connection. The approximate steps of the Louvain algorithm are as follows:

1. The algorithm starts its first phase with each vertex in its own community.
2. Vertices are moved into other communities, and modularity is calculated.
3. When the algorithm reaches a point where further vertex moves do not increase modularity, it finishes its first phase.
4. In its second phase, the communities resulting from the first phase are aggregated to form a simpler pseudograph where each vertex

---

[4]The meaning of 'high' and 'low' edge density is relative and really depends on the nature of the graph, and algorithms will do their best to find communities which maximize the difference between in-community density and cross-community density, even though some or all of these communities may not end up having particularly high edge density.

represents a community, where loop edges on a vertex are weighted by the total number of edges inside that community, and where edges between vertices are weighted by the total number of edges between those communities[5]. In this heuristic step, vertices are moved in this simpler graph with the aim of improving modularity. That is, communities may be combined if modularity is improved.

5. The first and second phases are repeated until modularity cannot be further improved.

A more recently developed community detection algorithm which improves on the Louvain algorithm is the Leiden algorithm. The Leiden algorithm operates similarly to Louvain, but has an additional refinement process at the end of the first phase which helps increase the options for improved modularity in the second phase. The Leiden algorithm will always achieve results as good as the Louvain algorithm, and in many cases may detect communities which are better connected than those detected by Louvain.

Both the Louvain and Leiden algorithms are good options for performing community detection in an organizational context. However, there are numerous other options, many of which are available in common data science packages. For example, the Girvan-Newman algorithm operates in a very different way by starting with an entire graph and progressively removing important edges to potentially reveal high modularity subgroups. For a more detailed reference on the Louvain and Leiden algorithms, see Traag et al. (2019) and for more general insight into a broader range of community detection algorithms, see Yang et al. (2016).

One important aspect of community detection which is often not understood is that community detection algorithms classify vertices into subgroups, but offer no direct insight into the *nature* of those subgroups. Further analytic techniques need to be applied to help describe the subgroups in a meaningful way. For example, the subgroups could be compared to known 'ground truth' characteristics of the network (such as department in the workfrance graph or class in the schoolfriends graph). We will examine this using an example later in this chapter.

7.1.4 Cliques

A **clique** is a subset of vertices in an undirected graph whose induced subgraph is complete. That is, the induced subgraph has an edge density of 1. This is best understood as the most intense possible type of community in an undirected graph. A **maximal clique** is a clique which cannot be extended by adding

---

[5]This also works with weighted edges, assuming that weights represent 'closeness' of connection, which they usually do in organizational contexts.

another vertex. A **largest clique** is a clique with the greatest number of vertices of all cliques in the graph.

In Figure 7.3, the following are maximal cliques: $B \longleftrightarrow C$, $A \longleftrightarrow C$, $C \longleftrightarrow E \longleftrightarrow F$ and $C \longleftrightarrow D \longleftrightarrow F$ because no other vertex can be added to these cliques without creating an incomplete graph. $C \longleftrightarrow E \longleftrightarrow F$ and $C \longleftrightarrow D \longleftrightarrow F$ are largest cliques because there is no clique in the graph that has more than three vertices.

Finding a single maximal clique in an undirected graph is not a complex problem and can be done quickly using a standard search algorithm starting on an arbitrary vertex. However, finding maximal cliques of a specified size, or all maximal cliques, as well as finding largest cliques, are problems whose complexity increases with the size and density of a graph. Care should be taken in attempting these algorithms on very large graphs.

> **Thinking ahead:** Go back to the graph of *Zachary's Karate Club* in Chapter 3. Can you identify some maximal cliques? What do you think is the size of the largest clique? Thinking about this will give you a sense of how hard the largest clique problem might be on very large graphs. We will use this as an example later in the chapter.

7.2 Finding components, communities and cliques using R

7.2.1 Finding connected components of disconnected graphs

To illustrate the `components()` function in `igraph` we will load up the `schoolfriends` edgelist data set from an earlier chapter. We will use reported friendships, create a directed graph and visualize it as in Figure 7.4.

```
library(igraph)
library(ggraph)
library(dplyr)

# get schoolfriends edgelist
schoolfriends_edgelist <- read.csv(
  "https://ona-book.org/data/schoolfriends_edgelist.csv"
)

# just use reported friendships
```

```
schoolfriends_reported <- schoolfriends_edgelist |>
  dplyr::filter(type == "reported")

# create directed graph
schoolfriends_rp <- igraph::graph_from_data_frame(
  schoolfriends_reported
)

# visualize
set.seed(123)
ggraph(schoolfriends_rp) +
  geom_edge_link(color = "grey",
                 arrow = arrow(length = unit(0.2, "cm"))) +
  geom_node_point(size = 2, color = "blue") +
  theme_void()
```

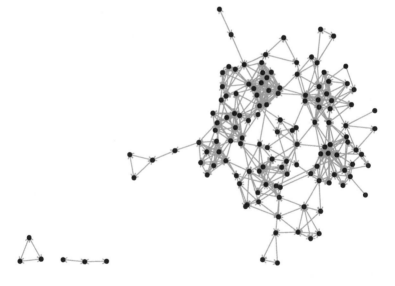

FIGURE 7.4: The directed graph of reported friendships from our French high school

We can see some connected components in this disconnected graph. We can use the components() function to classify the vertices into the connected components. This function generates a list containing the following vectors:

- membership, which is a vector assigning each vertex to a numbered component
- csize, which returns the size of each component

- no, which is the number of connected components

Let's verify the latter two:

```
# get weakly connected components (mode ignored if undirected)
schoolfriends_components <- igraph::components(schoolfriends_rp,
                                              mode = "weak")

# how many components?
schoolfriends_components$no
```

```
## [1] 3
```

```
# size of components
schoolfriends_components$csize
```

```
## [1] 128   3   3
```

We can use the membership to assign a component property and then visualize with the vertices colored by component, as in Figure 7.5.

```
# assign component property
V(schoolfriends_rp)$component <- schoolfriends_components$membership

# visualize
ggraph(schoolfriends_rp) +
  geom_edge_link(color = "grey",
                 arrow = arrow(length = unit(0.2, "cm"))) +
  geom_node_point(size = 2, aes(color = as.factor(component))) +
  labs(color = "Component") +
  theme_void()
```

> **Playing around:** Weakly connected components of a directed graph are easier to spot with the naked eye compared to strongly connected components. Why? Remind yourself of the definition of weakly connected components from earlier in this chapter. Try to repeat this analysis to visualize all strongly connected components in the reported schoolfriends graph and see the difference.

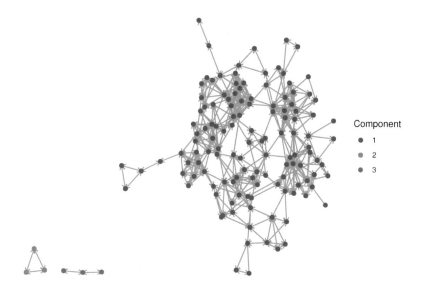

FIGURE 7.5: The reported 'schoolfriends' graph color coded by its (weakly) connected components

7.2.2 Partitioning and community detection in R

For the next few examples, we will return to *Zachary's Karate Club* network from Chapter 3. Let's load up and visualize that undirected graph and mark the known leading actors Mr Hi and John A with larger vertices, as in Figure 7.6.

```
# get karate edgelist and create undirected graph
karate_edges <- read.csv("https://ona-book.org/data/karate.csv")
karate <- igraph::graph_from_data_frame(karate_edges, directed = FALSE)

# color John A and Mr Hi differently
V(karate)$leader <- ifelse(
  V(karate)$name %in% c("Mr Hi", "John A"), 1, 0
)

# visualize
set.seed(123)
ggraph(karate, layout = "fr") +
  geom_edge_link(color = "grey") +
  geom_node_point(aes(size = as.factor(leader)), color = "blue",
                  show.legend = FALSE) +
  theme_void()
```

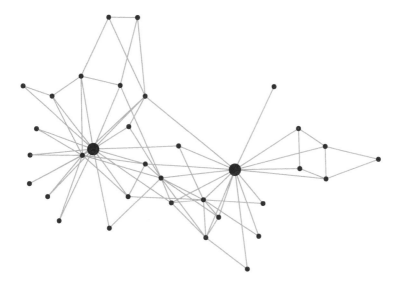

FIGURE 7.6: Zachary's Karate Club graph with Mr Hi and John A indicated with larger vertices

Minimum cuts in graphs can be found using the `min_cut()` function in `igraph`. This will return the number of edges in the minimum cut, unless you use the `value.only = FALSE` argument, in which case it will return more information on the cut,

```
igraph::min_cut(karate, value.only = FALSE)
```

```
## $value
## [1] 1
##
## $cut
## + 1/78 edge from 3d0e29c (vertex names):
## [1] Mr Hi--Actor 12
##
## $partition1
## + 1/34 vertex, named, from 3d0e29c:
## [1] Actor 12
##
## $partition2
## + 33/34 vertices, named, from 3d0e29c:
##  [1] Mr Hi   Actor 2  Actor 3  Actor 4  Actor 5  Actor 6  Actor 7  Actor 9  Actor 10 Actor 14
## [11] Actor 15 Actor 16 Actor 19 Actor 20 Actor 21 Actor 23 Actor 24 Actor 25 Actor 26 Actor 27
## [21] Actor 28 Actor 29 Actor 30 Actor 31 Actor 32 Actor 33 Actor 8  Actor 11 Actor 13 Actor 18
## [31] Actor 22 Actor 17 John A
```

We see that a minimum cut exists of size 1 between Mr Hi and Actor 12.

The Louvain community detection algorithm can be run using the `cluster_louvain()` function. `weights` can be added as an argument, or will be used by default if the graph has a `weight` edge attribute (set `weight = NA` to avoid this). This will produce a list of community groups. The best way to record the resulting community membership is to assign it as a vertex property using the `membership()` function.

```
# detect communities using Louvain
communities <- cluster_louvain(karate)

# assign as a vertex property
V(karate)$community <- membership(communities)
```

Before visualizing the communities, we can see how many they are and their size[6]:

```
sizes(communities)
```

```
## Community sizes
##  1  2  3  4
##  6 12 11  5
```

We have four detected communities of varying sizes. As before, we can color code to visualize these, as in Figure 7.7.

```
set.seed(123)
ggraph(karate, layout = "fr") +
  geom_edge_link(color =  "grey") +
  geom_node_point(aes(size = as.factor(leader),
                      color = as.factor(community)),
                  show.legend = FALSE) +
  theme_void()
```

> **Playing around:.** Try playing around with some of the other community detection methods available in `igraph` using the karate example. How different are the results? For example, try `cluster_edge_betweenness()` (the Girvan-Newman algorithm) or `cluster_infomap()` or any other methods that begin with `cluster`.

---

[6]We can also see the modularity of the partition by calling the `modularity()` function.

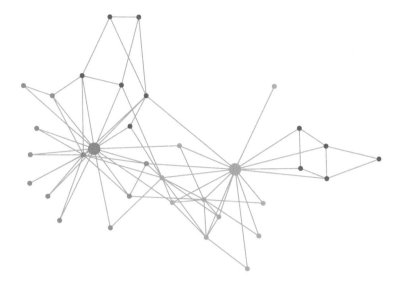

FIGURE 7.7: Communities of Zachary's Karate Club as detected by the
Louvain algorithm

7.2.3 Finding cliques in R

The cliques() and max_cliques() function in igraph identifies all cliques or
maximal cliques, respectively, with a specified maximum or minimum size if
desired. It is advisable to specify a size for cliques of interest because otherwise
a long list might be returned, including many single node cliques.

```
max_cliques(karate, min = 5, max = 5)
```

```
## [[1]]
## + 5/34 vertices, named, from 3d0e29c:
## [1] Actor 2  Mr Hi    Actor 4  Actor 3  Actor 14
##
## [[2]]
## + 5/34 vertices, named, from 3d0e29c:
## [1] Actor 2 Mr Hi   Actor 4 Actor 3 Actor 8
```

The largest_cliques() function finds all largest cliques in a graph.

```
largest_cliques(karate)
```

```
## [[1]]
```

```
## + 5/34 vertices, named, from 3d0e29c:
## [1] Actor 8 Mr Hi    Actor 2 Actor 3 Actor 4
##
## [[2]]
## + 5/34 vertices, named, from 3d0e29c:
## [1] Actor 4  Mr Hi     Actor 2  Actor 3  Actor 14
```

We see that the maximal cliques of size 5 that we identified are also the largest
cliques in the karate graph, and they have 4 out of 5 vertices in common. The
function clique_num() returns the size of the largest clique.

```
clique_num(karate)
```

```
## [1] 5
```

7.3   Finding components, communities and cliques using Python

7.3.1   Finding connected components using Python

For *undirected graphs*, the networkx function number_connected_components()
returns the number of connected components in the graph, while the
connected_components() function returns the vertices in each connected component.

For *directed graphs*, similar functions identify weakly and strongly connected
components. Let's use the reported friendships from the schoolfriends data
set as an example.

```
import pandas as pd
import networkx as nx

# get schoolfriends edgelist
schoolfriends_edges = pd.read_csv(
  "https://ona-book.org/data/schoolfriends_edgelist.csv"
)

# use only reported friendships
schoolfriends_reported = schoolfriends_edges[
  schoolfriends_edges.type == "reported"
]
```

```
# create directed graph
schoolfriends_rp = nx.from_pandas_edgelist(
  schoolfriends_reported,
  source = "from",
  target = "to",
  create_using=nx.DiGraph
)

# number of weakly connected components
nx.number_weakly_connected_components(schoolfriends_rp)
```

```
## 3
```

```
# create component subgraphs
components = nx.weakly_connected_components(schoolfriends_rp)

subgraphs = [schoolfriends_rp.subgraph(component).copy()
for component in components]

# size of subgraphs
[len(subgraph.nodes) for subgraph in subgraphs]
```

```
## [128, 3, 3]
```

```
# view nodes in one of the smaller components
subgraphs[2].nodes
```

```
## NodeView((366, 1485, 974))
```

7.3.2 Partitioning and community detection using Python

networkx has numerous algorithmic functions for exploring edge cuts on graphs, including to find the minimum edge cut. You can consult the reference documentation[7] to learn about the various functions available. Let's use the karate data set to demonstrate how to find a minimum cut.

```
# get karate edgelist
karate_edges = pd.read_csv("https://ona-book.org/data/karate.csv")
```

---

[7]https://networkx.org/documentation/stable/reference/algorithms/cuts.html

```
# create undirected network
karate = nx.from_pandas_edgelist(karate_edges, source = "from",
target = "to")

# find minimum cut
nx.minimum_edge_cut(karate)
```

```
## {('Actor 12', 'Mr Hi')}
```

```
# get minimum edge cut size
len(nx.minimum_edge_cut(karate))
```

```
## 1
```

Various built-in community detection algorithms are available in the
`networkx.community` module, such as the Girvan-Newman edge betweenness
algorithm. This generates communities by progressively removing edges with
the highest edge betweenness centrality. It returns an iterator object where the
first element is the result of the first edge removal, and subsequent elements
are the result of progressive edge removal.

```
# get communities based on girvan-newman and sort by no of communities
communities = sorted(
  nx.community.girvan_newman(karate),
  key = len
)

# view communities from first edge removal
pd.DataFrame(communities[0]).transpose()
```

```
##              0          1
## 0      Actor 7    Actor 9
## 1      Actor 8   Actor 21
## 2      Actor 2   Actor 28
## 3      Actor 4   Actor 15
## 4     Actor 14   Actor 10
## 5     Actor 18   Actor 30
## 6     Actor 12   Actor 26
## 7        Mr Hi   Actor 32
## 8     Actor 17   Actor 27
## 9     Actor 13   Actor 33
## 10     Actor 5   Actor 23
## 11    Actor 20    Actor 3
```

```
## 12   Actor 22   Actor 16
## 13    Actor 6   Actor 19
## 14   Actor 11   Actor 25
## 15       None   Actor 29
## 16       None     John A
## 17       None   Actor 31
## 18       None   Actor 24
```

We see that the first split leads to two communities, one around John A and the other around Mr Hi.

The cdlib package in Python contains a very wide range of community detection algorithms that work with the networkx package, including the Louvain and Leiden algorithms as well as many others. In this example, we create a Louvain partition of the karate graph using cdlib.

```
from cdlib import algorithms
import numpy as np
import matplotlib.cm as cm
import matplotlib.pyplot as plt

# get louvain partition which optimizes modularity
louvain_comms = algorithms.louvain(karate)
```

louvain_comms is a clustering object that has a lot of useful properties and methods. To see the communities, use the following:

```
pd.DataFrame(louvain_comms.communities).transpose()
```

```
##                0          1          2          3
## 0          Mr Hi    Actor 9   Actor 32    Actor 5
## 1        Actor 2   Actor 31   Actor 28    Actor 6
## 2        Actor 3   Actor 33   Actor 29    Actor 7
## 3        Actor 4     John A   Actor 24   Actor 11
## 4        Actor 8   Actor 15   Actor 26   Actor 17
## 5       Actor 12   Actor 16   Actor 25       None
## 6       Actor 13   Actor 19       None       None
## 7       Actor 14   Actor 21       None       None
## 8       Actor 18   Actor 23       None       None
## 9       Actor 20   Actor 30       None       None
## 10      Actor 22   Actor 27       None       None
## 11      Actor 10       None       None       None
```

We see four communities. The modularity of the resulting community structure can be calculated using the newman_girvan_modularity() method.

```
louvain_comms.newman_girvan_modularity()
```

```
## FitnessResult(min=None, max=None, score=0.4188034188034188, std=None)
```

To visualize the network community structure, we can create a color mapping against the communities, as in Figure 7.8.

```python
import matplotlib.pyplot as plt
from matplotlib import cm
from matplotlib.colors import ListedColormap, LinearSegmentedColormap

# create dict with labels only for Mr Hi and John A
node = list(karate.nodes)
labels = [i if i == "Mr Hi" or i == "John A" else "" \
for i in karate.nodes]
nodelabels = dict(zip(node, labels))

# create and order community mappings
communities = louvain_comms.to_node_community_map()
communities = [communities[k].pop() for k in node]

# create color map
pastel2 = cm.get_cmap('Pastel2', max(communities) + 1)

# visualize
np.random.seed(123)
nx.draw_spring(karate, labels = nodelabels, cmap = pastel2,
node_color = communities, edge_color = "grey")
plt.show()
```

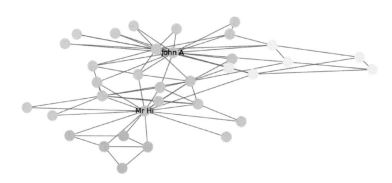

FIGURE 7.8: Best Louvain partition of Zachary's Karate Club graph

> **Playing around:** The options for community detection algorithms in the cdlib Python package are extensive. Consider playing around with some different algorithms. For example, you could try to visualize the community structure based on the Leiden algorithm. It's also worth spending a little time exploring the technical documentation for the cdlib package[8] to see the range of methods available.

7.3.3   Finding cliques in Python

All maximal cliques in a graph can be calculated using the `find_cliques()` function:

```
cliques = nx.find_cliques(karate)
maximal_cliques = sorted(cliques, key = len)

# get number of maximal cliques
len(maximal_cliques)
```

```
## 36
```

```
# get largest clique
maximal_cliques[len(maximal_cliques) - 1]
```

```
## ['Actor 2', 'Mr Hi', 'Actor 14', 'Actor 3', 'Actor 4']
```

Alternatively, there are functions that can calculate the number of cliques, the size of the largest clique, and can extract the graph of the largest clique.

```
nx.graph_number_of_cliques(karate)
```

```
## 36
```

```
nx.graph_clique_number(karate)
```

```
## 5
```

---

[8]https://cdlib.readthedocs.io/en/latest

7.4   Examples of uses

In this section we will illustrate the implementation and interpretation of community detection algorithms using our Facebook schoolfriends example, and introducing a new example related to political tweets in the Ontario province of Canada.

7.4.1   Detecting communities and cliques among Facebook friends

Let's reload our Facebook schoolfriends graph and remove any isolates so that we can investigate communities and cliques inside it.

```
# get schoolfriends data
schoolfriends_edgelist <- read.csv(
  "https://ona-book.org/data/schoolfriends_edgelist.csv"
)
schoolfriends_vertices <- read.csv(
  "https://ona-book.org/data/schoolfriends_vertices.csv"
)

# facebook friendships only
schoolfriends_facebook <- schoolfriends_edgelist |>
  dplyr::filter(type == "facebook")

# create undirected graph
schoolfriends_fb <- igraph::graph_from_data_frame(
  d = schoolfriends_facebook,
  vertices = schoolfriends_vertices,
  directed = FALSE
)

# remove isolates
isolates = which(degree(schoolfriends_fb) == 0)
schoolfriends_fb <- delete.vertices(schoolfriends_fb, isolates)
```

We now have a connected, undirected graph of 156 vertices, with class and gender as vertex properties. First, let's detemine the largest clique in the graph.

```
(cliques <- igraph::largest_cliques(schoolfriends_fb))
```

```
## [[1]]
## + 14/156 vertices, named, from 575e3fd:
##  [1] 525  797  466  376  638  841  1423 1218 769  440  125  325  694  245
##
## [[2]]
## + 14/156 vertices, named, from 575e3fd:
##  [1] 245  564  1218 440  466  376  841  1237 1423 769  624  125  325  694
##
## [[3]]
## + 14/156 vertices, named, from 575e3fd:
##  [1] 245  797  466  376  841  1423 1218 624  440  125  638  325  694  769
##
## [[4]]
## + 14/156 vertices, named, from 575e3fd:
##  [1] 245  797  466  376  841  1423 1218 624  440  125  638  325  694  1067
##
## [[5]]
## + 14/156 vertices, named, from 575e3fd:
##  [1] 245  1067 466  376  841  1237 1423 1218 624  440  125  638  325  694
##
## [[6]]
## + 14/156 vertices, named, from 575e3fd:
##  [1] 245  638  466  376  841  1237 1423 1218 769  624  440  125  325  694
```

We see 6 cliques of 14 individuals, all of which have considerable overlap. We can take a look at the class and gender of one of these cliques.

```
# subgraph for clique 6
clique6 <- igraph::induced_subgraph(schoolfriends_fb,
                                    vids = cliques[[6]])
```

```
(data.frame(
  id = V(clique6)$name,
  class = V(clique6)$class,
  gender = V(clique6)$gender
))
```

```
##        id class gender
## 1     466  MP*1      M
## 2     376  MP*1      M
## 3     638  MP*1      M
```

```
## 4     841   MP*1       M
## 5    1237   MP*2       M
## 6    1423   MP*2       M
## 7    1218   MP*2       M
## 8     769   PSI*       M
## 9     624   PSI*       M
## 10    440   PSI*       F
## 11    125   PSI*       F
## 12    325   PSI*       M
## 13    694    MP        F
## 14    245    MP        F
```

We see that this clique is distributed over four classes and is mostly male. Let's visualize where this clique sits in the full network, as in Figure 7.9.

```
# create clique property
V(schoolfriends_fb)$clique6 <- ifelse(
  V(schoolfriends_fb) %in% cliques[[6]], 1, 0
)

# visualize
set.seed(123)
ggraph(schoolfriends_fb, layout = "fr") +
  geom_edge_link(color = "grey", alpha = 0.7) +
  geom_node_point(size = 2, aes(color = as.factor(clique6)),
                  show.legend = FALSE) +
  theme_void()
```

Now let's use the Louvain algorithm to detect communities in our graph.

```
# get optimal louvain communities
communities <- igraph::cluster_louvain(schoolfriends_fb)

# assign community as a vertex property
V(schoolfriends_fb)$community <- membership(communities)

# how many communities?
length(unique(V(schoolfriends_fb)$community))
```

```
## [1] 6
```

Six communities have been identified. Let's compare the modularity of this community structure to the known ground truth communities of class and gender.

FIGURE 7.9: Facebook schoolfriends network with one of the largest cliques indicated

```
# modularity of louvain
modularity(schoolfriends_fb, V(schoolfriends_fb)$community)
```

```
## [1] 0.5284791
```

```
# modularity of class structure
modularity(schoolfriends_fb,
           as.integer(as.factor(V(schoolfriends_fb)$class)))
```

```
## [1] 0.317128
```

```
# modularity of gender structure
modularity(schoolfriends_fb,
           as.integer(as.factor(V(schoolfriends_fb)$gender)))
```

```
## [1] 0.06504432
```

This community structure is certainly a better indicator of connected Facebook subgroups than gender or class. We can visualize the class structure side-by-side with the Louvain community structure to try to interpret it, as in Figure 7.10.

```r
# use patchwork package for combining plots easily
library(patchwork)

# visualize louvain communities
set.seed(123)
g1 <- ggraph(schoolfriends_fb, layout = "fr") +
  geom_edge_link(color = "grey", alpha = 0.7) +
  geom_node_point(size = 2, aes(color = as.factor(community)),
                  show.legend = FALSE) +
  theme_void()

# visualize ground truth class communities
set.seed(123)
g2 <- ggraph(schoolfriends_fb, layout = "fr") +
  geom_edge_link(color = "grey", alpha = 0.7) +
  geom_node_point(size = 2, aes(color = class),
                  show.legend = FALSE) +
  theme_void()

# display side by side
g1 + g2
```

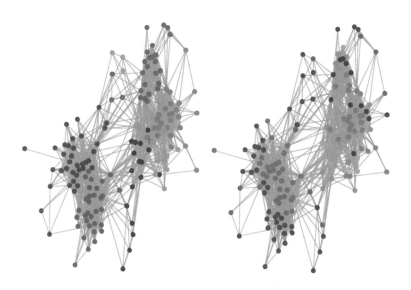

FIGURE 7.10: Optimal Louvain communities in the Facebook schoolfriends graph (left) versus ground truth class communities (right)

Visually, we can see that the Louvain community structure is a much better representation of dense friendship groups compared to the ground truth class structure, indicating that Facebook friendships tend to span across those class structures. We can also see that one of the Louvain communities contains the clique we identified earlier.

7.4.2 Detecting politically aligned communities on Twitter

The `ontariopol_edgelist` and `ontariopol_vertices` data sets represent tweeting activity between Ontario province politicians in Canada as captured in September 2021 and spanning several prior years of activity. Although the Twitter graph is a directed graph, we will set this network up as undirected, with two politicians connected if there has been an interaction between them by means of one mentioning the other in a tweet or one replying to a tweet from the other. The `weight` property represents the number of interactions and is therefore a measure of the connection strength.

```
# get edgelist and vertex data
ontariopol_edges <- read.csv(
  "https://ona-book.org/data/ontariopol_edgelist.csv"
)
ontariopol_vertices <- read.csv(
  "https://ona-book.org/data/ontariopol_vertices.csv"
)

# create undirected graph
(ontariopol <- igraph::graph_from_data_frame(
  d = ontariopol_edges,
  vertices = ontariopol_vertices,
  directed = FALSE
))
```

```
## IGRAPH ba7e394 UNW- 108 6095 --
## + attr: name (v/c), screen_name (v/c), party (v/c), weight (e/n)
## + edges from ba7e394 (vertex names):
##  [1] Deepak Anand--Doug Ford            Deepak Anand--Victor Fedeli
##  [3] Deepak Anand--Deepak Anand         Deepak Anand--Monte McNaughton
##  [5] Deepak Anand--Christine Elliott    Deepak Anand--Stephen Lecce
##  [7] Deepak Anand--Rod Phillips         Deepak Anand--Lisa MacLeod
##  [9] Deepak Anand--Michael Tibollo      Deepak Anand--Peter Bethlenfalvy
## [11] Deepak Anand--Raymond Sung Joon Cho Deepak Anand--Rudy Cuzzetto
## [13] Deepak Anand--Caroline Mulroney    Deepak Anand--Sheref Sabawy
## [15] Deepak Anand--Nina Tangri          Deepak Anand--Jill Dunlop
## + ... omitted several edges
```

We have an undirected, weighted graph, with `screen_name` and `party` vertex properties. First, we check if our graph is connected:

```
is.connected(ontariopol)
```

```
## [1] TRUE
```

Now we use the Louvain algorithm to detect an optimal community structure
in our graph. Since the graph has a `weight` property, our modularity calculations will include edge weight.

```
# find optimal communities
communities <- igraph::cluster_louvain(ontariopol)

# assign as vertex properties
V(ontariopol)$community <- membership(communities)

# how many communities
length(unique(V(ontariopol)$community))
```

```
## [1] 6
```

We see six commmunities. Let's compare the modularity of this community
structure to the ground truth political party structure.

```
# louvain modularity
modularity(ontariopol,
           membership = V(ontariopol)$community,
           weights = E(ontariopol)$weight)
```

```
## [1] 0.3904751
```

```
# political party modularity
modularity(ontariopol,
           membership = as.integer(as.factor(V(ontariopol)$party)),
           weights = E(ontariopol)$weight)
```

```
## [1] 0.382394
```

We see very similar modularity. Let's visualize the Louvain community and
party structure side-by-side, as in Figure 7.11.

```r
# visualize louvain communities
set.seed(123)
g1 <- ggraph(ontariopol, layout = "fr") +
  geom_edge_link(color = "grey", alpha = 0.7) +
  geom_node_point(size = 2, aes(color = as.factor(community))),
                  show.legend = FALSE) +
  theme_void()

# visualize ground truth political party communities
set.seed(123)
g2 <- ggraph(ontariopol, layout = "fr") +
  geom_edge_link(color = "grey", alpha = 0.7) +
  geom_node_point(size = 2, aes(color = party),
                  show.legend = FALSE) +
  theme_void()

# display side by side
g1 + g2
```

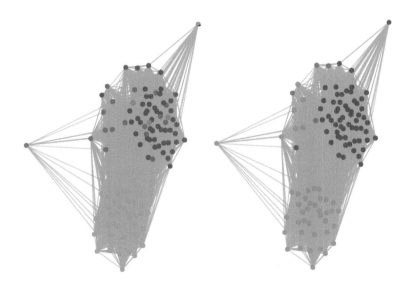

FIGURE 7.11: Twitter interaction of Ontario politicians segmented by their Louvain communities (left) and their ground truth political parties (right). Louvain does a good job of identifying political alignment.

We see very similar community structures, indicating that the Louvain algorithm has done a good job of identifying political party alignment from the tweet activity of the politicians. Using similar methods to our Facebook schoolfriends example in Section 7.4.1, we can also identify large cliques within the political parties, as in Figure 7.12.

```
# get largest cliques
cliques <- igraph::largest_cliques(ontariopol)

# there are 24 cliques of size 48 - choose one and visualize
# create clique property
V(ontariopol)$clique24 <- ifelse(
  V(ontariopol) %in% cliques[[24]], 1, 0
)

# visualize clique
set.seed(123)
g1 <- ggraph(ontariopol, layout = "fr") +
  geom_edge_link(color = "grey", alpha = 0.7) +
  geom_node_point(size = 2, aes(color = as.factor(clique24)),
                  show.legend = FALSE) +
  theme_void()

# visualize ground truth political parties
set.seed(123)
g2 <- ggraph(ontariopol, layout = "fr") +
  geom_edge_link(color = "grey", alpha = 0.5) +
  geom_node_point(size = 2, aes(color = party)) +
  labs(color = "Party (Right hand graph)") +
  theme_void()

g1 + g2
```

Playing around: In both of the examples in this section, consider extending the work to identify key important or influential nodes within communities using your learning from Chapter 6. Remember that the Twitter graph is a directed graph and this may impact calculations of centrality, so consider moving back to a directed graph for these calculations. Also, try investigating what happens when you seek optimal *unweighted* Louvain communities in the `ontariopol` graph.

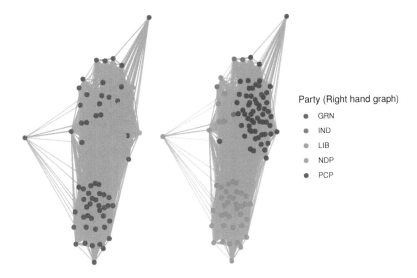

FIGURE 7.12: Large Twitter clique of 48 politicians (left). Comparison with party membership (right) reveals this to be a PCP clique.

7.5 Learning exercises

7.5.1 Discussion questions

1. What does it mean when an undirected graph is described as a connected graph? Provide similar definitions for a weakly and strongly connected directed graph.
2. By starting with a random vertex, design a set of algorithmic steps that would determine all connected components of an undirected graph.
3. What is a vertex partition of a graph? Describe how a partition arises from a series of edge cuts in a graph.
4. What is meant by a vertex clustering of a graph?
5. What is meant by a community of vertices? What objective are we usually trying to achieve when we detect communities in a graph?
6. Describe your understanding of the term 'modularity' as it relates to community detection in graphs.
7. Name a common community detection algorithm and describe how it works.
8. What do we mean by the term 'unsupervised' when we describe a community detection process?

9.   What is meant by the term 'clique' in an undirected graph?
10. What is a maximal clique and a largest clique in a graph? Are maximal cliques always largest cliques? Why or why not?

7.5.2   Data exercises

For Exercises 1-3, load the `wikivote` edgelist from the `onadata` package or download it from the internet[9]. Recall that this data set represents votes from Wikipedia members to other Wikipedia members to nominate the `to` member to administrator status. Create a directed graph from this data set. Be careful with trying to visualize this graph, as it is large.

1.   Determine how many weakly connected components there are in this graph. How large is the largest component?
2.   Determine how many strongly connected components there are in this graph. How large is the largest component?
3.   Describe how you would explain and interpret the difference between your results for Questions 1 and 2.

For Exercises 4-10, load the `email_edgelist` and `email_vertices` data sets from the `onadata` package or download them from the internet[10]. This data set represents a network of emails sent between members of a large research institution. The department of each member is included in the vertex data set. Create an undirected graph from this data[11].

4.   Determine the connected components of this network and reduce the network to its largest connected component.
5.   Use the Louvain algorithm to determine a vertex partition/community structure with optimal modularity in this network.
6.   Compare the modularity of the Louvain community structure with that of the ground truth department structure.
7.   Visualize the graph color-coded by the Louvain community, and then visualize the graph separately color-coded by the ground truth department. Compare the visualizations. Can you describe any of the Louvain communities in terms of departments?
8.   Create a dataframe containing the community and department for each vertex. Manipulate this dataframe to show the percentage of

---

[9] https://ona-book.org/data/wikivote.csv

[10] https://ona-book.org/daya/email_edgelist.csv and https://ona-book.org/data/email_vertices.csv

[11] Note that the visualizations in these exercises might be demanding on low-memory/low-CPU machines. Proceed with caution.

individuals from each department in each community. Try to visualize this using a heatmap or other style of visualization and try to use this to describe the communities in terms of departments.

9. Find the largest clique size in the graph. How many such largest cliques are there? What do you think a clique represents in this context?

10. Try to visualize the members of these cliques in the context of the entire graph. What can you conclude?

Extension: These questions require the use of the Leiden community detection algorithm, which you may recall from earlier in this chapter is guaranteed to find a partition which at least matches the modularity of a Louvain partition, and can often improve it. If you are a Python programmer, the Leiden algorithm is easily used from the cdlib package. If you are an R programmer, you will need to use the leiden package, which uses a Python implementation of the algorithm inside R. You may need to be familiar with the reticulate package[12] to ensure that an appropriate Python environment is available inside your R session.

11. Use the Leiden community detection algorithm to find a vertex partition with optimal modularity. How many communities does the Leiden algorithm detect?

12. Compare the Leiden partition modularity to the Louvain partition modularity.

13. Try to use visualization or data exploration methods to determine the main differences between the Leiden and Louvain partitions.

---

[12]https://rstudio.github.io/reticulate/

8

Assortativity and Similarity

In this chapter we will round off our study of important graph concepts and metrics by looking at two new concepts which a people network analyst will often have good reason to study. The first concept is assortativity, and this is described as the tendency of vertices to connect or 'attach' to vertices with similar properties in a graph. This is effectively a measure of homophily in a network. Highly assortative networks are more robust to destructive events like the loss of vertices, but because of their concentration they can be inefficient in terms of information flow, and in organizational settings they can be problematic for diverse interaction and experience.

The second concept we will look at is vertex and graph similarity. In certain networks where information on vertex properties is not available, it may make sense to infer that two vertices are similar in some way if their immediate networks are very similar. The concept of similarity can be also extended to entire graphs. In the simplest case, we may be looking at the same set of vertices but using different definitions of connection, and we want a measure of whether those different definitions produce substantially the same network or an entirely different network. As organizations start to mine many different forms of data to define connection (email, calendar, timesheet, document collaboration to name a few), it is becoming more and more important to understand the similarities or differences between the networks generated by these data sources.

8.1 Assortativity in networks

We have already seen in previous chapters that it is natural to want to study the extent to which vertices with similar ground truth properties are more densely connected in a graph. In Chapter 7, we looked at how politicians representing the same political parties connect to each other over Twitter, or how schoolchildren in the same class connect over Facebook. In the exercises at the end of that chapter, we looked at how researcher communities form over email either within or between ground truth research departments.

DOI: 10.1201/9781003266815-8

The **assortativity coefficient** of a graph is a measure of the extent to which vertices with the same properties connect to each other. It is a relatively recently defined metric and is defined slightly differently according to whether the property of interest is categorical (e.g., department or political party) or numeric (e.g., degree centrality). See Newman (2002) for a full description and mathematical definition.

The assortativity coefficient of a graph ranges between -1 and 1, just like a correlation coefficient. Assortativity coefficients close to 1 indicate that there is very high likelihood of two vertices with the same property being connected. This is called an *assortative network*. Assortativity coefficients close to -1 indicate that there is very low likelihood of two vertices with the same property being connected. This is called a *disassortative network*. Networks with assortativity coefficients close to zero are neither assortative nor disassortative and are usually described as having *neutral assortativity*.

8.1.1 Categorical or nominal assortativity

Let's look at categorical assortativity first by bringing back two examples from the previous chapter. First, we look at our Facebook schoolfriends network and calculate the assortativity by class. In R, we can use the `assortativity_nominal()` function to calculate categorical assortativity (see the end of this chapter for Python implementations). Note that these functions expect a numeric vector to indicate the category membership.

```
library(igraph)

# get data
schoolfriends_edgelist <- read.csv(
  "https://ona-book.org/data/schoolfriends_edgelist.csv"
)
schoolfriends_vertices <- read.csv(
  "https://ona-book.org/data/schoolfriends_vertices.csv"
)

# create undirected Facebook friendships graph
schoolfriends_fb <- igraph::graph_from_data_frame(
  d = schoolfriends_edgelist |>
    dplyr::filter(type == "facebook"),
  vertices = schoolfriends_vertices,
  directed = FALSE
)

# calculate assortativity by class for Facebook friendships
igraph::assortativity_nominal(
```

```
  schoolfriends_fb,
  as.integer(as.factor(V(schoolfriends_fb)$class))
)
```

```
## [1] 0.3833667
```

This suggests moderate assortativity, or moderate likelihood that students in the same class will be Facebook friends. Now let's compare to 'real' reported friendships.

```
# create directed graph of reported friendships
schoolfriends_rp <- igraph::graph_from_data_frame(
  d = schoolfriends_edgelist |>
    dplyr::filter(type == "reported"),
  vertices = schoolfriends_vertices
)
```

```
# calculate assortativity by class for reported friendships
igraph::assortativity_nominal(
  schoolfriends_rp,
  as.integer(as.factor(V(schoolfriends_fb)$class))
)
```

```
## [1] 0.7188919
```

We see substantially higher assortativity by class for reported friendships, indicating that being in the same class is more strongly associated with developing a reported school friendship.

> **Playing around:** You may remember the concept of modularity which we introduced in Chapter 7. For categorical vertex properties, modularity and assortativity effectively measure similar concepts. Calculate the modularity for the Facebook schoolfriends by class and compare it to the assortativity. Also, play around with some prior data sets and calculate the assortativity of some of the communities we detected in Chapter 7. Recall also our example from Chapter 5 where we divided up the workfrance population to have tables with a good mix of different departments. If you completed that exercise, you may be interested to compare the assortativity of that population by department versus by table to get a measure of how successful you were at creating diverse tables.

8.1.2   Degree assortativity

The most common form of numerical assortativity is degree assortativity. A high degree assortativity is a measure of preferential attachment in organizations, where highly connected vertices are connected with each other and a large number of vertices with low degree make up the remainder of the network.

Again, let's use our schoolfriends networks as an example to calculate degree assortativity in R.

```
# degree assortativity of Facebook friendships (undirected)
igraph::assortativity_degree(schoolfriends_fb)
```

```
## [1] 0.02462444
```

```
# degree assortativity of reported friendships (directed)
igraph::assortativity_degree(schoolfriends_rp)
```

```
## [1] 0.3098123
```

We see that real-life friendships are moderately assortative in this data, whereas Facebook friendships are approximately neutral. This indicates that more popular students have a stronger tendency in real-life to be friends with other popular students.

Although it is a relatively recent concept, assortativity is a useful measure in understanding people or organizational networks. Highly assortative networks demonstrate resilience in that knowledge, community and other social capital are concentrated in a strong core, and disruptions such as departures of actors from those networks are less likely to affect the network as a whole. However, such networks also demonstrate characteristics which are counterproductive to diversity and inclusion and can represent challenging environments for new entrants to adjust to.

It has been thought that social networks are unlike most other real-life networks in that they are degree assortative. However, recent research has begun to question this. Although it does seem to be the case that social networks are more assortative than non-social networks, research on various data sets where the connection between individuals is direct (rather than inferred from joint membership of a group) suggests that social networks are likely neutrally assortative (Fisher et al. (2017)). This is a research topic of great interest currently in social network analysis.

8.2   Vertex similarity

Often we are not lucky enough to have really rich ground truth information on the vertices in a network. This is particularly the case if we need to analyze people networks under anonymization constraints. Nevertheless, as we have seen with examples in previous chapters like the workfrance graph and the ontariopol graph, computational methods allow us to infer conclusions about vertices and groups of vertices that can often be good estimates of the ground truth properties of those vertices. In some networks, we can conclude that vertices are similar in some way if they share very similar immediate connections. For example, in our workfrance graph, if two vertices have first degree networks that overlap to a large degree, it would not be unreasonable to infer a likelihood that those two vertices are from the same department.

The **vertex similarity coefficient** of a pair of vertices is a measure of how similar are the immediate networks of those two vertices. Imagine we have two vertices v_1 and v_2 in an unweighted graph G. There are three common ways to calculate the vertex similarity of v_1 and v_2, as follows:

1. The *Jaccard similarity coefficient* is the number of vertices who are neighbors of *both* v_1 and v_2 divided by the number of vertices who are neighbors of *at least one of* v_1 and v_2.
2. The *dice similarity coefficient* is twice the number of vertices who are neighbors of *both* v_1 and v_2 divided by the sum of the degree centralities of v_1 and v_2. Thus, common neighbors are double counted in this method.
3. The *inverse log-weighted similarity coefficient* is the sum of the inverse logs of the degrees of the common neighbors of v_1 and v_2. This definition asserts that common neighbors that have high degree in the network are 'less valuable' in detecting similarity because there is a higher likelihood that they would be a common neighbor simply by chance.

To illustrate these three types of vertex similarity coefficients and show how they are calculated in R, let's bring back our G_{14} unweighted graph from Chapters 5 and 6, and visualize it again in Figure 8.1.

```
library(igraph)
library(ggraph)
library(dplyr)

# download edgelist and create unweighted graph
g14_edgelist <- read.csv("https://ona-book.org/data/g14_edgelist.csv")
```

```
g14 <- igraph::graph_from_data_frame(d = g14_edgelist |>
                                     dplyr::select(from, to),
                             directed = FALSE)
```

```
# visualize
set.seed(123)
(g14viz <- ggraph(g14, layout = "lgl") +
    geom_edge_link(color = "grey") +
    geom_node_label(aes(label = name), fill = "lightblue") +
    theme_void())
```

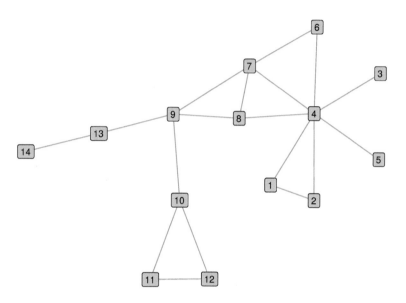

FIGURE 8.1: It's our old friend G_{14} again

Let's look at Vertices 7 and 8 in G_{14}. To calculate the Jaccard similarity coefficient, we note that Vertices 4 and 9 are the two common neighbors of these vertices, and that Vertices 4, 6, 7, 8 and 9 are all neighbors of at least one of Vertices 7 and 8. Therefore, we should see a Jaccard similarity coefficient of 0.4. We use the similarity() function in igraph whose default is to calculate Jaccard similarity.

```
igraph::similarity(g14, vids = c("7", "8"))
```

```
##      [,1] [,2]
## [1,]  1.0  0.4
## [2,]  0.4  1.0
```

We see in the off-diagonal components of this matrix confirmation of a Jaccard similarity coefficient of 0.4.

To calculate the dice similarity coefficient, we note that the sum of the degrees of Vertices 7 and 8 is 7; therefore, the dice similarity should equal $\frac{4}{7}$ or 0.571.

```
igraph::similarity(g14, vids = c("7", "8"), method = "dice")
```

```
##             [,1]      [,2]
## [1,] 1.0000000 0.5714286
## [2,] 0.5714286 1.0000000
```

Finally, to calculate the inverse log weighted similarity coefficient, we sum the inverse of the logs of the degrees of the common neighbors of Vertices 4 and 8, which is $\frac{1}{\ln 7} + \frac{1}{\ln 4}$, which calculates to 1.235.

The output of this similarity() function variant returns the similarity of the selected vertices with all vertices in the network—try it if you like. In order to extract the specific similarity for Vertices 7 and 8, we should ensure to label the rows and columns of the matrix by vertex name before extracting a specific value from it.

```
# get invlogweighted similarity
invsim <- igraph::similarity(g14, method = "invlogweighted")

# rows and cols should be labelled by vertex name before extracting
colnames(invsim) <- V(g14)$name
rownames(invsim) <- V(g14)$name

# extract value for vertices 7 and 8
invsim["7", "8"]
```

```
## [1] 1.235246
```

> **Playing around:** Go back to some of our prior examples from Chapter 7 where we detected communities of more densely connected vertices in graphs like schoolfriends and ontariopol. Play around with calculating the similarity between pairs of vertices inside communities versus between communities and think about whether the results make sense.

8.3   Graph similarity

The general question of whether two graphs which contain vertices representing different entities still exhibit similar internal patterns and structures is of great interest in computer science and image recognition. The *graph isomorphism* problem, for example, is a computational problem concerned with finding a function that exactly maps the vertices of one graph onto other[1].

In organizational network analysis we are usually more concerned with comparing graphs where the vertices represent the same entities (usually people), and where the vertex set is identical but where the edge set may be different. An example of this is our `schoolfriends` data set from earlier in this chapter, where the vertices are the same set of high school students, but where the edge sets are different according to whether the friendships are Facebook friendships or reported friendships. In this situation, we can use a common set similarity metric from set theory to determine how similar our graphs are.

Let $G_1 = (V, E_1)$ and $G_2 = (V, E_2)$ be two graphs with the same vertex set. The *Jaccard similarity* of G_1 and G_2 is the number of edges in *both* E_1 and E_2 divided by the number of edges in *at least one* of E_1 and E_2.

Note that a Jaccard similarity of 1 means that both graphs have identical edge sets and so are identical in structure, and a similarity of 0 means that both graphs have no edges in common. Let's try this on our `schoolfriends` graphs. To do a fair comparison, we will redefine our Facebook schoolfriends graph to be a directed graph where edges always go in both directions.

```
# create directed version of Facebook graph
schoolfriends_fb_dir <- igraph::as.directed(schoolfriends_fb)
```

We can create a handy function to calculate the Jaccard similarity of the edge sets of two graphs. Note that the `igraph` package has special operators `%s%` for the intersection of two graphs (that is, all vertices and edges that both graphs have in common), and `%u%` for the union of two graphs (that is, all unique vertices and edges in both graphs combined).

```
# function for jaccard similarity of edge sets
jaccard_edgeset_similarity <- function(G1, G2) {
  inter <- length(E(G1 %s% G2))
  un <- length(E(G1 %u% G2))
```

---

[1]The question of whether the graph isomorphism problem can be solved in polynomial time is one of a number of high-profile open graph problems currently.

```
  if (un == 0) {
    0
  } else {
    inter/un
  }
}


# test
jaccard_edgeset_similarity(schoolfriends_fb_dir, schoolfriends_rp)


## [1] 0.09727385
```

We see that there is only about 10% similarity between the Facebook friendships and the 'real' reported friendships.

8.4 Calculating assortativity and similarity in Python

To demonstrate assortativity functions, we load up the schoolfriends data sets.

```
import networkx as nx
import pandas as pd

# load data
# get data
schoolfriends_edgelist = pd.read_csv(
  "https://ona-book.org/data/schoolfriends_edgelist.csv"
)
schoolfriends_vertices = pd.read_csv(
  "https://ona-book.org/data/schoolfriends_vertices.csv"
)

# create undirected facebook graph
schoolfriends_fb = nx.from_pandas_edgelist(
  df = schoolfriends_edgelist[
    schoolfriends_edgelist.type == 'facebook'
  ],
  source = "from",
  target = "to"
```

```
)

# create directed reported graph
schoolfriends_rp = nx.from_pandas_edgelist(
  df = schoolfriends_edgelist[
    schoolfriends_edgelist.type == 'reported'
  ],
  source = "from",
  target = "to",
  create_using=nx.DiGraph()
)

# add class vertex attribute to both graphs
class_attr = dict(zip(schoolfriends_vertices['id'],
schoolfriends_vertices['class']))
nx.set_node_attributes(schoolfriends_fb, name = "class",
values = class_attr)
nx.set_node_attributes(schoolfriends_rp, name = "class",
values = class_attr)
```

The following functions can be used to calculate categorical assortativity and degree assortativity, respectively.

```
nx.attribute_assortativity_coefficient(schoolfriends_fb, "class")

## 0.38336668753682646

nx.attribute_assortativity_coefficient(schoolfriends_rp, "class")

## 0.7188918572576617

nx.degree_assortativity_coefficient(schoolfriends_fb)

## 0.024624435635859483

nx.degree_assortativity_coefficient(schoolfriends_rp)

## 0.30981226480406543
```

To calculate Jaccard similarity between two vertices, we can use the `jaccard_coefficient()` function in networkx. In this example, we calculate the Jaccard coefficients for two pairs of vertices in `schoolfriends_fb`.

```
jaccards = nx.jaccard_coefficient(G = schoolfriends_fb,
ebunch = [(883, 132), (63, 991)])
sorted(jaccards)
```

```
## [(63, 991, 0.15384615384615385), (883, 132, 0.30612244897959184)]
```

Dice similarity and inverse log weighted similarity coefficients can be calculated by creating functions.

```
# function for dice similarity
def dice_coefficient(G, ebunch = None):
    def dicesim(u, v):
        total_degree = nx.degree(G, u) + nx.degree(G, v)
        if total_degree == 0:
            return 0
        return 2*len(list(nx.common_neighbors(G, u, v))) / total_degree

    if ebunch is None:
        ebunch = nx.non_edges(G)
    return ((u, v, dicesim(u, v)) for u, v in ebunch)
```

```
# test
dice = dice_coefficient(G = schoolfriends_fb,
ebunch = [(883, 132), (63, 991)])
sorted(dice)
```

```
## [(63, 991, 0.26666666666666666), (883, 132, 0.46875)]
```

```
import math
```

```
# function for inverse log weighted similarity
def invlogweight_coefficient(G, ebunch = None):
    def invlogwsim(u, v):
        logw = [1/math.log(nx.degree(G, w))
                for w in nx.common_neighbors(G, u, v)]
        if logw == 0:
            return 0
        return sum(i for i in logw)

    if ebunch is None:
        ebunch = nx.non_edges(G)
```

```
    return ((u, v, invlogwsim(u, v)) for u, v in ebunch)
```

```
# test
invlogw = invlogweight_coefficient(G = schoolfriends_fb,
ebunch = [(883, 132), (63, 991)])
sorted(invlogw)
```

```
## [(63, 991, 0.5728002621049868), (883, 132, 4.566433503199232)]
```

Finally, to calculate Jaccard similarity of two edge sets, a simple function can be written:

```
# create function for Jaccard edge set similarity
def jaccard_edgeset_similarity(G1, G2):
  setG1 = set(G1.edges)
  intersection = len(setG1.intersection(G2.edges))
  union = len(setG1.union(G2.edges))

  if union == 0:
    return 0
  return intersection/union
```

```
# recreate schoolfriends_fb as directed graph to compare
schoolfriends_fb_dir = schoolfriends_fb.to_directed()
```

```
# test
jaccard_edgeset_similarity(schoolfriends_fb_dir, schoolfriends_rp)
```

```
## 0.09727385377942999
```

8.5 Learning exercises

8.5.1 Discussion questions

1. Describe the meaning of the term 'assortativity' for vertices in a graph.
2. Describe the meaning of degree assortativity and discuss how it relates to the concept of preferential attachment.

3. Describe why assortativity and modularity are similar concepts in graph theory.
4. Describe the concept of vertex similarity and define two measures of vertex similarity.
5. Describe a method to compare the similarity of two graphs with the same vertex sets.

8.5.2 Data exercises

1. Calculate the gender assortativity coefficient in the two schoolfriends graphs. What would you conclude from this?
2. Calculate the department assortativity coefficient in the workfrance graph from earlier chapters.
3. Calculate the degree assortativity coefficient of the workfrance and the ontariopol graphs from previous chapters. How would you describe the meaning of the difference between the two?
4. Choose pairs of vertices from the same department in the workfrance graph and calculate their Jaccard similarity coefficients. Then choose pairs from different departments and do the same. Do the results make sense? Why?
5. Find the three vertices with highest degree centrality in the workfrance graph, and calculate some pairwise similarity coefficients for them. Now do the same with three vertices with relatively low degree centrality. Do the results make sense? Why?

9

Graphs as Databases

Over the course of the early chapters of this book, we established a certain workflow for doing graph analysis, as follows:

1. If necessary, transform existing transactional data into a graph-like structure that better allows the analysis of relationships in the data (Chapter 4).
2. Load the transformed data into (temporary) graph structures inside data science languages like R or Python (Chapter 2).
3. Create visualizations, perform analysis or run algorithms based on those temporary structures (Chapter 3 and Chapters 5 to 8).

This workflow is perfectly fine for one-off or temporary network analysis, such as an academic project or an experimental analytic effort. However, for organizations whose use of graph methods is maturing, it will become wasteful, inefficient and unnecessarily repetitive to ask analysts to follow this workflow for repeated similar analyses. We have already seen in Chapter 4 that the steps involved in transforming rectangular data into a graph-like structure are far from trivial. Therefore, as the use of graphs for analytic purposes matures, it becomes natural to ask whether the data can be persisted in a graph-like structure in order to be permanently available in that structure for rapid querying or easier, faster analysis.

In this chapter we look at how organizations can persist data in a graph structure for more efficient analysis and data query. This is a rapidly developing field, and many leading organizations have started implementing graph databases in recent years. There are a variety of technologies available, and no single technology is dominant. We will start with an overview of the space of graph database technology and then proceed to show illustrative examples of one particular well-developed technology—*Neo4J* graph databases—including how to work with these graph databases in R and in Python. While this chapter is not intended to be a full reference on graph databases, by the end of this chapter readers should have a good sense of the basics of how these powerful emerging technologies operate, and how they can be used to make network analysis faster and easier to perform.

DOI: 10.1201/9781003266815-9

9.1   Graph database technology

Graph databases store data so that finding *relationships* is the primary priority.
This contrasts with traditional databases where finding transactions is the
primary priority. Most commonly, graph databases take one of two forms:
labelled-property graphs or resource description frameworks (RDFs)[1].

9.1.1   Labelled-property graphs

Labelled-property graphs are very similar in structure to the way we have
learned about graphs in this book. Entities such as products, customers, employees or organizational units are stored in nodes, and relationships such
as 'purchased,' 'member of,' 'worked with' or 'met with' are stored in edges.
Nodes and edges can contain defined properties allowing users to filter data
effectively. These node and edge structures are usually encoded by means of
simple JSON documents. This type of graph database is simple and efficient,
and also very intuitive to query. However, flexibility can be limited and the
upfront design of the graph needs to be considered carefully, because changes
to the structure of the database via the introduction of new nodes and new
relationships may not be straightforward. For organizational network analysis,
such databases are a good choice, however, because of their ease of use and
because data structures within organizations are generally quite predictable
and manageable. *Neo4J* is an example of a labelled-property graph database
and is the most popular at the time of the writing of this book.

One of the features of labelled-property graphs which make them easier to
use in general is the ability to write queries using intuitive query languages.
The *Cypher* query language for Neo4J graph databases is a good example.
A common graph database used for teaching Cypher is the `movies` database,
which contains information on relationships between a small number of people
in the entertainment industry and the movies they have participated in. Figure
9.1 is a schema diagram of the types of nodes and relationships stored in this
graph database.

We can see that there are two types of nodes: `Person` and `Movie`. We can also see
that a `Person` can follow another `Person`, while there are five relationship types
between a `Person` and a `Movie`. Cypher uses ASCII art to make queries easier
to understand and write. Nodes are written in parentheses such as `(p:Person)`
and relationships are written in lines or arrows such as `-[:ACTED_IN]->`. The
following Cypher query will return the graph of all people who acted in movies

---

[1] It should be noted that graph database technologies are now emerging that can support
both of these forms, most notably AWS Neptune.

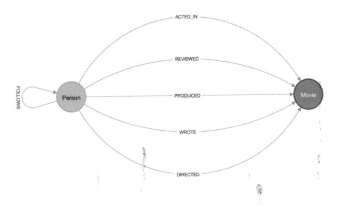

FIGURE 9.1: Graph schema of the `movies` database

in the database which were directed by Clint Eastwood, with the results displayed in Figure 9.2.

```
MATCH (p1:Person)-[:ACTED_IN]->(m:Movie)
MATCH (m:Movie)<-[:DIRECTED]-(p2:Person {name: "Clint Eastwood"})
RETURN p1, m
```

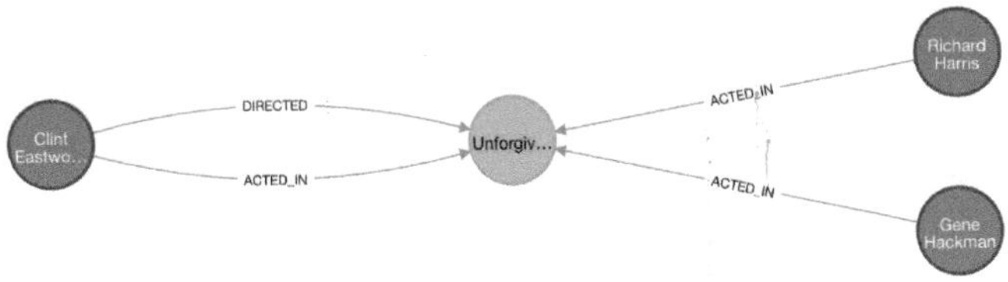

FIGURE 9.2: Graph of actors in movies directed by Clint Eastwood from `movies` graph database

Each node or relationship may contain properties which can be accessed and returned in queries. For example, `Movie` nodes have `title` and `released` properties, while `Person` nodes have a `name` property. This query will return the actor name, movie title and movie release data, and the result looks like Figure 9.3.

```
MATCH (p1:Person)-[:ACTED_IN]->(m:Movie)
MATCH (m:Movie)<-[:DIRECTED]-(p2:Person {name: "Clint Eastwood"})
RETURN p1.name AS actor, m.title AS movie, m.released AS released
```

"actor"	"movie"	"released"
"Clint Eastwood"	"Unforgiven"	1992
"Gene Hackman"	"Unforgiven"	1992
"Richard Harris"	"Unforgiven"	1992

FIGURE 9.3: Results of a query to find the names of actors, movie title and release date for movies directed by Clint Eastwood in the `movies` database

> **Thinking ahead:** Neo4J offers a free, sandbox web-based environment through which to learn about its graph database structure and to learn how to write Cypher queries. It includes some interesting graph data sets related to social media analysis, crime investigation, fraud detection, sport and many others. You can start projects in this sandbox and interact with them over the web for a limited period (after which you need to restart a project). You can access the sandbox at `https://neo4j.com/sandbox`. Later in this chapter, we will go into more detail about working with Neo4J graph databases including how to interact with them in R and in Python, and how to run queries and algorithms against them.

9.1.2   Resource description frameworks

Resource description frameworks (RDFs) are highly flexible graph database models that allow the hierarchical 'spawning' of new information in a graph by means of the addition of new nodes. This permits the graph to build more easily organically, because there is no need to worry about whether a given node property already exists in the graph—it can simply be added into a new node that is pointed to by the parent node. For example, imagine that a graph contains nodes that represent people, and imagine that we have some information on the preferred names of those people. Imagine that we have this information for some but not all people, and that some people have a preferred name but others do not. In an RDF, we can create new 'property edge' called `hasPreferredName` which directs to a new node containing the preferred name of the individual.

This high level of flexibility makes RDFs a great choice for ontologies or knowledge graphs for which their development will be unpredictable and will grow organically over time. The low level simplicity of RDFs is the engine behind this flexibility, but this can translate into a complex query language at a high level, making RDFs challenging to deal with for those without specialized knowledge of them. In particular, it can often be necessary to 'dictate the traversal route' of the graph in the query language of an RDF, which will require an extensive knowledge of the graph's structure.

An example of an open, widely used RDF graph is the graph that underlies the Wikipedia online encyclopedia, known as *Wikidata*[2]. This graph gives structure and connection to the various components of Wikipedia's content. It helps organize common hierarchical elements of articles and helps link related articles as well as the resources inside those articles such as photos, hyperlinks and so on. As Wikipedia is constantly developing and being added to by a thriving community, this underlying graph needs an extremely high degree of flexibility to support it.

The *Wikidata Query Service (WDQS)* allows this graph to be queried directly using SPARQL, the standard query language for RDFs. Queries can be submitted at `https://query.wikidata.org/`, or sent to an API endpoint by an application[3]. Here is an example that will return the top 10 countries of the world in terms of the number of current female city mayors recorded in Wikidata.

```
SELECT ?countryLabel (count(*) AS ?count)
WHERE
{
    ?city wdt:P31/wdt:P279* wd:Q515 .
    ?city p:P6 ?hog .
    ?hog ps:P6 ?mayor .
    ?mayor wdt:P21 wd:Q6581072 .
    FILTER NOT EXISTS { ?hog pq:P582 ?x }
    ?city wdt:P17 ?country .

    SERVICE wikibase:label {
        bd:serviceParam wikibase:language "en" .
    }
}
GROUP BY ?countryLabel
ORDER BY DESC(?count)
LIMIT 10
```

---

[2]https://www.wikidata.org/

[3]For example, the author of this book has developed an R package called `wikifacts` which contains a function to submit queries to Wikidata and retrieve the results as a dataframe.

Briefly described, the WHERE component of this query instructs a graph traversal as follows:

1. Follow property edges that are 'instances of cities' or 'subclasses of cities' (call the resulting nodes city)
2. Follow 'head of government' property edges from city nodes (call the resulting nodes hog)
3. Follow to retrieve the value of the hog nodes (call this mayor)
4. mayor must have a 'sex or gender' property edge that directs to 'female'
5. Filter results so that hog has no 'end date' property edge going from it (that is, current heads of government)
6. Follow 'country' property edges from remaining city nodes (call the resulting nodes country)
7. Get the English labels of the country nodes.

This is the core of the query—the remainder simply counts the occurrences of the different country labels and then ranks them in descending order and returns the top 10. You can see how this query requires quite detailed instruction on how to traverse the graph and also needs a very detailed knowledge of a bewildering array of codes for properties and values. RDFs are beautiful and extremely powerful relationship storage engines, but there is a high expertise bar to their use.

> **Playing around:** The query and traversal complexity of RDFs should not be a barrier to you playing around with them. The Wikidata Query Service (WDQS) has a ton of resources to help you understand how to construct interesting queries. For a start, try submitting the above query to WDQS and check the result. If you thought that was fun, some key resources include a long list of example queries[4] and a Query Builder[5] which can help non-SPARQL experts to build their own queries.

9.2 Example: how to work with a Neo4J graph database

In this section we will briefly review some ways to work with a Neo4J graph database in order to illustrate how data can be moved into a persistent graph

---

[4] https://www.wikidata.org/wiki/Wikidata:SPARQL_query_service/queries/examples
[5] https://query.wikidata.org/querybuilder/?uselang=en

structure for regular query and analysis. First we will look at how to interact with the database via a web browser interface. Then we will look at how to load and query data programmatically via R and Python.

In order to follow the instructions in this section, you will need to set up a free Neo4J Aura graph database. This is a limited instance of a Neo4J graph database hosted on the cloud and offered to developers and learners for free. To do this, follow these steps:

1. Go to the Neo4J Aura site at `https://neo4j.com/cloud/aura/` and click 'Start Free.'
2. Register for free database in a region of your choice and give your database a name.
3. Make a record of your database URI, your username and your password. In the following instructions, we will refer to these as `your_URI`, `your_username` and `your_password`.

In the following examples, we will load our `ontariopol` data set of the Ontario state politician Twitter network from Chapter 7 into a Neo4J graph database and do some querying against the database.

9.2.1 Using the browser interface

The easiest way to interact with the database is using the browser interface, similar to the Neo4J sandbox mentioned earlier. This is especially useful for beginners who do not need to interact with the database programatically from other applications or data science languages.

Navigate to your free database instance by visiting the Neo4J Aura site, selecting 'Databases' from the menu, finding your free database and selecting 'Open with Neo4J Browser.' After logging in with your credentials, you should be in the browser interface, which looks like Figure 9.4.

Cypher queries can be entered in the box at the top[6]. To break a line without submitting the query, press Shift+Enter. To submit the query, press Ctrl+Enter or click the play icon. Before we can start submitting queries, we need to load some data into the database. Among many formats, data can be loaded into Neo4J from an online `csv` file. Use the following query to load all the vertices from our `ontariopol` data set.

```
LOAD CSV WITH HEADERS
FROM 'https://ona-book.org/data/ontariopol_vertices.csv'
AS row
```

---

[6]Multiple queries can be submitted together providing they are separated by a semicolon. Generally, it is good practice to always end a query with a semicolon.

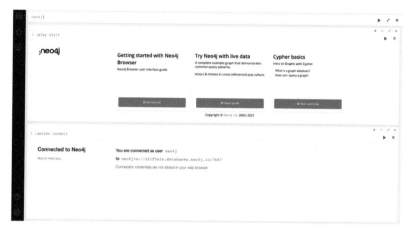

FIGURE 9.4: The Neo4J browser interface

```
MERGE (p:Person {
  personId: row.id,
  screenName: row.screen_name,
  name: row.name,
  party: row.party
});
```

This query instructs the database to retrieve the data from the specified URL address. It further instructs the database to create nodes called `Person` nodes from each row of the data. Each `Person` node should contain four properties: `personId`, `screenName`, `name` and `party` loaded from the `id`, `screen_name`, `name` and `party` fields, respectively.

This will load all our `Person` nodes. You can check that these have been loaded by running this new query:

```
MATCH (p:Person)
RETURN p.name;
```

This query should return the `name` property of all `Person` nodes in the graph. Now we need to add the edges using this query:

```
LOAD CSV WITH HEADERS
FROM 'https://ona-book.org/data/ontariopol_edgelist.csv'
AS row
MATCH (p1:Person {personId:row.from}), (p2:Person {personId:row.to})
CREATE (p1)-[:INTERACTED_WITH {weight: toInteger(row.weight)}]-> (p2);
```

This query instructs the database to load the data from the specified online URL. For each row of the data, it instructs the database to find the Person nodes with personId property corresponding to the from and to fields, to create a *directed* edge called INTERACTED_WITH between these nodes and to give the edge an integer value weight property extracted from the weight field.

We can now look at our database schema using the following query:

```
CALL db.schema.visualization();
```

This should show a very simple schema with one node type and one edge type. By clicking on the database icon in the top left, you should see a further information panel, which should confirm the details of the nodes, the relationships and the properties in the graph, as in Figure 9.5.

Congratulations! You've loaded the data into the graph database. Now let's run a query to find the top 5 politicians who interacted with Christine Elliott based on weight (excluding Christine Elliott herself).

```
MATCH (p:Person)-[i:INTERACTED_WITH]->({name: "Christine Elliott"})
WHERE p.name <> "Christine Elliott"
RETURN p.name as name, i.weight as weight
ORDER BY weight DESC
LIMIT 5;
```

This should return a list of 5 with Robin Martin at the top with a weight of 872. As another example, we can try to find out all interactions between LIB party politicians and IND party politicians.

```
MATCH (p1:Person {party: 'LIB'})-[INTERACTED_WITH]->(p2:Person {party:
"IND"})
RETURN p1.name AS LIB_name, p2.name AS IND_name;
```

This should return 4 interactions. You can also try some procedures from Neo4J's APOC (Awesome Procedures on Cypher) library. For example, try this to receive information on the distribution of the degrees of the nodes in the graph.

```
CALL apoc.stats.degrees()
```

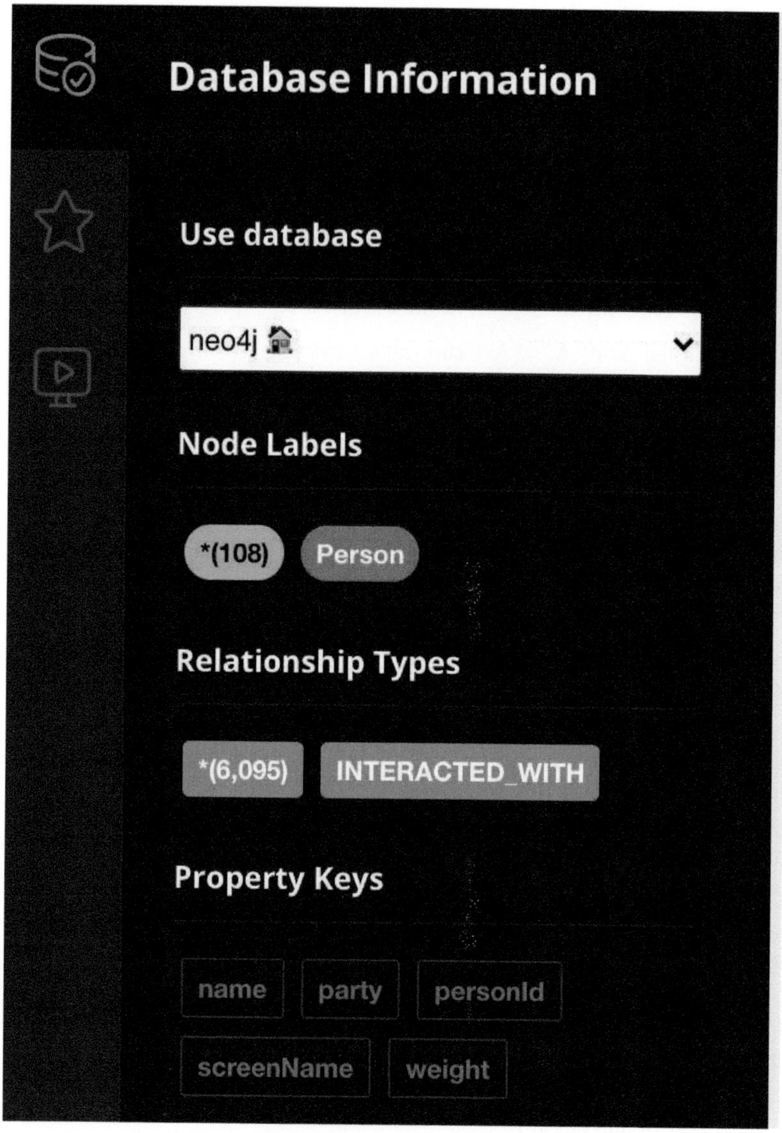

FIGURE 9.5: The database information panel

> **Playing around:** Awesome Procedures on Cypher (APOC) is an add-on library which, in its full form, has a very wide range of useful procedures for calculating statistics, finding paths, running search algorithms and much more. As of the time of writing, only a limited number of APOC procedures are available on the free cloud database version we are using here. To see a list of all available APOC procedures, run the query `CALL apoc.help('apoc')`. If you are interested in the full range of APOC procedures, you can consider installing the Neo4J Desktop product on your local machine for free from the Neo4J website. *APOC Full* can be installed as an add-on inside the Desktop version, as well as the GDS (Graph Data Science) library, which contains a wide range of graph algorithms including many of the methods we have covered earlier in this book.

9.2.2 Working with Neo4J using R

The `neo4jshell` package in R allows you to submit queries to a Neo4J database and retrieve results, among other things[7]. This package requires the `cypher-shell` command line utility to be installed on your system. You can install the `cypher-shell` command line utility standalone by downloading and installing from the Neo4J downloads page[8]. Another option is to download and install the full and free Neo4J community server, which will include `cypher-shell`, from the community server download page[9].

For the `neo4j_query()` query function to work most smoothly, you should ensure the directory containing the `cypher-shell` executable is in your system `PATH` environment variable. Otherwise, you will need to constantly quote the full path to the `cypher-shell` executable in the `shell_path` argument of the function.

Assuming you have configured `cypher-shell` on your system, it is very easy to submit queries to your Neo4J instance and retrieve the results as a dataframe. The first step is to configure your Neo4J connection as a list in R.

```
neo4j_conn <- list(
  address = "your_URI",
  uid = "your_username",
  pwd = "your_password"
)
```

---

[7] In full disclosure, this package was developed by the author of this book.

[8] https://neo4j.com/download-center/#cyphershell

[9] https://neo4j.com/download-center/#community

In the examples below, we assume that the data has already been loaded to the database using the queries in Section 9.2.1. If not, you can load the data from R by submitting the same queries using the neo4j_query() function. Assuming the data has already been loaded, we can submit a query to the database and retrieve the results as a dataframe. Let's submit a query to find out the first degree incoming network of all IND party politicians.

```
# write cypher query
query <- "
MATCH (p:Person)-[:INTERACTED_WITH]->({party: 'IND'})
RETURN DISTINCT p.name AS name, p.party as party;
"


# submit to server and retrieve results as dataframe
results <- neo4jshell::neo4j_query(con = neo4j_conn, qry = query)

# view first few results
head(results)
```

```
##                  name party
## 1   Ernie Hardeman    PCP
## 2      Kinga Surma    PCP
## 3 Randy Pettapiece    PCP
## 4      Gila Martow    PCP
## 5      Sara Singh    NDP
## 6     Robin Martin    PCP
```

In a similar way we can submit an APOC procedure to obtain statistics about the graph. This query gets statistics on the out-degree of the nodes of the graph.

```
# get out-degree stats
stats <- neo4jshell::neo4j_query(
  con = neo4j_conn,
  qry = "CALL apoc.stats.degrees('>');"
)

# extract max, min and mean
stats[c("min", "max", "mean"), ]
```

```
## [1] "7"                    "80"              "56.43518518518518"
```

9.2.3 Working with Neo4J using Python

The py2neo package allows interaction with Neo4J servers from Python. No preconfiguration is required. Connection is established by means of a Graph() object.

```python
import pandas as pd
from py2neo import Graph
import os

# create  connection
neo4j_conn = Graph(
    "your_URI",
    auth = ("your_username", "your_password")
)
```

Again, we assume that data has already been loaded to the graph. If this is not the case, submit the data load queries from Section 9.2.1 in the same way as the following examples.

Results from queries will be returned as a list of dicts, which can be converted into the required format.

```python
# write cypher query
query = """
MATCH (p:Person)-[:INTERACTED_WITH]->({party: 'IND'})
RETURN DISTINCT p.name AS name, p.party as party;
"""

# submit to server and retrieve results as list of dicts
results = neo4j_conn.run(query).data()

# convert results to pandas DataFrame and view first few rows
pd.DataFrame(results).head()
```

```
##                 name party
## 0    Ernie Hardeman   PCP
## 1       Kinga Surma   PCP
## 2  Randy Pettapiece   PCP
## 3       Gila Martow   PCP
## 4        Sara Singh   NDP
```

To run APOC procedures:

```
# submit APOC procedure
stats = neo4j_conn.run("CALL apoc.stats.degrees('>');").data()

# convert results to pandas DataFrame
pd.DataFrame(stats)
```

```
##    type direction  total  p50  p75  p90  p95  p99  p999  max  min       mean
## 0  None  OUTGOING   6095   59   63   70   71   77    80   80    7  56.435185
```

9.3   Moving to persistent graph data in organizations

The material in this chapter is intended as a brief introduction to the idea of persisting data in a graph database. For organizations that are repeatedly conducting analysis on connections and relationships, this is a natural step to make such analysis more 'oven ready.' Common transformations which need to be done on data in traditional rectangular databases in order to allow the analysis of connections can be done automatically at regular intervals (weekly, monthly or whatever makes sense based on reporting cadences) and incrementally added to the graph database. An automated ETL (Extract, Transform, Load) process can be set up in R, Python or another platform and timed to run on servers at specified intervals to extract the data from the rectangular databases, perform the necessary transformations to create the data on vertices, edges and properties and then load the data to the graph database.

It should be noted that a graph database is extremely flexible in its ability to store many types of data for many use cases in the same schema. Imagine, for example that we wanted to add the data from our schoolfriends graph to the same graph schema where we loaded the ontariopol data. These are completely different networks, but they can easily coexist in the same graph database. There are many options for how the database could be designed to facilitate this. For example, instead of a single Person node, there could be different Politician and Student nodes. Or we could add a type property to a Person node which could have the value politician or student. Or we could create new Politician and Student nodes and have edges with the relationship IS_A connecting them in a more RDF-like approach.

In all of these cases, the two networks can live in the same database but never interfere with each other, and this model can be scaled arbitrarily as long as it is designed appropriately[10]. This plethora of options means that graph

---

[10]Alternatively, if different network data is being used for completely different use cases,

databases often require more up-front schema design consideration compared to traditional databases. Changes in the organization's data that inevitably occur over time will need to be added to the schema, and some designs will make it more or less easy to do this.

9.4   Learning exercises

9.4.1   Discussion questions

1. Why are graph databases an attractive option for organizations that are regularly performing analysis on connections?
2. Describe labelled-property graphs and resource description frameworks (RDFs). Can you explain some differences between them as graph database technologies, including some pros and cons of their use?
3. Find some examples of real-life use cases of RDFs. Why are RDFs good choices for these use cases?
4. Search some examples of labelled-property graph technologies. What query languages does each use?
5. Describe how Cypher queries are constructed intuitively using ASCII art. Can you find any other query languages that use ASCII art? How similar or different are these languages?

9.4.2   Data exercises

For exercises related to Neo4J, try completing this in the browser and also using either R or Python. Remember that if you are loading data to the graph, be careful to ensure that any previous load of the same data is deleted before reload. If you need to, you can search for help online for Cypher deletion queries, but note that edges must be deleted before nodes.

1. Try to write a SPARQL query and submit it to Wikidata to find the winners of the first ten Eurovision Song Contests. Try a similar query to find the winners of all FIFA World Cups.
2. Write and submit a Cypher query on the `ontariopol` data loaded to Neo4J to find all interactions *from* PCP party politicians *to* LIB party politicians with a weight of greater than 10.

---

many graph database products also offer multitenancy, allowing you to host separate graph databases on the same database server.

3. Write and submit an APOC procedure on the `ontariopol` data loaded to Neo4J to obtain the in-degree statistics of the graph.

4. Using the online vertex and edge set for the `schoolfriends` data set[11], create a new set of nodes in the Neo4J graph called `Student` nodes. Give these nodes a `name`, `studentClass` and `studentGender` property from the data sets.

5. Create *undirected* edges for the Facebook friendships in the data and call the relationship `FACEBOOK_FRIENDS`. Create *directed* edges for the reported friendships and call the relationship `REPORTED_FRIEND`.

6. Write and submit a Cypher query to find all Facebook friends of node 883, and a similar query to find all those who reported node 883 as a friend.

7. Write and submit an APOC procedure to find the node degree statistics for the Facebook friendships. Write and submit separate procedures for the incoming and outgoing reported friendships.

---

[11] https://ona-book.org/data/schoolfriends_edgelist.csv and https://ona-book.org/data/schoolfriends_vertices.csv

10

Further Exercises for Practice

In this chapter we present a series of further exercises supplemental to the end-of-chapter exercises in this book. While the prior exercises were focused on specific techniques and methodologies, the purpose of these exercises is to apply a broad range of network analysis techniques to a problem. To encourage critical thinking, the guidance for these exercises is more limited and directional rather than specific in nature. A big part of becoming a competent network analyst is the ability to understand real world questions and translate them into an appropriate analytic approach before executing the techniques involved in that approach. These exercises will encourage you to do both of these, and you could also consider extending your work past the given questions in each example to investigate other aspects of the networks which might interest you.

To this end, the reader is encouraged to tackle these exercises by documenting them appropriately using an R Markdown document or a Jupyter Notebook. There are two very important advantages to working from a vertical document from the very beginning of your work. First, your analytic decisions and methodological approach are captured well, meaning it is easy to revisit and adjust the work later, or to pick up where you last left it. Second, you are forced to think about the communication of your work to 'laypeople' who may not be interested in the intricacies of the code, but will be interested in understanding how you went about solving the problem more broadly. For your work to have true impact, you need to be able to explain it well to varied audiences. The examples in this chapter will help you exercise those muscles.

10.1 Friendships among Scottish teenage girls

Load the `s50_edges` and `s50_vertices` data sets from the `ona_data` package or download them from the internet[1]. This data extract comes from a study

---

[1]https://ona-book.org/data/s50_edges.csv and https://ona-book.org/data/s50_vertices.csv

of a group of Scottish teenage girls in the 1990s and as part of the Teenage Friends and Lifestyle Study[2].

The edgelist represents pairs of subjects whom the researchers deemed to be friends with each other. The vertex data set contains information on a number of factors related to each subject:

- smoke represents the frequency with which the subject smoked cigarettes, where 1 means never, 2 means occasionally and 3 means regularly
- alcohol represents the frequency with which the subject drank alcohol, ranging from 1 (never) to 5 (more than once a week)
- drugs represents the frequency with which the subject took cannabis, ranging from 1 (never) to 4 (regularly)
- sport represents the frequency with which the subject participated in sporting activities, where 1 means not regularly and 2 means regularly

1. Create a graph object and a network visualization from this data. Use visualization techniques to investigate the degree to which different lifestyle factors influence the friendships of the subjects in this study. Bear in mind that the lifestyle properties of the vertices are on differing scales and consider how you could compare them fairly when judging the influence they have on friendships.

2. Consider how to use mathematical measures to illustrate how the lifestyle factors influence the formation of friendships among the subjects. Which measures would you use? Calculate these measures and determine what conclusions you can make from the results.

3. Use appropriate methodologies to find more intensely connected subgroups than those represented by the disconnected components of this graph. Use visualization techniques to compare those subgroups to the ground truth lifestyle properties of the vertices. Calculate similar mathematical measures as in Exercise 2 to compare your new subgroup structure to that of the ground truth lifestyle factors. What can you conclude?

---

[2]Many papers have been published around this study, for example Pearson & Michell (2000).

10.2   Interactions between dolphins in Doubtful Sound, New Zealand

Load the `dolphins` data set from the `onadata` package or download it from the internet[3]. This edgelist represents a network of dolphins monitored by researchers in Doubtful Sound, New Zealand[4]. An edge between two dolphins indicates that researchers observed them interacting frequently.

1. Visualize this network and use your visualization to hypothesize which dolphins play an important role in the overall connectedness of the population.

2. Use appropriate metrics to quantify the importance of each dolphin in connecting other dolphins in this network. Adjust your visualization to illustrate this metric.

3. Use appropriate methodologies to identify communities of dolphins that interact more densely. Use appropriate metrics to rank the interaction density of each community you identify.

4. Identify the most central dolphins for each of the communities you identify.

5. Do you think there is any evidence of preferential attachment among dolphins in this population. Why? Use an appropriate metric to confirm or reject your hypothesis.

10.3   Character interaction in Victor Hugo's novel *Les Misérables*

Load the `lesmis` data set from the `onadata` package or download it from the internet[5]. This edgelist represents the network of characters in the novel *Les Misérables* by Victor Hugo[6]. An edge exists between two characters if they interact with each other in the book, and the `weight` column indicates the number of interactions.

---

[3]https://ona-book.org/data/dolphins.csv
[4]Lusseau et al. (2003).
[5]https://ona-book.org/data/lesmis.csv
[6]This data set is taken from Knuth (1993).

1. Using appropriate measures, find some of the most central characters in the book and see if this aligns with your memory of the book or with an online synopsis if you have not read it.

2. Find the largest cliques in the character network. Research the members online to see if you can associate these cliques with the plot of the book.

3. Use an appropriate method to identify communities of characters and find the most central character for each community. Ask yourself how well aligned this is with the plot of the book (or ask someone who knows the book). How do the communities change if you consider the weight of the connection between characters?

4. Visualize the network in a way that identifies the communities. Consider ways to further enhance the visualization. For example, how might you illustrate connection weight?

5. Do you think that interactions between characters in a novel would be degree assortative, degree disassortative, or neutral? Use an appropriate metric to confirm or reject your hypothesis in the case of this novel.

10.4 Communication between criminals involved in a drug importation operation

Load the `caviar_start`, `caviar_middle` and `caviar_end` data sets from the `ona_data` package or download them from the internet[7]. These data sets are formed from Operation Caviar, a 2-year international covert police investigation into the illegal importation of hash and cocaine in Montreal[8]. During this investigation, illegal shipments were seized, but police did not make any arrests, instead choosing to covertly track the communication between suspects via wiretaps.

These edgelists represent the flow of communication as of the first seizure, the fifth seizure and the eleventh and final seizure after which arrests were made. The edge weights represent the frequency of calls from one suspect to the other. As you analyze this data, consider what is possible in treating the network as directed versus undirected.

1. Visualize the development of this network over the three stages provided. Consider ways to illustrate the importance of various

---

[7]https://ona-book.org/caviar_start.csv, https://ona-book.org/caviar_middle.csv and https://ona-book.org/caviar_end.csv

[8]This is taken from Morselli (2009).

participants. For example, how can you show what happens to important initial participants as the investigation develops?

2. Compare your visualizations and use them to try to describe how the network has developed. Remember that participants will have been aware of police attention because their shipments were seized. What information can you determine from your visualizations that helps you understand how the network has adapted?

3. Consider how you can use specific metrics to help illustrate and support any of the conclusions you make from Question 2. For example, how can you illustrate changes in the overall complexity of the communication between participants? What measures might help you understand the different roles of individuals as receivers of information versus suppliers of information?

4. By changing the type of the network object if you need to, consider ways to identify communication subgroups, and determine who may be considered ringleaders of the criminal operation based on this.

5. Imagine you are supporting the investigation team as a crime analyst after the final seizure, but before arrests are to be made. Write a report with all of your conclusions from this analysis and with supporting visualizations and metrics. Focus your report firstly on the characteristics of the final network and which participants should be prioritized for arrest or may be important as informants. Secondly, provide insight into how the network has developed to try to evade law enforcement over the course of the investigation.

10.5 Academic collaboration between network scientists

Load the `netscience` data set from the `onadata` package or download it from the internet[9]. This edgelist represents collaboration between 1,589 academics working in the field of network science[10]. An edge exists if the two individuals have collaborated through co-authoring at least one paper, and the edge weight in this network is a measure of the strength of the collaboration[11].

---

[9] https://ona-book.org/data/netscience.csv
[10] Published in Newman (2001).
[11] Here, the edge weight considers the total number of papers co-authored, but also normalizes for the total number of authors on a co-authored paper, so that more exclusive collaboration drives higher weight.

1. Visualize this network and describe its structure.

2. Find the largest group in the network where each individual has collaborated with each other individual. Use visualization techniques to illustrate where precisely in the network this group lies.

3. Identify the most central individuals for each of the five largest connected components using a variety of measures. Determine the extent to which the degree centrality of two individuals in this network influences their likelihood of co-authoring.

4. Focus on the largest connected component of this network and identify subgroups of more intense collaboration within it. Visualize this component with the subgroups illustrated.

5. Identify a pair of scientists in the largest connected component who have the largest distance between them. Identify a path to connect these two scientists through intermediate collaborators.

10.6   Other sources of data for practice

Numerous public sources of data for graph and network analysis are available where you can find resources for further practice if you need to, and many of the data sets in this book are drawn from these sources. If you are interested in exploring them, here is a list of some of the better ones:

• The Stanford Large Network Dataset Collection (http://snap.stanford.edu/data/index.html) is part of SNAP, the Stanford Network Analysis Project, and contains a wide range of large network data sets of various types.

• CASOS, the Center for Computational Analysis of Social and Organizational Systems at Carnegie Mellon University (http://www.casos.cs.cmu.edu/) contains a large collection of classic and modern social network analysis data sets.

• SocioPatterns—a research collaboration which focuses on face-to-face and close proximity interactions between people—has numerous interesting data sets on its website at http://www.sociopatterns.org/.

• The Network Data Repository (https://networkrepository.com/) has a huge range of network data sets across a very wide array of disciplines.

Graph data can be found in a variety of different formats to reflect different computational tools used for graphs over the years. In the vast majority of cases, R and Python will have packages which can work the relevant format.

For example, files with a `.gml` extension can be loaded directly in `igraph` as a graph object using the `read_graph()` function with the argument `format = "gml"` and `networkx` has a similar function called `read_gml()`.

References

Althoff, T., Danescu-Niculescu-Mizil, C., & Jurafsky, D. (2014). *How to ask for a favor: A case study on the success of altruistic requests.* https://arxiv.org/pdf/1405.3282.pdf

Broido, A. D., & Clauset, A. (2019). Scale-free networks are rare. In *Nature Communications.* https://www.nature.com/articles/s41467-019-08746-5

Feld, S. L., & Carter, W. C. (1998). When desegregation reduces interracial contact: A class size paradox for weak ties. In *American Journal of Sociology* (No. 5; Vol. 103, pp. 1165–1186).

Fisher, D. N., Silk, M. J., & Franks, D. W. (2017). The perceived assortativity of social networks: Methodological problems and solutions. *CoRR.* http://arxiv.org/abs/1701.08671

Génois, M., & Barrat, A. (2018). Can co-location be used as a proxy for face-to-face contacts? In *EPJ Data Science.* https://arxiv.org/pdf/1712.06346.pdf

Hafnaoui, I., Nicolescu, G., & Beltrame, G. (2019). Timing information propagation in interactive networks. In *Scientific Reports.* https://www.nature.com/articles/s41598-019-40801-5

Holt-Lunstad, J. (2018). Fostering social connection in the workplace. In *American Journal of Health Promotion* (No. 5; Vol. 32, pp. 1307–1312).

Holt-Lunstad, J., Smith, T. B., Baker, M., Harris, T., & Stephenson, D. (2015). Loneliness and social isolation as risk factors for mortality: A meta-analytic review. In *Perspectives on Psychological Science* (No. 2; Vol. 10, pp. 227–237).

Knuth, D. E. (1993). *The stanford GraphBase: A platform for combinatorial computing.* ACM Press.

Lu, Z., Wahlström, J., & Nehorai, A. (2018). Community detection in complex networks via clique conductance. In *Scientific Reports.* https://www.nature.com/articles/s41598-018-23932-z

Lusseau, D., Schneider, K., Boisseau, O. J., Haase, P., Slooten, E., & Dawson, S. M. (2003). The bottlenose dolphin community of doubtful sound features a large proportion of long-lasting associations. In *Behavioral Ecology and Sociobiology* (Vol. 54, pp. 396–405).

McNulty, K. (2021). *Handbook of regression modeling in people analytics.* CRC Press. https://peopleanalytics-regression-book.org/

Morselli, C. (2009). *Inside criminal networks.* Springer.

Newman, M. E. J. (2001). Scientific collaboration networks. II. Shortest paths, weighted networks, and centrality. *Phys. Rev. E.* https://link.aps.org/doi/10.1103/PhysRevE.64.016132

Newman, M. E. J. (2002). Assortative mixing in networks. *Physical Review Letters.* https://arxiv.org/pdf/cond-mat/0205405.pdf

Olguin, D., Waber, B. N., Kim, T., Mohan, A., Ara, K., & Pentland, A. (2009). Sensible organizations: Technology and methodology for automatically measuring organizational behavior. In *IEEE transactions on systems, man, and cybernetics. Part B, Cybernetics* (Vol. 39, pp. 43–55).

Paoletti, T. (2006). Leonard euler's solution to the konigsberg bridge problem. In *Convergence.* https://www.maa.org/press/periodicals/convergence/leonard-eulers-solution-to-the-konigsberg-bridge-problem

Pearson, M. A., & Michell, L. (2000). Smoke rings: Social network analysis of friendship groups, smoking and drug-taking. In *Drugs: Education, Prevention and Policy* (No. 1; Vol. 7, pp. 21–37).

Rath, T. (2006). *Vital friends: The people you can't afford to live without.* Gallup Press.

Solly, M. (2020). Before chain letters swept the internet, they raised funds for orphans and sent messages from god. *Smithsonian Magazine.* https://www.smithsonianmag.com/history/chain-letters-swept-internet-they-raised-funds-orphans-and-conveyed-messages-god/

Stoer, M., & Wagner, F. (1997). A simple min-cut algorithm. In *Journal of the ACM* (No. 4; Vol. 44, pp. 585–591).

Traag, V. A., Waltman, L., & van Eck, N. J. (2019). From louvain to leiden: Guaranteeing well-connected communities. *Scientific Reports.* https://www.nature.com/articles/s41598-019-41695-z

Travers, J., & Milgram, S. (1969). An experimental study of the small world problem. *Sociometry.* http://snap.stanford.edu/class/cs224w-readings/travers69smallworld.pdf

Ugander, J., Karrer, B., Backstrom, L., & Marlow, C. (2011). *The anatomy of the facebook social graph.* https://arxiv.org/pdf/1111.4503.pdf

Wickham, H. (2016). *ggplot2: Elegant graphics for data analysis.* https://ggplot2-book.org/

Yang, Z., Algesheimer, R., & Tessone, C. J. (2016). A comparative analysis of community detection algorithms on artificial networks. *Scientific Reports.* https://www.nature.com/articles/srep30750

Zachary, W. W. (1977). An information flow model for conflict and fission in small groups. In *Journal of Anthropological Research* (Vol. 33, pp. 452–473).

Glossary

adjacency matrix A representation of a graph as a square matrix indexed by the vertices, where the (i, j)-th entry is the weight of the edge from vertex i to vertex j or zero if such an edge does not exist. Weights are considered to be 1 for unweighted graphs.

adjacent vertices Two vertices which are connected by an edge in a graph.

assortativity The extent to which vertices with a given property are more likely to connect to vertices with the same property.

authority score The authority score of a vertex in a directed graph is the incoming eigenvector centrality of that vertex.

betweenness centrality The betweenness centrality of a vertex is the proportion of times it lies on the shortest path between all other pairs of vertices in the graph. It is a measure of the role of the vertex in the overall connectedness of the graph.

bipartite graph A graph consisting of two distinct sets of vertices such that no two vertices in the same set are adjacent.

breadth-first search A graph traversal method which moves through all neighboring vertices of a given vertex before moving to neighbors of neighbors.

centrality A general term for the importance of a vertex in the connective structure of a graph. It can be defined in a variety of ways.

clique A subset of vertices in a graph whose induced subgraph is a complete graph.

closeness centrality The closeness centrality of a vertex is the inverse of the sum of the distances from that vertex to all other vertices in the graph. It is a measure of how efficiently other vertices can be reached from that vertex.

clustering The process of partitioning a graph into subsets of vertices with high density, strongly associated with community detection.

community A subset of vertices in a graph which are considered to have a relatively dense connected structure.

community detection An algorithmic process to partition a graph into subsets of vertices in order to maximize the connectedness within subsets and minimize the connectedness between subsets. Common algorithms for community detection include the Louvain, Leiden and Girvan-Newman algorithms.

complete graph A graph where all pairs of vertices are connected. Otherwise stated, a graph with an edge density of 1.

connected component A subset of vertices in a graph whose induced subgraph is connected.

connected graph A graph where a path exists between all pairs of vertices.

cut A set of edges in a connected graph whose removal would split the graph into distinct connected components.

Cypher query language An increasingly popular query language developed for Neo4J graph databases which uses ASCII art to denote nodes and edges.

degree assortativity Assortativity based on the degree centrality of vertices.

degree centrality The degree centrality (or simply the degree) of a vertex is the number of edges connected to it in the graph. It is a common measure of the vertex's importance.

density (edge density) The number of edges in a graph expressed as a proportion of the total possible number of edges in the graph, most commonly used in the description of simple graphs. A higher density graph means greater likelihood of connection between any pair of its vertices.

depth-first search A graph traversal method which selects a neighboring vertex of a given vertex and moves as far down the resulting path as possible before returning to the starting point and visiting another neighboring vertex.

diameter The largest distance between any pair of vertices in a graph.

distance The length of the shortest path between two vertices in a graph.

edge An element of the edge set of a graph, representing a connection between two vertices.

edgelist A representation of a graph as a list of edges (pairs of vertices in the edge set), often with other information such as edge weight.

edge weight A common name for a numeric edge property.

edge subgraph A graph formed from an edge subset of a larger graph and the vertices connected by that edge subset.

ego size The n-th order ego size of a vertex is the number of vertices in its n-th order ego network.

ego network The n-th order ego network of a vertex is a set consisting of that vertex plus all vertices that are at distance at most n from it.

eigenvector centrality The eigenvector centrality (or eigencentrality) of a vertex is calculated using the unique largest eigenvalue and corresponding eigenvector of the adjacency matrix of the graph. It is a measure of the influence of a vertex in the sense that it is connected to other vertices that are important in the network. Also known as relative centrality or prestige.

force-directed layout A popular and aesthetically pleasing layout of vertices which is calculated by means of physical simulation algorithms. Force-directed algorithms are good at finding layouts where the edges are of similar length and where as few edges cross as possible.

graph A mathematical structure consisting of a set of vertices and a separate set of pairs of vertices, known as edges.

graph similarity The extent to which two graphs have a similar structure. In simpler situations, this reduces to the similarity of the edge sets of two graphs with the same vertex sets.

graph traversal An algorithmic process of visiting, checking and updating vertices in a graph, commonly used in graph search or shortest path problems.

graph database A persistent data storage system that is structured similar to a graph, with a vertex set and an edge set.

hairball A common phenomenon in the visualization of complex graphs, where a group of densely connected vertices resemble a ball or clump of hair.

hub score The hub score of a vertex in a directed graph is the outgoing eigenvector centrality of that vertex.

induced subgraph A graph formed from a vertex subset of a larger graph and all edges connecting the vertices in the vertex subset, also called vertex subgraph or simply subgraph.

isolate A vertex which is not connected to any other vertices in a graph, also known as a singleton.

k-partite graph A graph consisting of k distinct sets of vertices such that no two vertices in the same set are adjacent.

labelled-property graph A form of graph database where the nodes and edges contain defined properties. These tend to be easier to query but are less flexible in handling rapidly changing data structures.

layout A positioning of the vertices in a graph visualization, usually calculated by means of a selected algorithm.

loop edge An edge that starts and ends on the same vertex.

maximal clique A clique where the addition of any other vertex would render it no longer a clique.

minimum cut A cut for which no other cut exists with fewer edges.

modularity For a partition of a graph, the modularity measures the extent to which in-group density is greater than what would be expected by chance. Modularity is an important measure in community detection as high modularity indicates a strong community structure.

multigraph A graph where more than one edge can exist between any pair of vertices.

network A group or system of interconnected entities (people or things), usually modeled using a graph.

nominal assortativity Assortativity based on a categorical property of vertices.

partition A division of the vertices of a graph into mutually exclusive subsets.

path A route from one vertex to another using edges in the graph.

path length The sum of the weights of the edges on a path between two vertices in a graph. If it is an unweighted graph, then the edge weights are taken as 1.

preferential attachment A phenomenon observed in some real world networks where vertices are more likely to connect to high degree (or popular) vertices.

pseudograph A graph where loop edges are allowed.

random seed A value used in programming to control and replicate random number generation. In graph layouts, this is used to ensure that a layout can be reproduced by others.

regex Regular expression syntax, a common syntax used to search text for certain patterns or strings.

resource description framework (RDF) A form of graph database which allows new entities and relationships be 'spawned' flexibly. RDFs are more flexible in handling rapidly changing data structures, but querying is more complex.

scale-free network A network where the degrees of the vertices obey a power law distribution with certain parameters. Such networks exist rarely but are of interest because they can be the result of rapid network growth with preferential attachment.

scraping A process whereby elements of text are extracted from electronic documents.

shortest path algorithms A class of graph traversal algorithms designed to find the shortest length paths between vertices, including Dijkstra, Bellman-Ford, Johnson and Floyd-Warshall.

simple path (or acyclic path) A path between two vertices in a graph where no vertex is repeated.

simple graph A graph where there is no more than one edge between any two vertices and where there are no loop edges.

SPARQL The standard query language for resource description framework (RDF) graph databases.

sparse graph A graph considered to have low edge density.

strongly connected A directed graph is said to be strongly connected if there is a directed path between all pairs of vertices in the graph.

temporal network A network whose characteristics can change over time.

tree A connected graph where there is only one path between any pair of vertices. When visualized, such a graph has a tree structure.

unilaterally connected A directed graph is said to be unilaterally connected when there is a path in any direction between all pairs of vertices in the graph.

vertex similarity The extent to which two vertices have similar neighboring vertices. Measured using Jaccard, dice or log-weighted similarity coefficients.

vertex or edge property Information that is attached to or stored in the vertices or edges of a graph.

vertex (or node) An element of the vertex set of a graph, representing an entity (person or thing) which may or may not be connected to other entities.

weakly connected A directed graph is said to be weakly connected if it is connected when viewed as an undirected graph.

Index

adjacency list, 28
adjacency matrix, 27
    creating a graph from, 30, 38
    sparse form, 27
adjacent vertices, 16
aesthetic mappings (in `ggraph`), 58
algorithm
    A*, 125
    Bellman-Ford, 125
    Dijkstra, 125
    Floyd-Warshall, 125
    force-directed, 51
    Fruchterman-Reingold, 53
    Girvan-Newman, 174, 184
    graph search, 119
    Johnson's, 125
    Kamada-Kawai, 53, 76
    Leiden, 174, 187
    Louvain, 62, 173, 190, 194
    shortest path, 125
APOC procedures, 223
ASCII art, 216
assortativity, 201
    calculating in Python, 210
    calculating in R, 202–204
    coefficient, 201
    degree, 204
    nominal, 202

Bacon number, 128
belongingness, 6
betweenness centrality, *see* centrality
bipartite graph, *see* graph
breadth-first search, 121

centrality, 9, 25, 40, 128, 147
    authority score, 152

betweenness, 9, 51, 150
    calculating in Python, 154–156
    calculating in R, 152–154
    closeness, 9, 149
    considering edge weights, 152
    degree, 4, 9, 43, 51, 149
    eigenvector, 9, 151
    hub score, 152
    illustrating visually, 157–159
clique (in a graph), 22, 174
    calculating in Python, 187
    calculating in R, 181
closeness centrality, *see* centrality
community, 25, 169, 173
community detection, 8, 62, 173
    calculating in Python, 184
    calculating in R, 179
community discovery, *see* community
    detection
complete graph, *see* graph
connected component, 170
    calculating in Python, 182
    calculating in R, 175
cut (of a graph), 172
    calculating in Python, 183
    calculating in R, 179
cut size, 172
Cypher query language, 216

data sets
    `caviar`, 234
    `chinook`, 84
    `dolphins`, 233
    `email`, 198
    `eu_referendum`, 72
    `friends_tv`, 146
    `g14`, 119, 147, 205

For Product Safety Concerns and Information please contact our
EU representative GPSR@taylorandfrancis.com Taylor & Francis
Verlag GmbH, Kaufingerstraße 24, 80331 München, Germany